D0935381

# IMAGES AND IDEAS IN
# CHINESE CLASSICAL PROSE

# Images and Ideas in
# Chinese Classical Prose

*Studies of Four Masters*

YU-SHIH CHEN

Stanford University Press

1988          Stanford, California

Stanford University Press
Stanford, California
© 1988 by the Board of Trustees of the
Leland Stanford Junior University
Printed in the United States of America

CIP data appear at the end of the book

Published with the assistance of U.S.-China Industrial Exchange, Inc.

*Frontispiece:* A detail from the eight-panel painting by Ch'iao Chung-ch'ang (twelfth century) illustrating Su Shih's "Rhymeprose on the Red Cliff," showing Su Shih visited by two Taoist priests in a dream. The Chinese characters are taken from the last lines of Part II of the Rhymeprose: "Presently my guests left, and I too returned home to bed.... The Taoist priests looked back and laughed." Photograph courtesy of the Nelson-Atkins Museum of Art, Kansas City, Missouri (Nelson Fund).

To my mother, Tsuh-min Lee

# PREFACE

THE PROSE WRITINGS of the T'ang and Sung dynasties known today under the rubric of *ku-wen* (classical prose) are recognized as one of the treasures of Chinese literature. Yet critical study of these works began only in the first half of the twentieth century. Then, such scholars and literary historians as Kuo Shao-yü (1893–1984) and Lo Ken-tse (1900?–1960) introduced the concept of a "classical-prose movement," summarized the salient features of its theories, and mapped its stylistic and conceptual development from the sixth to the twelfth century.

The attention of these scholars was captured by the protest that began early in the sixth century against the excessive formalism of the then-current *p'ien-wen* (parallel prose), which used predominantly four- and six-word phrases and was characterized by an emphasis on verbal parallelism, tonal euphony, and frequency of allusions. The protest, according to these scholars, took the form of a call for a return to the more vigorous, free prose of pre-Ch'in times. An ideological basis was soon developed to support this call: Confucianism and the Six Classics furnished the norms for both government and literature. In his writings, Han Yü, the principal exponent of the classical-prose revival, fully explored the Six Classics for their political, intellectual, and literary implications. Orthodoxy became the issue. The principles inherent in the Six

Classics were to be reactivated in the public and private spheres of human activity—in government and religion, as well as in philosophy and literature—on the ground that the Classics represented the orthodox tradition in China. Buddhism, Taoism, and parallel prose, the forms of thought and writings in vogue at the time, Han Yü regarded as heresies. A formidable polemicist, Han Yü gave the fullest and most forceful articulation to the mainstream ideas of the classical-prose movement (hereafter "*ku-wen* movement"). After his death, the movement lost its vitality and thrust, and parallel prose regained its dominance. Not until the middle of the eleventh century did a revived *ku-wen* movement succeed in realizing the goals of its T'ang predecessors. The Sung advocates of *ku-wen* consolidated the preeminent position of Confucian orthodoxy in government and society and established a free prose modeled on pre-Ch'in and T'ang classical-prose writings as the official medium of prose composition for centuries to come.

The concept of the *ku-wen* movement as developed by Kuo and Lo has generally been accepted since the publication of their histories of Chinese literary criticism. No basic advance has been made beyond their view that the theories and writings of the T'ang-Sung proponents of *ku-wen* constitute a homogeneous whole. In this study I approach these writings from a somewhat different premise and draw different conclusions about the nature of the writings, theories, practices, and achievements of the *ku-wen* movement, and I begin to develop a tentative theory of *ku-wen* as a literary genre.

The main body of this study (Chapters 1–4) is devoted to a close analysis of the theories and practices of four *ku-wen* masters: Han Yü (768–824) and Liu Tsung-yüan (773–819) of the T'ang period and Ou-yang Hsiu (1007–72) and Su Shih (1036–1101) of the Sung period. The study shows, first, that T'ang and Sung *ku-wen* theories and practices were not as homogeneous as they were made to appear in the histories of Kuo and Lo; second, that there was a basic shift in perspective between the T'ang and Sung *ku-wen* masters from the unique to the universal; and third, that the Sung advocates of *ku-wen* absorbed the T'ang ideals of uniqueness and originality (Han Yü's "lofty" [*kao*] and "extraordinary" [*ch'i*]) into their antithetical concepts of universality and simplicity (Ou-yang Hsiu's "common" [*ch'ang*] and "simple" [*chien, yi*]). In the process, they created prose works distinct in temperament, style, and philosophical orientation from those of their T'ang predecessors. In these chapters, I explore the divergences between the *ku-wen* masters in matters of ideas and stylistics, especially their individual perception of what the "way" (*tao*) is, how it can be successfully transmitted, and what the distinguishing features of its written medium of transmission, *wen*, are. (Chinese characters for terms can be found in the Glossary; characters for proper names are in the Index.)

The overall emphasis of this study falls therefore on the diversity of the individual *ku-wen* masters rather than on the homogeneity of the movement. As we progress from the T'ang to the Sung, we shall see that the authors of theories and practices of *ku-wen* not only shifted their perspective from the unique to the universal, but they also found a place for a lyrical voice in *ku-wen*, thus effecting a change in theoretical orientation from the political to the poetic. By Su Shih's time, the basic concerns of *ku-wen* had moved increasingly away from questions of history, nature, and political government (*tao*) to analysis of an author's own perceptive mind (*yi*) and of the art of representation (*fa*). For the first time, Chinese prose turns away from the utilitarian or the didactic toward a concern with artistic representation itself.

Although I do not have the space in the present work to do so, analysis of this shift in theoretical orientation from *tao* to *fa* can be pursued in relation to prose writers after the Sung. It is now apparent that the obsession of Ming prose writers with *fa* continued a trend present in Su Shih.

Nor have I chosen to treat to any significant extent the role of either Buddhism or parallel prose in the theories and practices of the four *ku-wen* masters. It is well known that they were all subject to Buddhist influences and that Ou-yang Hsiu and Su Shih both wrote parallel prose well. These questions are not of immediate relevance to this particular study, but would of course be an integral part of a comprehensive history of Chinese prose style and of the intellectual history of this period.

Three chapters of this book developed from articles published over a period of ten years: "Han Yü as a *Ku-wen* Stylist," *Tsing-hua Journal of Chinese Studies*, n.s. 7, no. 1 (Aug. 1968); "Change and Continuation in Su Shih's Theory of Literature: A Note on His *Ch'ih-pi-fu*," *Monumenta Serica*, 31 (1974–75); and "The Literary

Theory and Practice of Ou-yang Hsiu," in Adele A. Rickett, ed., *Chinese Approaches to Literature from Confucius to Liang Ch'i-ch'ao*, copyright © 1978 by Princeton University Press, reprinted by permission of Princeton University Press. These have all been revised, expanded, and reworked to show contrasts in the philosophical views of the individual writers as well as in the theories of literature and art that they to some extent shared.

In the expanded chapter on Han Yü (Chapter 1), for instance, new data were brought to bear on a reinterpretation of his personal relationship with his junior colleague Liu Tsung-yüan, which has traditionally been regarded as one of animosity. Here the old interpretation is reexamined to show that the two advocated similar political and literary reforms. This new understanding has necessitated a new look at a number of their well-known works. It has also made possible a different comparison of their views on *tao* and *wen*, which I have attempted to do at the end of the chapter on Liu Tsung-yüan (Chapter 2).

The chapter on Su Shih (Chapter 4) has been reworked into nearly twice the length of the original article. I have here pursued his involvement with his Neo-Confucian contemporaries and with their concepts of *ch'i* (material energy), *shu* (mathematical principles), and *li* (the principle underlying physical nature). The result is used to provide an intellectual context for a new translation of his two *Ch'ih-pi fu* ("Rhymeprose on the Red Cliff"). Su Shih's literary manipulation in the two *fu* of the concepts of number, time, and change comes through vividly, though somewhat playfully, in his use of the singular and plural and in his riddle of one crane turning into two Taoists in the second *fu*. I have also tried to specify how Su Shih departs from Ou-yang Hsiu in his view of *ku-wen* and how his ideas of *li*, *shu*, and *ch'i* link him more with Liu Tsung-yüan than with Ou-yang Hsiu.

By devoting a book to the theory and art of *ku-wen*, I hope to restore a balance to the study of the literature of the T'ang and Sung periods, which, at least in the West, tend to be regarded as an age of poetry (T'ang *shih* and Sung *tz'u*). Other kinds of literary activity were going on, and the four masters, all of them major poets as well, took their prose writings in *ku-wen* seriously, leaving a heritage of masterpieces read by every subsequent Chinese writer as models to be emulated even as they looked to the poets of the period for their inspiration. Since it is also my intent in this book to clarify rather than to criticize the views, practices, and art of the masters, I have in my discussion relied more on the works of the masters themselves than on modern secondary sources. It is my belief that before undertaking criticism, one needs to understand what a writer says. There has been so little written in the West on *ku-wen* that the preliminary task of clarification is as difficult as it is essential. This task has been more than sufficient for the present book.

I wish to take this opportunity to thank my thesis adviser, Professor Hans Frankel, who first suggested the topic of Han Yü to me and under whose supervision I completed my thesis on Han Yü's theory and practice of *ku-wen*. My particular gratitude goes to Professor James R. Hightower, who read numerous versions of the different chapters and did his best to rid them of the more fatal flaws in argument and style. Dr. Achilles Fang laid the foundation of my research skill in Chinese studies; to him, I owe the affectionate gratitude of a former graduate student. Professor Yu-kung Kao encouraged the publication of my research in T'ang-Sung *ku-wen* as a book and supplied throughout the years the necessary momentum behind my effort with his unflagging faith in its possible merit. Professor Andrew Plaks read the complete manuscript when it was first finished and made invaluable suggestions for the improvement of its critical framework. I also wish to thank Timothy Connor and Kathleen Perry, whose indefatigable editorial attention to the substantive and stylistic details gave the book its present form.

There is one special person who throughout my academic career has supported me in ways as bountiful as nature; to him, I owe thanks that are beyond the power of words. Professor C. T. Hsia's forceful humanistic spirit is present in all my academic endeavors. His is a spirit that inspires without interfering, a spirit that is in the purest May Fourth tradition.

Finally, I wish to thank the Harvard-Yenching Library for granting me free and convenient access to its vast collection of classical Chinese literature over the years. Its generous loan policy played a vital role in the coming together of this book.

Y.C.

# CONTENTS

# IMAGES AND IDEAS IN
# CHINESE CLASSICAL PROSE

# INTRODUCTION

## The T'ang *Ku-wen* Movement

THE TERM *ku-wen yün-tung* ("*ku-wen* movement") refers to a literary movement that flourished between the mid-sixth and the mid-ninth centuries. Two themes dominate its 300-year history: revolt against the prevalent parallel-prose tradition of the Six Dynasties period and a revival of classical ideals in literature. In this chapter, I review the development of these two themes in the three phases of the *ku-wen* movement—the initial utilitarian, the intermediate classical, and the culminating polemical phases—and place the *ku-wen* theories and practices of Han Yü and Liu Tsung-yüan, which are representative of the culminating polemical phase and whose analysis begins the study of T'ang-Sung *ku-wen* writings in this book, in their proper historical perspective.

### The Utilitarian Phase

According to the twentieth-century scholar Lo Ken-tse, the *ku-wen* movement began with Su Ch'o (498–546), a minister of the Western Wei dynasty who in 545 rejected parallel prose and drafted an edict called the "Great Announcement" in the style of the ancient *Shu ching* (Classic of documents).[1] In this initial phase, the predominant theme was revolt, and the theme of revival lay dormant. Its principal advocates were court historians and drafters of imperial decrees, people concerned more with the political and ideological use of literature than with belletristic problems of literary values and ideals. Reacting against parallel prose, a euphuistic prose style that used most of the devices peculiar to Chinese poetry—notably metrical, grammatical, and phonic parallelism—and the values it embodied,[2] these advocates regarded their own position as a challenge to that tradition. Li E's memorial to Emperor Wen of Sui (r. 581–605) on frivolity of style (584) was a famous manifesto of this challenge.[3]

In the "Memorial," Li E condemned parallel prose for its corruption of the morals of the government and of the people. The rules of parallel-prose composition, he contended, overemphasized the formal aspects of style and encouraged the pursuit of literary art as an end in itself. This style had subverted the true purpose of literature, which since antiquity had been to promote good government and foster civilizing influences. This subversion had caused rulers to "neglect the great principle of proper relations between ruler and ruled," the literati and officials to become petty-minded and dissolute, and states—notably Wei (220–65), Chin (265–420), and the Southern Dynasties (420–589)—to disintegrate and fall.

Implicit in Li E's criticism was the idea that literature, lacking its own ideals, must find them in political and social institutions. This utilitarian theory of literature, as it has been called, was also espoused by the early T'ang historians, but they went one step further than Li E in constructing a theory: they proposed, above and beyond their criticism of the parallel-prose tradition, the first new idea of an alternative style; namely, the idea of "balance between plainness and adornment in literary expression" (*wen-chih pin-pin*).[4]

*Wen-chih pin-pin* had classical roots, but adapting a classical style for contemporary use was not the same as reviving the classical style itself in contemporary writing. These two approaches to classicism underscore the difference between the utilitarianism of the historians in the first phase of the *ku-wen* movement and the classicism of the poets and literary writers of its second phase. The early T'ang historians saw the differences in literary style between one age and another as being related to practical considerations in each age. Their stylistic idea of *wen-chih pin-pin*, therefore, in spite of its classical roots, did not invoke classicism as its basic criterion of value; rather, it was oriented toward practical use. Su Ch'o's imitation of the *Shu ching*'s style, for example, was severely criticized by the historians; its archaism was considered "too plain."[5] Leaning too heavily on "blunt actuality," it upset the balance of *wen-chih pin-pin* and, for that reason, was not entirely adequate for use.

Fifty years later, the historiographer Liu Chih-chi (661–721) introduced two additional criteria, "linguistic usage" (*yen*) and "contemporaneity" (*shih*), thereby initiating another attack on slavish imitation of a classical style. His views, especially his criticism of anachronistic imitation, have interest for this study because they were to recur in different forms in Han Yü's *ku-wen* theory.

According to Liu Chih-chi, no style is timeless. Time and circumstances change, and gradually the use and value of any particular style also change. Imitation of the style of the classical masters, simply because they are classic, has no solid basis. In refusing to acknowledge change in language and in disregarding contemporary usage, such imitators combine dissimilar linguistic usages and create unnecessary complications for the reader. In Liu's opinion, reproducing the "appearance" (*mao*) of a classical master is an undesirable, "low" (*hsia*) form of imitation. One should strive, rather, to imitate the "heart" and "spirit" (*hsin*) that underlie classical writings.[6]

Liu Chih-chi's criticism was essentially directed at the writing of history, but its influence was far wider. His arguments against the use of classical style and his linguistic criteria of "genuineness" (*chen*), "purity" (*ch'un*), and "artificiality" (*wei*) were soon restated by Tan Chu (725–70) and his school of *Ch'un-ch'iu* (Spring and autumn annals) criticism and widely adopted as the basis for textual criticism of the classics by the intellectuals of the period following the An Lu-shan rebellion (755–63).[7] Liu's skepticism and rationalism strongly influenced the intelligentsia of the post-rebellion world. Han Yü, as well as Liu Tsung-yüan, was affected by this general atmosphere of rationality and skeptical thought, and both demonstrated in a number of their works that they were familiar with the technique of textual criticism.[8] Each in his own way incorporated certain of these techniques into his *ku-wen* theory of literature.

To sum up, the first phase of the *ku-wen* movement began with a revolt against the parallel-prose tradition. In the century from Li E to Liu Chih-chi, a didactic theory of literature and a utilitarian outlook on style culminated in a rationalistic school of classical scholarship. In the sense that their criticism of parallel prose and their didactic view of literature were shared by later mainstream *ku-wen* theorists of the second and the third phases, the principal spokesmen of this phase can be seen as precursors of the *ku-wen* movement. But they differed from the mainstream theorists in their emphasis on rationality, practicality, and conformity to contemporary customs instead of classicism. Their principal contribution was to provide later, more literary writers with a critical self-consciousness. Their polemic against the parallel-prose tradition was assimilated by the *ku-wen* movement. Indirectly, they also contributed to literary reform and to the establishment of an alternative literary tradition. Their efforts provided a precedent for later writers to depart from a rigid style of expression.

## The Classical Phase

Just as rationality characterized the initial phase of the *ku-wen* movement, idealism was the dominant trait of its second phase. Between the time of the early T'ang historians and the appearance of the leading classicists of the second phase—Hsiao Ying-shih (717–68) and Li Hua (ca. 710–67)—the impulse toward the revival of classicism was already apparent in the writings of such prose stylists and poets as Ch'en Tzu-ang (661–701), Li Po (701–62), and the "four outstanding writers of the early T'ang period" (*ch'u T'ang ssu chieh*)—Wang Po (647–75), Yang Chiung (650–95), Lo Pin-wang (d. 684), and Lu Chao-lin (ca. 641–80).

Ch'en Tzu-ang and Li Po first enunciated the theme of classical revival, looking back to the "unsullied and unspoiled sincerity" of the classical style, and earnestly proposed reviving the long-lost principle or "way" (*tao*) of the *Shih ching* (Classic of poetry).[9] Yang Chiung and Wang Po discoursed passionately on the "way of literature" (*wen tao*), lamented its degeneration during the Six Dynasties, and appealed to "principled writers" to rehabilitate it.[10] Later, Hsiao Ying-shih and Li Hua boldly identified themselves with the "principled writers" of whom Yang Chiung and Wang Po had written and began to campaign for a concrete program to implement this idea. Thus, the *ku-wen* movement emerged full-fledged when Hsiao Ying-shih and Li Hua became spokesmen for a classical revival and undertook to realize it in their own writings.

These poets and writers of the second, classical phase accepted the historians' practical view of literature and for the most part conceded that literature functioned as the vehicle for government. They differed, however, on the question of what makes literature timeless. To these classicists, political utility was not the only aspect of thought that informed the production of the Classics. Classical literature itself, in its formal aspects, provided an ideal to be striven after—a way of *being* the vehicle for government that was never merely subordinate to the "way" of government and was to be distinguished from the latter. In other words, the Classics, even as they served government, developed their own history and their own values—of genres, of style, and of ideas—independent of any question of utility.

Li Hua set forth his views in his preface to the collected works of Ts'ui Mien (673–739):

> The significance of literature rises out of writers, but its mood of joy or sorrow is conditioned by its time. That the significance of literature should rise out of the writer is the purport of the Six Classics. And that its mood is conditioned by its time means that one rejoices in the times of [rulers like] King Wen and King Wu [of the Chou dynasty, 1255–1122 B.C.] but grieves in the times of King Yu and King Li [of the Chou].... The writings of our Master [Confucius, 551–479 B.C.] were first transmitted by [his disciples] Yen [Yen Yen or Tzu-yu, b. 506 B.C.] and Shang [Pu Shang or Tzu-hsia, 507–420? B.C.]. When Yen and Shang died, K'ung Chi [or Tzu-ssu, d. ca. 407 B.C.] and Meng K'o [Mencius, 372–289 B.C.] wrote, and they succeeded to the tradition of the Six Classics. The writings of Ch'ü P'ing [Ch'ü Yüan, 343–277 B.C.] and Sung Yü [fl. 298–265 B.C.], on the other hand, are sad and mournful, diffuse and astray. The way (*tao*) of the Six Classics became obscured. In the ages following, those who were able to write did not know the way, and those who knew the way were unable to realize it in their works. As a consequence, the principle of literature deteriorated and disappeared from the world.[11]

Li Hua here specifically identified the literature of the classical age with the Six Classics and its *tao* with the timeless *tao* of all writings. This identification of the Six Classics with the *tao*, the ideal, and the classic in literature marked a turning point in the development of the *ku-wen* movement in the T'ang. From this moment on, the movement began to diverge from its former practical criteria of judging literature by its effect in the political world and to base itself on an internal criterion: approximation of the ideals of the Six Classics. In thus holding up the Six Classics as the ideal, the goal, and the model for all writers, Li Hua and Hsiao Ying-shih distinguished their *ku-wen* theory, with its clear-cut classical orientation, from that of the early T'ang historians. Classicism became the new basis for literary reform. Li Hua's idea of a direct line of descent from Confucius and the Six Classics to Tzu-ssu and Mencius was the precursor of a central issue in Han Yü's theory of literature.[12]

Before the *ku-wen* movement entered its final, polemical phase as represented by Han Yü, two important stylists—Tu-ku Chi (744–96) and Yüan Chieh (723–72)—and two original theorists—Liang Su (753–93) and Liu Mien (fl. 779–97)—introduced a new dimension into the movement. These four men were part of the contemporary literary and intellectual world, and they provided a context for the literary theory and stylistic practice of Han Yü himself.

Tu-ku Chi and Yüan Chieh are considered the leading classical stylists of the second half of the eighth century, although they did not contribute much in the way of original literary theory. As a theorist, Tu-ku Chi is remembered for his famous preface to the collected works of Li Hua, in which he criticized the frivolity of parallel prose in much the same terms as Li E and made his criticism memorable by rendering the utter flimsiness of that style quite evident by means of the exquisite image of a "boat of magnolia-wood" with "ostrich-feather oars."[13] His and Yüan Chieh's contribution to the *ku-wen* movement lay essentially in their role as creative writers and stylists. They promoted the use of a free *ku-wen* style and consolidated its status as the new literary medium. The writings of Tu-ku Chi, in particular, anticipated Han Yü thematically and stylistically in their brisk criticism of historical writings and of historical personages, in their intense concern for moral character, and above all, in their taste for the sublime and the extraordinary as manifested in nature and the human world.

Liang Su, acknowledged by his contemporaries as the leader of the new stylistic movement around 790,[14] introduced the important concept of *ch'i* ("energy" or "vital force"), giving a new metaphysical dimension to *ku-wen* theory, which previously had been more politically and morally oriented. His concept of *ch'i* differed from that formulated centuries before by Ts'ao P'i (188–226). According to Liang Su,

> Literature has its original root in the *tao*. When it loses its foothold in the *tao*, it can be buoyed up with *ch'i*. If *ch'i* is inadequate, then it can be embellished with rhetoric. For the *tao* is able to comprehend *ch'i*, and *ch'i* in turn comprehends the art of rhetoric. When the art of rhetoric is not properly practiced, literature comes to grief.[15]

*Ch'i*, as conceived by Ts'ao P'i in his "Discourse on Literature," referred to a set of physiological qualities with which each individual is endowed at birth and which therefore cannot be changed at will.[16] The term corresponds roughly to the concept of "humors" in medieval Western physiology—a concept used primarily to rationalize qualitative differences in dispositions and natural endowments.

Liang Su's concept of *ch'i* has little in common with this older usage. It is, however, strongly reminiscent of the concept as used in contemporary Buddhist cosmogony.[17] Being a learned Buddhist lay disciple, Liang Su absorbed the concept and practiced it in his new stylistic movement.[18] The immediate consequence of the adoption of this metaphysical idea was that the essential "classicism"—or the *tao* of the Six Classics—of *ku-wen* theory suddenly lost its standing as the norm of good literature. Political, social, and literary ideals had to be redefined in terms of a total vision of the metaphysical reality of man and his world. Liu Mien's discourses on literature reflect this total vision and thus become the first comprehensive defense of classical ideals in terms of the current metaphysical ideas of "universal mind" (*hsin*) and "emotions" (*ch'ing*).[19]

Liu Mien's defense can be summarized under three points.[20] First, he professes the concept that the "universal mind" of heaven and earth is immanent in human emotions. "For heaven generated [*sheng*] man, who generated [*sheng*] his emotions." The saints and sages of the classical age perceived the truth and made human emotions the natural basis for their teachings. In teaching the principles of "human-heartedness" (*jen*) and "righteousness" (*yi*) and the highest fulfillment of human emotions in rites and rituals, the saints and sages affirmed their perception of the universal mind as accessible to all. The *tao* does not transcend human emotions but is one with them; the saints and sages were not without emotions but had reached the ultimate reality and had made peace with it. Second, he states that human emotion is the natural basis of literature. But in literature it assumes the form of experiences such as joy and sorrow. Man feels joy or sorrow in response to the order or disorder he perceives in society. Thus literature, rather than determining the condition of society, is itself determined by the moral state of that society as expressed through the intermediate emotional response of the writer. To effect a change in the character and the function of literature, one must therefore first change the mores of society. Third, the problem of *ch'i* in literary writing has a social aspect: only when society encourages the cultivation of a special talent does the *ch'i* come to life in a writer to produce good literature.

Literature, according to Liu Mien's theory, does not derive its significance from promoting the *tao* of government, as in the practical theory of Li E and the early T'ang historians; nor is it a self-sufficient ideal that contains its own *tao* (presumably manifesting the *tao* of government also), as Hsiao Ying-shih and Li Hua perceived in the Six Classics. From Liu Mien's point of view, both literature and government are vehicles of the ultimate *tao* of the universe, the proper function of which, whether in politics, literature, or elsewhere, depends on a proper conception of that ultimate *tao* and on unfailing cultivation of this *tao*. Once the *tao* of literature was dissociated from the concept of political order and from the classical literary ideal and became a metaphysical truth, the stage was set for Han Yü and his Confucian polemics.

## The Polemical Phase: Han Yü

Han Yü's theory of literature appears in its most coherent form in his "Letter in Answer to Li Yi" (801).[21] As the best statement of the theory of literature of the *ku-wen* school at its culmination, it is translated here in full.

The twenty-sixth day of the sixth month, Yü addresses Mr. Li.
The language of your letter is very elevated. Yet how humbly and respectfully you have presented your questions! Since you presented them in such a fashion, how could I not want to tell you what I know? The principles of *tao* and *te* [i.e., the Confucian ethos] have long been in decline, and how much the more has literature, which is the external expression of that ethos.[22] How can someone, whom I would consider as having caught sight of only the gate and

wall of Confucius's palace but not having entered the premises, know right and wrong?[23] At any rate, I cannot but tell you what I know. What you have said about literary achievement is correct.[24] What you have done and what you expect are quite in line. But I wonder whether your aim is to surpass ordinary people and become esteemed by them or to attain the same height of achievement as the ancient masters. If all that you wish is to surpass others and be esteemed by them, you have already surpassed and may be so esteemed. But if you wish to attain the height of achievement of the ancient masters, then you must not expect quick results, nor should you be lured away by what is advantageous and profitable. Nurture the root and await the fruit;[25] add oil to the lamp and expect it to burn bright. Where the roots thrive, the fruit will be good; where oil abounds, light will be radiant. When a man lives by human-heartedness and righteousness, his words will be gentle and graceful.

However, there are difficulties along the way. Take my own case: I do not know whether I have arrived at perfection or not. All I can say is that I have been devoting myself to this pursuit for more than twenty years. At first I dared not read any book that was not from the Three Dynasties or the Two Hans; I dared not harbor any idea that was not from the sages. I lived as if in a state of forgetfulness; I behaved as if I were lost. Now I looked serious as if I were deliberating; now I looked vague as if I were confused. When I selected from my mind ideas to express through my pen, I insisted on expunging all clichés. How excruciatingly difficult it was, full of creaking and squeaking! As to how I looked to others, I was impervious to their ridicule. I went on like this for many years, still unchanging.

After that, I was able to distinguish the genuine from the false in the ancient works, as well as those that, though genuine, were still not wholly so,[26] as clearly as black from white; and I applied myself to eliminating them. Gradually I succeeded. Then, when I selected from my mind ideas to express through my pen, they came flowing forth. As to how I looked to others, I was happy when they laughed at me, and I was troubled when they praised me, for I was afraid that I still harbored some of their ideas. It went on like this for several years. After that, ideas gushed forth in a flood. Still, I feared that there might be impurities among them. I confronted them and held them at bay; I scrutinized them with a composed mind. Only when I found them all pure did I give them full rein. Even so, I must cultivate the *tao*:[27] I walk the path of human-heartedness and righteousness and linger at the source—the *Shih ching* and the *Shu ching*—lest I lose the path, lest I be cut off from the source. This I shall have to do until the end of my days. The vital force [*ch'i*] is like water, and language is like something floating on it.[28] When a body of water is large, anything floats, will float, regardless of its size. So it is with the vital force and language; if the vital force is abundant, then, whether speech be short or long, its tone proud or humble, it will be appropriate. Even if one has achieved this, dare he say that he is near perfection? Even if he be near perfection, will it make him acceptable to others? Even so, he who wishes to be accepted by others, is he not like a utensil?[29] His acceptability depends on others. Things are different with a gentleman: his thoughts have principles and his conduct has direction [*fang*].[30] When he is in office, he extends his way [*tao*] to others; when he is out of office, he teaches it to his students and transmits it in writing as a model for later generations. When a man can conduct himself like this, will he not be pleased with himself? Or rather, will he not find anything pleasing in so doing?

Few are the men that aspire to the ancients, for those who aspire to the ancients are invariably neglected by their contemporaries. I myself truly delight in such men and sympathize with them, tirelessly praising them so as to offer them encouragement. I do not [like Confucius] presume to judge what or who is to be commended, and what or who is to be spurned. Many have asked my opinion. I deem, from what you wrote, that you are not bent on profit, and so I have written to you freely and openly.

In 800, the year before the "Letter to Li Yi" was written, Han Yü had ended a long, unsuccessful career as adviser on the staff of various regional military governors and had returned to Ch'ang-an to try his luck again at the court.[31] His appointment as an academician in the Ssu-men Academy in 801 brought him neither power nor prestige. Li Yi, a young candidate for the *chin-shih* degree, was in Ch'ang-an waiting to take his examination the next year. He was doing what a degree candidate customarily did in such circumstances: presenting influential men with samples of his literary skill to solicit their recommendations to the examiners.[32] Han Yü was approached by Li Yi, and the letter was his first response.[33] Han Yü admonished Li Yi to cultivate correct literary ideals, and he warned against shortcuts to success. The letter is important; not merely a response to the circumstances that prompted it, it is a manifesto of Han Yü's own theory of literature.

The literary theory advanced in the letter is in part a continuation of the past development of *ku-wen* theory: many of the ideas expressed in it originated in the writings of former critics and *ku-wen* theorists. Han Yü's ideas that literature is the expression of *tao* and *te* and that a writer must aspire to the same ideals that the classical masters exemplified in their writings carry on the classical didactic tradition of Hsiao Ying-shih and Li Hua. In his distinction between the genuine and the false among the ancient writings, he echoes Liu Chih-chi, Tan Chu, and the classical scholars of his own time. In his casual references to "vital spirit" and "language," he joins the powerful literati Liang Su and Ch'üan Te-yü (759–819), appropriating perhaps unconsciously the same Buddhist source of inspiration. And in his concept of "cultivation," the vital relationship between *tao* and *wen*, there is a reminder not only of Mencius but even more of Han Yü's senior contemporary Liu Mien. In terms of the historical sources of his ideas, Han Yü may appear to be a rather unoriginal thinker.

However, Han Yü does not use these ideas unchanged. His two most important transformations are found in the concepts of the genuine (*chen*) and the false (*wei*) and of *tao* and *te*. *Chen* and *wei* were originally used in reference to the date and authorship of a classical text and the establishment of its authenticity, but Han Yü invokes political orthodoxy and applies them to the problem of *tao*. Han Yü's conceptions of *tao* and *te* also differ from those of his *ku-wen* predecessors; to him they are not only classical ideals but specifically the ideals of the Confucian school. By interpreting *tao* and *te* as strictly Confucian, Han Yü is anticipating his later use of the Confucian *tao* and *te* as weapons against what he regards as the misappropriation of these terms by Taoism and Buddhism.[34] With this single-minded transformation of the older ideas of the *ku-wen* movement into weapons against heterodoxy, Han Yü cast the *ku-wen* movement off from its historical moorings and launched it into the hitherto uncharted realm of militant Confucianism. In the perspective of Han Yü's personal development and that of the entire *ku-wen* movement, the "Letter to Li Yi" marks an important departure from preceding *ku-wen* theory.

This departure constitutes the smaller part of Han Yü's original contribution to the development of *ku-wen* theory in the T'ang. The larger part is the literary program he designed for a methodical cultivation of the *ku-wen* ideal. The "Letter to Li Yi" is the only document that contains a full statement of that program. Its full significance can best be grasped when viewed in conjunction with the literary theory of Liu Mien.

Liu Mien's theory of *ku-wen* was the most comprehensive of those we have yet encountered because it included nearly all of the essential points previous theorists had raised. It began with a belief in the oneness of the "heart" of heaven and earth—which is the *tao*—and the emotion of man, and it ended with the observation that the proper function of literature depends much on a writer's understanding and cultivation of the ultimate *tao*. All that was lacking in this theory was a concrete program. Liu Mien did not anticipate Han Yü in discriminating between the true (Confucian) *tao* and the false (Taoist and Buddhist) *tao*. Han Yü supplemented Liu Mien's theory by providing the means by which to realize the ultimate goal of the advocates of *ku-wen*: the integration of *tao* and *wen*.

Han Yü's program consisted of three steps: first, to master the Classics in order to "expurgate all clichés"; second, to discriminate between the true and false among classical writings in order to purify one's own writings of all that is "false" (*wei*) and "impure" (*tsa*); and third, to maintain constant communion with the *tao* and its classical expression to prevent any relapse. In other words, whereas Liu Mien and the earlier *ku-wen* theorists emphasized the importance of the proper concept of the goal and function of literature but left the problem of style more or less to the realm of individual talent (*ts'ai*), Han Yü was the first to theorize about the art of *ku-wen* style, to standardize its artistic tenets, and to suggest a discipline for its mastery.

"Truth" and "purity"—full conformity to the spirit and the style of the Confucian classics—were the two new ideals Han Yü contributed to the *ku-wen* movement. His achievement as a literary theorist was to weld a vital link between fidelity to the Confucian school of thought and the purity of style of the Six Classics. His "Letter to Li Yi" should be regarded not as merely another document on *ku-wen* theory (which he largely assumed and only sketchily describes) but as the only document on the fundamental principles and theory of *ku-wen* style. This letter is Han Yü's guide for all would-be *ku-wen* writers who aspire to the literary realization of the true *tao*. The stylistic principles he developed later in his literary career can be put in perspective by referring back to this earlier statement. Taken in sequence, those principles bespeak an increasing awareness on Han Yü's part of the intricate technical problems involved in executing his program. In Chapter 1 of this study, I examine the precise manner in which he set about solving those problems, how his literary techniques were related to his overall theory, and to what extent he succeeded in realizing his goal in individual works.

# I

# HAN YÜ

## Classicism as Orthodoxy

OF HAN YÜ, Su Shih wrote: "His writings quickened literature from a languor that had lasted through eight dynasties; his *tao* saved all mankind from drowning [in heresies]."[1] Han Yü played a unique role in both the literary and the intellectual history of China. First, he was an epoch-making theorist whose doctrine of the union of *tao* (the "way") and *wen* ("literature") sounded the death knell of the excessively formal art of parallel-prose writing that had dominated the preceding centuries, thus heralding a new age of didacticism in literature.[2] Second, he created a prose style, which he called *ku-wen*, that has since become identified with the classic and orthodox in traditional Chinese writings.[3] Third, as an essayist, he was principally responsible for elevating the essay, which had for the most part served a utilitarian function, to the status of pure literature. From the time of Han Yü onward, essay writing was conceived, executed, and consciously criticized as literature.[4] Finally, he has a secure place in intellectual history as the founder and inspirer of the Confucian revival movement, which culminated in the Neo-Confucianism of the Sung dynasty. His work changed the cultural outlook of China.[5]

Han Yü's ideology and his theory of classicism in literature are the core of this intellectual and literary movement.[6] Han Yü employed various terms, methods, and techniques in his prose works to realize his classical ideal and to effect a "literary transformation" consonant with his anti-Buddhist and anti-Taoist ideology.[7] Concomitant with this broader literary transformation was an evolution in his own prose style and his theoretical conception of this style. This stylistic evolution was informed by changes in his personal, moral, and spiritual attitudes.

Han Yü's works diverge from those of his predecessors in two closely related aspects. One is the change in context and meaning of such critical terms as "clichés" (*ch'en tz'u*), "false" (*wei*), and "impure" (*tsa*); the other is the emergence of new, positive literary ideals and criteria that are literary counterparts to Han Yü's ideological goals, as we saw in the "Letter in Answer to Li Yi," translated in the preceding chapter. With Han Yü's assertion that Confucianism represented the true *tao*, the terms "clichés," "false," and "impure" no longer refer only to the trite expressions, formal pretensions, and trivial, unseemly topics of the parallel-prose tradition; the range of criticism, by implication, has been expanded to include censure of Taoism and Buddhism. The characterizations "false" and "clichéd" can easily be extended to all Taoist and Buddhist literature. Similarly, the impurities that need to be purged are no longer just the formal patterns required by the parallel-prose style but all non-Confucian expressions. Han Yü has extended the domain of *ku-wen* to a new, moral sphere.

Han Yü's essential contributions to the *ku-wen* movement as a literary theorist were his insistence on a strict Confucian interpretation of the true *tao* and the predication of his stylistic ideal of purity on Confucian ideology. Nearly all the principles of style that he developed later in his literary career spring from this early ideal, and they derive a certain unity of inspiration from this perspective.

Han Yü's writings reflect his own *ku-wen* programs with varying degrees of clarity and focus, as the following analyses of some representative examples of his work demonstrate: the "Letter Written While Attending the Civil Service Examination" (793), the "Valediction to Li Yüan on His Return to Meander Valley" (801), the "Memorial Inscription on the Pacification of the Huai-hsi Rebellion" (818), and the "Stele Inscription on the Lo-ch'ih Shrine in Liu-chou" (823).[8] Punctuated by his two exiles to the southern frontier (803 and 819), these four works span 30 years of Han Yü's literary career and can be considered illustrative of three stages in his stylistic development.

## The Principle of Uniqueness (1): Originality Through Imitation

The "Letter Written While Attending the Civil Service Examination" (hereafter the "Examination Letter") and the "Valediction to Li Yüan on His Return to Meander Valley (hereafter the "Li Yüan Valediction") were written before Han Yü's first southern exile.[9] They are best studied as embodiments of the doctrines of the first stage of his *ku-wen* program—namely, "learning from the ancients" and "expurgation of all clichés."

By "learning" (*hsüeh,* "to learn," "to study"; or *shih,* "to model oneself after," "to hold as a teacher"), Han Yü meant more than imitating the language of the ancients. As he expressed it in another early work, the "Letter in Answer to Liu Cheng-fu":

> If someone should ask me whom one should take as a model in literary writings, I would respectfully answer that one should take the ancient sages and worthies as one's models. If he should point out, "But the works of the ancient sages and worthies are preserved in variant wordings; which wording should I accept?" I would respectfully answer that he should take the ideas as his model and not the wording.[10]

To Han Yü, "learning from the ancients" is ideally a meeting of the mind. This discipline differs qualitatively from imitation: a true act of "learning" does not "take as a model" the text created by a great mind; rather it "takes as a model" the mind itself, the ideas expressed in the text.

Further on in the same letter, Han Yü resorts to historical and practical examples to prove that *ch'i* ("the extraordinary") is a desirable object of learning and a sign of true greatness:

> Men take no notice of the hundred and one objects they see day and night. But when they see something extraordinary, they notice it and talk about it. Is the case of literature any different? Many men of the Han dynasty were competent in letters, but only Ssu-ma Hsiang-ju, the Grand Historian [Ssu-ma Ch'ien], and Liu Hsiang were considered outstanding. This is because it is those who apply

themselves long and hard who are remembered by posterity. As to those who drift with the times and do not hold any distinction of originality, they may not be criticized by their contemporaries, but their names will certainly not be perpetuated by later generations. For every one of your sundry household articles you have no doubt some use, but the items that you consider precious must have something extraordinary about them. Why should a gentleman's attitude toward literature be any different?

This emphasis on the importance of the extraordinary is in line with the doctrine of "expurgating all clichés" expressed in the "Letter to Li Yi." But the "Letter in Answer to Liu Cheng-fu" defines in more specific terms what Han Yü considered to be central to the great classical writings and what, at this stage of his literary development, seemed the most important quality one should strive for. It also constitutes the principle underlying the "Examination Letter" and the "Li Yüan Valediction."

*Letter Written While Attending the Civil Service Examination*

By the shore of the celestial pool, by the strand of the great river, they say there lurks a strange creature. It is not of the same species as ordinary creatures with scales or shells. When it is in the water, it controls the wind and the rain and rises up to the sky without any difficulty. But when it is out of the water, be it a matter of yards, feet, or even inches, even when there are no high mountains or wild expanses, nine times out of ten it becomes stranded and cannot betake itself to the water, and thus it becomes the laughing stock of the otters and beavers.

Should a great personage take pity on it in its plight and give it a push or a turn, all that is necessary is a jerk of the arm and a kick of the foot. But this creature, proud of being different from the rest, says to itself, "I have no wish to die in the sand and mud, but it is not my intention to bow my head, droop my ears, wag my tail, and beg for pity." As a result, great personages pass by without noticing the creature right under their noses; and there is no knowing whether it will live or die. Now another great personage stands before it. This time the creature raises its head and utters a great howl, and waits to see what will happen. There is no telling whether the great personage may not take pity on its plight and, unmindful of the effort required by a jerk of the arm and a kick of the foot, transport it to the limpid waves. Whether or not he pities it is a matter of fate. To raise a great howl while knowing it is determined by fate is itself fated. My present plight is not unlike the plight of that strange creature. Hence I am making this appeal, oblivious to all proper manners. May Your Honor give the appeal your sympathetic consideration.

The "Examination Letter" bears a salutation; otherwise we might not recognize it as a letter. It is practically a parable, much in the style and spirit of the *Chuang-tzu*.[11] Indeed, some critics of Han Yü have taken the work as an imitation of the parables in the *Chuang-tzu* and considered the mixture of epistolary form with parable as proof of Han Yü's predilection for the extraordinary.[12] However, we must not forget that Han Yü's writing, though striving for the extraordinary, usually has an ideological dimension. The "Examination Letter" is also an objective lesson in expurgating the clichés that pervaded the parables, fables, and supernatural tales of its day. Han Yü's adaptation of the classical parable in the "Examination Letter" and his recreation of an archaic form and style were not intended merely to be extraordinary.

Li Chia-yen, in a study published in 1934, pointed out that the classical revival advocated by Han Yü was not merely a literary revolt against the parallel-prose tradition of the Southern Dynasties; more specifically, it was an ideological revolt against the Buddhist influences present in that literature,[13] influences, it might be added, that did not cease with the fall of the Southern Dynasties. Certainly, the beginnings of the *ku-wen* movement in the early T'ang did bring changes in the manner of contemporary writing, but the Buddhist voice in literary expression was by no means silenced. And Taoism, with the patronage of the ruling Li family, who claimed Lao-tzu as their ancestor,[14] suddenly rose in political status and gained a more favorable position in its long-standing rivalry with Buddhism in the spheres of philosophy, religion, social concerns, and literature. Many eminent writers of the century who claimed to be political or literary reformers of the Confucian school were at the same time followers of Buddhism or Taoism. Li Po (701–62), for instance, sang as enthusiastically about the Taoist quest for immortality as he did about the revival of the classical ideals of *chen* ("genuineness") and *ch'un* ("purity") in literature.[15]

The poetry of Wang Wei (699–759) was known for its Ch'an spirit. Po Chü-yi (772–846), publicly a Confucian scholar, a political reformer, and a classicist, was a Buddhist in private. Among *ku-wen* theorists were such T'ien-t'ai Buddhist disciples as Li Hua and Liang Su and such Taoist erudites as Tu-ku Chi. To these theorists, Taoism, Buddhism, and Confucianism presented no problem of incompatibility. Rather, these schools represented three different systems of values and of models for personal fulfillment, which, at various times and under different circumstances, could be cultivated singly or together in perfect harmony.

Contemporary with this Buddhist and Taoist influence in high literary society was the inundation of the world of popular literature by Buddhist and Taoist writings. *Pien-wen* ("transformation texts"), for instance, were a well-known literary vehicle of popular T'ang Buddhism. *Ch'uan-ch'i* ("tales of marvels"), a prose form that matured in the eighth century, made much use of Buddhist and Taoist myths. Compilations of literary and popular anecdotes were filled with omens, portents, and magical exploits illustrating the potency of Taoist and Buddhist magic and the supernatural power of priests and monks.[16] Indeed, the entire category of *hsiao-shuo* ("small talk" or "fiction") writings was encumbered with all the Taoist and Buddhist extravagances that Han Yü deplored. The entire literary milieu was suffused with what he considered heterodox influences, and it is not surprising that he was attacking more than merely the already embattled literary tradition of parallel prose. Han Yü in fact never initiated any heavy-handed attack on the parallel-prose style per se or as a vehicle of Buddhist religion. Writers at that time who showed a propensity toward Buddhism, Taoism, or syncretism in their outlook were no longer parallel-prose writers but classical stylists of the newest vintage. In other words, the decadence of the parallel-prose tradition had become a stale issue by Han Yü's time; it had lost pertinence either as the literary or the ideological antithesis to the *ku-wen* movement. What was "false" to Han Yü was not so much the parallel-prose tradition as the non-Confucian Taoist and Buddhist traditions, and what was "impure" was not the extravagant emphasis on the formal beauty of various parallelisms but the Taoist and Buddhist elements in current writings. Han Yü's reiteration of the classical-revival theme, therefore, should be clearly distinguished from the classical-revival movement of Hsiao Ying-shih and Li Hua. This is a reform movement within the *ku-wen* movement itself, as opposed to the previous reform movement, which had principally been a reaction against the parallel-prose tradition.

Han Yü's adaptation of the classical parable in his "Examination Letter" was "extraordinary" in both literary and ideological terms. From the literary point of view, its style ran counter to many of the formal features of parallel prose. From the ideological point of view, the letter turned away from the more superstitious expression of the Buddhist and Taoist myths and made the parable conform in form and function to its classical archetype.

To counter the influence of parallel prose, Han Yü offered the classical parable as an artistic device to demonstrate his doctrines of "learning from the ancients" and "expurgating all clichés." For each cliché of parallelism, the "Examination Letter" proposes an alternative by directing attention to a classical antecedent.[17] Thus, while eschewing ornate literary allusions, Han Yü created a parable. In describing the monster, instead of relying on elegant variation of synonyms and symmetry of syntax, he deliberately employed archaisms and crude repetition of words and phrases: *kuai-wu* ("strange creature," "marvelous creature"), *shih wu* ("this creature"), *ch'i* ("it"), *ch'i te shui* ("when it is in the water"), *ch'i pu-chi shui* ("when it is out of the water"), and *pu-neng tzu chih hu shui* ("cannot betake itself to the water"). And instead of the regulated four-six rhythm of parallel prose, he used a great number of particles—*kai, ku, jan*—designed to disrupt the four-six beat and create in its place a free-flowing cadence.[18]

In the process of reconciling the form and function of the parable to those of the archetype, Han Yü conscientiously underlines the illustrative or symbolic aspect of his supernatural creature and departs from the conventional practice of *hsiao-shuo*. In T'ang-*hsiao-shuo*, supernatural beings similar to the one in Han Yü's "Examination Letter" were often presented as real and were generally regarded by the people and officials alike as portents of fortune or calamity. The latter believed that Taoist priests and Buddhist monks, especially those of the Tantric sect,[19] possessed magical power over these supernatural beings and often asked them to use this power to avert calamities, exorcise evil spirits, and secure blessings such as timely rain. The conventional *hsiao-shuo* and pseudo-historical records, in recording such events, affirmed the super-human power of Taoist priests and Buddhist monks and became an influential literary medium for spreading superstition. Han Yü's illustrative parable, with its final self-interpretation as a metaphor rather than a realistic account, is, however, a *hsiao-shuo* cleansed of superstition. When Han Yü employed the form and style of a classical parable in the "Examination Letter," not only was he trying to achieve the "extraordinary" in the technical sense, but he was also trying, by means of his nonconventional treatment, by example, to "expurgate" current Taoist and Buddhist "clichés" from *hsiao-shuo* writing. In this sense, Han Yü's predilection for the extraordinary cannot be interpreted as a matter of style alone: it is intimately related both to his doctrine of "learning from the ancients" and to his anti–Buddhist and anti–Taoist ideology.

In several other early works, Han Yü made the same attempt to transform the ordinary into the extraordinary and the contemporary into the classical, with varying degrees of ingenuity. These works aroused little admiration and incurred much criticism. P'ei Tu (765–839), a statesman and friend of Han Yü's, criticized him for his "frivolous" treatment of literature.[20] According to Ch'ien Mu, Chang Chi's (766–829) criticism of Han Yü's taste for "mixed unreal stories" as "infamous" was specifically directed at these works.[21] The feeling persisted that Han Yü's repeated failures in the civil service examinations and his inability to find official employment were partly a result of his circulation of examples of such work in a misguided effort to impress examiners.[22]

Aside from its stylistic and doctrinal interest, the "Examination Letter" is not a successful presentation of Han Yü's ideal of the "extraordinary." The imitative act here, unsustained by elevating context, tends to lapse into the very mimicry Han Yü expressly wished to avoid. What is "extraordinary" about the "Examination Letter" is obviously its manner of expression—that is, its choice of such eccentric characters as the "strange creature" and "beavers and otters" and the adoption of pseudo–archaic language. The personal plight that these characters illustrate is not "extraordinary" in itself. The creature, pitifully caught between its own arrogance and its urgent need for help, has neither the disinterested wisdom nor the compensating innocence of an animal in a true classical parable. At the time that he wrote the "Examination Letter," Han Yü evidently was perceptive enough to see the need for and the possibility of achieving the effect of "extraordinariness" through "imitation of the ancients" and "expurgating all clichés," but his conceptual power and literary skills were not adequate to give form to his theoretical vision. Eight years later, when he made another attempt at the "extraordinary" in his "Li Yüan Valediction," we see an artist emerging, with all his former zest for novelty and audacity intact but free of gaucherie and crudeness.

In form, the "Li Yüan Valediction" is a *hsü* ("preface"). The *hsü*, in its earliest form, was an introductory essay to a book or a chapter in a book. Its purpose, according to the Ch'ing dynasty scholar Chang Hsüeh-ch'eng (1738–1801), was "to evince the aim and scope of a work, not to make a display of its own beauty and elegance."[23] The most notable early examples of this kind of *hsü* are K'ung An-kuo's (fl. 2d century B.C.) preface to the *Shu ching*, P'u Tzu-hsia's (507–420? B.C.) "Great Preface" to the *Shih ching*, and Ssu-ma Ch'ien's (145?–186? B.C.) prefaces to the *Shih chi* and its individual chapters, all written in the Han dynasty.[24]

In the same period, another type of preface, more literary than scholarly in nature, developed together with the *fu* ("rhymeprose") genre. Conceived as a prologue rather than an essay, it was meant to set the scene in the reader's imagination for the rhapsodic descriptions to follow, not to characterize the work. Yet the *hsü* achieved the status of a minor literary genre in its own right during the third and fourth centuries A.D. Often introductory to collections of occasional poems—the product of a new fashion for social gatherings among literary coteries—this type of preface was intensely personal. Famous examples, such as the Preface to the *Chin-ku Poems* by Shih Ch'ung (d. 300) and the Preface to the *Lan-t'ing Poems* by Wang Hsi-chih (321–79),[25] came to be read and anthologized separately for their own brilliance. For that reason, and because of their use during social gatherings, such prefaces are frequently confused with the *sung-hsü* ("valediction"), which shares with the earlier form its use on social occasions but dispenses altogether with its poems.[26]

In retrospect, we can say that the *sung-hsü* is a distinct, minor prose form that emerged early in the T'ang dynasty and that it differs from its predecessors in two basic respects: it is a totally independent composition (it is not prefatory to anything), and it is always addressed to a particular person.[27] In most cases, the *sung-hsü* written before Han Yü are dull and stereotyped: in many examples of this minor prose form, hyperbole and literary allusion dramatize the farewell party and exalt the site of both the leave-taking and the destination.[28]

Let us now consider Han Yü's "Valediction to Li Yüan on His Return to Meander Valley" (801) to see how he managed to ex-purgate the clichés that had developed in that prose form.[29]

To the south of T'ai-hang Mountain is the P'an ["meander"] Valley, where the springs are sweet and the soil fertile. Meadows and groves abound and thrive, but the inhabitants are few. Some say the valley is named *P'an* because it winds between two mountain ranges. Others say that, being secluded and sequestered, the valley is a place where recluses meander [*p'an*]. My friend Li Yüan lives there.

This is what Yüan says: "I know what that man, whom people call a great man, is like. He is the one who bestows benefits on the people and whose renown dazzles his time. When he presides over the court, he summons and dismisses the court officials and assists the emperor in issuing ordinances. When he is on tour, flags and banners are carried high and bows and arrows are brandished in array, armed men march shouting in front and the retinue follows filling the streets, while the attendants, each bearing his assigned object, gallop at full speed down both sides of the road. When pleased, he metes out rewards; when angered, he metes out punishment. Talented and able men crowd before him, discoursing about the past and present and drawing attention to his illustrious virtue; and his ears are not irritated by listening. His women—with arched eyebrows and plump cheeks, clear voices and attractive figures, elegant appearance and gracious disposition, their weightless gowns fluttering and their long sleeves used as veils, their faces powdered fair and [eyebrows] painted dark—live idly in their lodgings arranged in rows, each jealous of the other because of favors granted and each proud of her special position; each competing with her charm in order to win the lord's attention. This is the comportment of the great man when he ingratiates himself with the emperor and is in a position to wield his power over the empire.[30] It is not that I abhor this way of life and therefore have fled it. In fact, such things are a matter of fate, and one cannot come by them by luck.

"[When a great man is not visited by good fortune], he is disposed to live in indigence and reside in the countryside and to ascend the high hills and gaze into the distance, to spend the day sitting under the luxuriant foliage of a tree and to clean himself bathing in the limpid spring, to pick the mountain fruits and berries, so pleasing to the palate, and to catch fish in the stream, so fresh and edible. He has no regular hours of rising or retiring but does as he pleases. How much better it is to suffer no condemnation later than to receive all the compliments at the outset, and how much better to have no worries at heart than to enjoy the pleasures of the body. Unencumbered by carriages and robes and untouched by torturing knives and saws, unaware of order and chaos, and uninformed about promotions and demotions—this is how a great man lives when good fortune does not come his way. I will do the same. What a contrast between this way of life and the way of those who wait at the gates of dignitaries and scurry along the road of posts and power, who falter before they proceed and stammer before they speak, who live in filth and feel no shame, and who violate the law and are condemned to capital punishment. Even if such people should be lucky enough to keep going until they die of old age, how striking is the contrast between the way of life of the worthy and that of the unworthy."

Han Yü of Ch'ang-li heard Li Yüan's speech and considered it great. Offering him a toast, he sang this song for him:

In Meander Valley your palace stands.
The Meander soil is good for tilling.
The Meander springs are good for bathing and strolling.
The Meander seclusion bars contention from your abode.
Recessed and withdrawn, what an expanse it embraces;
Coiling and winding, the roads lead hither and thither.

Ah! the pleasures of Meander, pleasures pure and carefree.
Tigers and leopards keep their tracks at a distance;
Reptiles and dragons skulk and hide.
Spirits and gods are ever watchful to ward off wicked
    things.
Eating and drinking, one lives long in good health.
With nothing lacking, what is there more to wish for?
Grease my carriage, feed my horse.
Let me join you in Meander, to spend my life in indolent
    idleness.

The title indicates four traditional motifs of the *sung-hsü*: the leave-taking, the destination, the return to that destination as a ful-fillment, and the author's farewell gesture. A conventional treat-ment of the first two motifs would require conventional compli-ments, couched in terms expressing recognized social values and enumerating official achievements, and allusions to ancient sages and eminent figures. Han Yü has avoided both of these stereotypes. Instead of dramatizing Meander Valley by means of hyperbole, he adopts with startling simplicity the lucid style of the *yu-chi* ("records of excursions"). Meander Valley, unlike the bank of the winding stream where the Lan-t'ing gathering took place, has no historical or mythical glamor, and so Han Yü merely enumerates in his introduction a few simple facts about the location of the valley and its legends and inhabitants. The details are specific but not trivial. Although certain details are rendered ambiguous by the repetitious use of "some say," they are not fanciful distortions of fact paraded as time-honored local lore.[31] The tempo thus created is at once brisk and exciting; the style artistically transcends all the flatness inherent in the subject itself.

After this brief introduction, Han Yü passes on to a description of the farewell party, to Li Yüan and his "return."[32] Here, he succeeds in eulogizing without falling into overworked and meaningless compliments, in commending Li Yüan's voluntary retirement without casting him in the conventional image of an eccentric disdainfully keeping himself aloof from the mundane world.[33] Han Yü achieves this delicate balance by means of a unique artistic device: he lets Li Yüan speak for himself. The second unit of the "Li Yüan Valediction" is a long soliloquy. The diction in the soliloquy is strongly reminiscent of Mencius, recalling Han Yü's early intellectual allegiance.[34] The same artful device of diverting the audience's attention from familiar subject matter to stylistic innovation that is found in the parable of the "Examination Letter" is exercised here. The age-old conflict of court and country is dramatically transformed into two lively, absorbing, antithetical portraits of what constitutes a "great man."

The third and last part of the preface begins with a song epilogue, sung by Han Yü, who approves and praises the choice his friend has made. In this passage, Han Yü introduces his most surprising technical innovation: he adapts the meter and diction of the two oldest and most venerated Chinese poetic traditions to his work. The first half of the song, written in the meter and style of the *Shih ching* odes, celebrates with borrowed austerity the bucolic setting of Meander Valley. The second half of the song, written in the meter and style of the *Ch'u tz'u*, appropriates the religious solemnity of its model and invokes divine blessings on Li Yüan and on his life in the valley. The shift in the middle from the *Shih ching* meter to the *Ch'u tz'u* meter (between "Coiling and winding, the roads lead hither and thither" and "Ah! the pleasures of Meander, pleasures pure and carefree") emphasizes a subtle transition in the lyric content of the piece and impressionistically magnifies the desired "extraordinary" effect of Han Yü's stylistic innovation. The song concludes on the climactic note of return (*kuei*) and is poetically resolved in Han Yü's accompanying gesture of farewell: he offers to join his friend in his idyllic abode.

The "Li Yüan Valediction," the culminating expression of Han Yü's early style, is a work of sheer literary virtuosity. The poetry manifests an extraordinary suppleness as Han Yü imitates and integrates his ancient models into a personal mastery of writing that is not present in his earlier works. Here Han Yü proves not only that he can handle a minor literary form with ease and grace but, more significantly, that he is able to liberate the form from the stiffness and formality that had encrusted it for more than a century. The archaism, the dramatic soliloquy, the graceful song, all coalesce in the "Li Yüan Valediction" to give expression to Han Yü's originality and artistic mastery. Together they constitute the realization of Han Yü's aspiration to create a unique "ancient-prose" style, a style in the image of the ancient works but impressive for its own extraordinary effect.

Su Shih, an ardent admirer of Han Yü's literary genius, is said to have remarked of the "Li Yüan Valediction":

> His Excellency Ou-yang Wen-chung-kung [Hsiu] said that the Chin dynasty had no literature except "The Return" by T'ao Yüan-ming [365–427]. And I would say that the T'ang dynasty had no literature except Han T'ui-chih's "Valediction to Li Yüan on His Return to Meander Valley." All my life I have wanted to imitate that work. But every time I picked up my brush, I hesitated. I laughed to myself and said, "Why not let T'ui-chih remain peerless." [35]

Thus did Su Shih, himself a great literary innovator and a consummate stylist, pay tribute to the first sign of Han Yü's genius. In placing Han Yü's "Li Yüan Valediction" by the side of T'ao Yüan-ming's "The Return," Su Shih certainly was not thinking of the emotional maturity or spiritual depth of the work. In neither respect can the "Li Yüan Valediction" be compared to "The Return." Su Shih probably juxtaposed the two works because of their similar expressions of feelings of intense joy at liberation from official life. In the "Li Yüan Valediction," the reader can sense the genuine delight that the author felt toward his subject. This delight, this harmony of the spirit with its external expression, ultimately transforms Han Yü the writer into Han Yü the poet.

Their largely experimental character notwithstanding, the "Examination Letter" and the "Li Yüan Valediction" represent the victories Han Yü won against his literary and ideological adversaries. Although their ingenuity and their whimsical, deft touch fall short of the austere grandeur that was to typify Han Yü's fully developed prose style, they reveal the same creative genius and the same vision of *ku-wen*.

## The Principle of Uniqueness (2): The Awakening of Art

The interval of 17 years between the "Li Yüan Valediction" and the "Memorial Inscription on the Pacification of the Huai-hsi Rebellion" (hereafter the "Huai-hsi Inscription") was an eventful one in Han Yü's personal and official life. This period was also formative in his second stage of development as a *ku-wen* stylist. Just as the first stage of Han Yü's literary achievement can be summarized by invoking his doctrines of "learning from the ancients" and "expurgation of all clichés," so the second stage can be characterized by another of his doctrines, that of *tz'u-shih hsiang-ch'eng* ("expression appropriate to the topic").[36] The doctrine of *tz'u-shih hsiang-ch'eng* was a direct product of Han Yü's emotional experience with *ch'iung* ("at the end of one's resources") during this part of his life and his resultant new outlook on *kung* ("craft," "artistry").[37]

In those 17 years, Han Yü experienced many adversities and much personal growth. In 801, after years of bitter and desperate waiting, he finally received his first official appointment in the capital as an academician in the Ssu-men Academy; in 802, he was made a censor. But in the following year, his outspokenness against those in power at the court brought his first banishment to the extreme south.[38] When Emperor Hsien-tsung ascended the throne in 805, Han Yü was summoned back to the capital, only to be shunted from post to post during the next few years. If the uncertainty of his position upset his equilibrium, it also contributed to his intellectual maturation. His banishment to the south, oddly enough, was an enriching experience; it afforded him opportunities to reflect on his ideals of the life of a Confucian scholar. Reality there challenged him to summon the strength and courage to transform the ideals into action. The southern climate was stimulating in an adverse way. The southern people, who did not observe Confucian social etiquette, strengthened Han Yü's conviction of the values and excellences of Confucian society and the superiority of Confucian culture. The Taoist priests and Buddhist monks, probably the only intellectuals in this region and certainly the predominant influence in the lives of the common folk, particularly fascinated Han Yü with their religious eloquence and repelled him with their heretical doctrines and practices. In his frequent exchanges with these priests and monks, his instinct for polemic was sharpened. The leisure of banishment enabled him to mobilize his forces against the Taoist and Buddhist heresies. His prose style, and his intellectual vigor, underwent a significant change. In his well-known polemical writings of this period, such as "On the True Way" and "On the True Nature of Man,"[39] his earlier poetic innovations gave way to the vigorous logic of argument expressed in an equally vigorous prose.

These polemical encounters challenged Han Yü's conceptual powers and literary skills in a way totally different from that of his previous skirmishes with the parable form or with the clichés of parallel prose. The vital struggle of ideas called for a different style. In this battle, his purpose was not to create values through "extraordinary" stylistic innovations, but to use language so that it would convey fully, forcefully, and convincingly the system of ideas he was defending.

As these practical considerations were urging Han Yü toward a more craftsmanlike view of style, his emotional experience was demanding a concomitant change in his general outlook on life and literature.

Before his exile, Han Yü had toyed with the metaphysical question of the birth of literature. At that point in his career as a writer, the genesis of literature had seemed intimately related to some displacement of the individual in his world: people wrote when they lost their equanimity; this process seemed as natural as the surging of water agitated by the wind. In the same way, literary excellence was a natural phenomenon. Those who were born more gifted naturally wrote with more skill. Han Yü had advanced this theory of literature as the natural voice of genius in his "Valediction to Meng Tung-yeh" (801),[40] at a time when he was advocating the theory of conscientiously imitating the ancients and cultivating one's literary sensibility in the "Letter to Li Yi."

Han Yü's experience during his southern banishment made clear to him that neither genius nor strict conformance to orthodoxy was sufficient for the production of great literature. He had learned by then, from the caprice of the emperor and the treachery of his fellow officials,[41] what such a displacement could signify in a person's life. Through his own experience, he came to understand how the practical misery of a life in exile and the disheartening prospect of never regaining the emperor's favor could exaggerate the loss of personal equanimity and develop into a metaphysical sense of ch'iung, of having reached the end of his resources. Contrary to his earlier theory of literary creativity, the immediate result of this pervasive sense of ch'iung did not lead to a spontaneous flow of masterpieces. Rather, such a state of mind seemed to spell defeat—defeat of his own person and defeat of the higher principles that he had championed. The term ch'iung occurred frequently in Han Yü's writings immediately following the banishment, and the concept reoriented his theory of literature.[42]

At first, Han Yü was extremely bitter about this debilitating state of ch'iung, full of resentment and self-pity; but gradually he began to analyze the condition with greater detachment. He discovered that the crippling effect of ch'iung was only local and temporary; his principles and his values were still intact and would remain unaffected by material conditions. He could strive for these values and even attain them once his situation had changed for the better. Meanwhile, he saw no reason why he could not continue to live by his principles despite his unjust and cruel repudiation, which, after all, reflected more the blindness of others than his own unworthiness. Thus persuaded by pride and reason, Han Yü even found a certain satisfaction in fighting for an unseasonable cause and defending the right in its dark hours. As a result, he was able to accept ch'iung and even resigned himself to it with a certain self-irony, as can be seen in his essay "Seeing off Ch'iung" (811).[43] This essay contains an imaginary dialogue between the author and the five demons of ch'iung—ch'iung in wisdom, learning, literature, fate, and friendship. He attempts to send them away, but they refuse to leave. They mock him and say,

> You know our names and all that we do. But to drive us out is a
> great stupidity, though it may seem a small bit of cleverness. How
> long does a man live in this world? We will make you a name that
> will not be forgotten for a hundred generations. It is the mind that
> distinguishes the mean man from the gentleman. Only when you
> are at odds with the world are you in touch with Heaven.

His intense struggle with the realities of *ch'iung* taught Han Yü a
profound moral lesson. He finally realized that he should not have
considered his material success or failure as the measure of the
worth of his values. It is the mind, the inner power to abide by
one's values in spite of external degradation or glory, that distinguishes a principled man from an unprincipled one.

Once reconciled to the discrepancy between his fate and his aspirations, Han Yü was able to see not only where he stood in regard
to principles and ideals but, furthermore, where he and these principles and ideals stood in the context of his time and his world. He
became keenly aware that facts and events are not only inarticulate
but frequently misleading because people tend to judge men and
their actions on the basis of material advancement or failure.
Therefore, the duty of a writer, as the moral spokesman of his time,
is to distinguish the right from the wrong and from that which,
though right, still falls short of the highest order. Having sharpened
his intellectual and literary skills in the battle of ideas against his
Taoist and Buddhist opponents, and having passed through a
moral and spiritual crisis in his struggle against the demon *ch'iung*,
Han Yü experienced in his life what he had earlier posited in words
as the second stage in the development of a writer: "Then I was
able to discern truth and falsehood in the ancient works, as well as
those which, though true, still fell short of perfection...and I applied myself diligently to the elimination of them [the false and
inferior]." [44]

A preoccupation with artistry, the means of expressing his literary and moral vision, displaced Han Yü's earlier single-minded
pursuit of the "extraordinary." The "Eulogy of Po-yi," [45] written
when this new principle first obsessed him, expresses a more universal conception of *kung*—literary art—which he later defined as
the doctrine of *tz'u-shih hsiang-ch'eng*. The "Eulogy of Po-yi" de-

scribes a "great man," and its values resemble those of the "Li Yüan Valediction." But there the resemblance stops. Conceptually and stylistically, these two works represent two different mentalities. In the "Li Yüan Valediction," Han Yü at first stresses the moral quality of Li Yüan's "return" but then intertwines the aesthetic with the moral and confusedly supplies an artistic instead of a moral justification for Li Yüan's act. The tranquillity, purity, and delight with which he portrays Li Yüan's voluntary retirement from public life grossly misrepresent the true stoic spirit of this retreat. In the "Eulogy of Po-yi," there is no such confusion. Han Yü has discovered that people like Po-yi, Li Yüan, and himself, who prefer to live by their "heart," could never base their choice to retire on the aesthetic view that he had previously celebrated. Such a choice, when made, is profoundly moral and should be presented as a manifestation of the spiritual superiority of the man and of his unusual courage. For this reason, the style of the "Eulogy of Po-yi" differs perceptibly from that of the "Li Yüan Valediction." There is no ponderous poetic intrusion; instead, Han Yü confines himself to statements that demonstrate the nature and moral stature of Po-yi's personality. The eulogy makes use not of freedom of expression but of control, not of ingenious variations but of terse definitions and purposeful repetitions, not of exquisite sentiment or poetic exultation but of sober and well-reasoned criticism.

However, if the "Li Yüan Valediction" is representative of Han Yü's first stage of literary achievement and a culminating expression of the stylistic principles that he advocated at that stage, the "Eulogy of Po-yi" gives only a limited demonstration of what can be achieved with his new conception of literary art—that of *tz'u-shih hsiang-ch'eng*. Not until he wrote the "Huai-hsi Inscription" did Han Yü find a subject magnificent enough to serve as a full measure of the literary potential of this new principle.

Han Yü wrote the "Huai-hsi Inscription" to celebrate the success of the famous Huai-hsi expedition of 815–17, which marked an upturn in the fortunes of the T'ang dynasty. At the end of the An Lu-shan rebellion (755–63), the provinces of China were run by regional military governors who chose their own successors and were ready to rise against the central government if it threatened their autonomy. The emperors Tai-tsung (r. 762–79) and Te-tsung (r. 779–805), through a combination of diplomacy and military

force, had reasserted central authority over most of the provinces.[46] When the emperor Hsien-tsung (r. 805–20) refused to con-
firm the position of a self-appointed successor to the governorship
of Huai-hsi, that province rose in rebellion. When, after three years
of fighting, the imperial armies were successful, the court and the
nation were overjoyed. Commemoration of the triumph with an
inscription carved on stone was deemed appropriate, and Han Yü
was assigned to compose the text, which he presented to the throne
early in 818.

The "Huai-hsi Inscription" soon came under attack for historical
inaccuracy.[47] Han Yü's account of the expedition was condemned
as deliberately de-emphasizing the role of Li Su, the general who
had actually won the victory, and giving excessive credit to P'ei
Tu, the chief minister who had held overall responsibility for pros-
ecuting the war and on whose staff Han Yü had served. Li Su, son
of a famous general and son-in-law of an imperial princess, carried
his complaint to the throne. The emperor ordered Han Yü's text
removed from the stele and ordered the Han-lin scholar Tuan
Wen-ch'ang (773–835) to compose a new one.

Ironically, later generations learned of the Huai-hsi expedition
not from Tuan Wen-ch'ang's accurate account, but from Han Yü's
brilliant if distorted version. Su Shih took note of this in one of his
two "Little Poems Found at the Lin-chiang Post Station":[48]

> The success of the Huai-hsi expedition crowned the glory of
>     T'ang.
> And the text of *Li-pu* [Han Yü] shines like the sun and the
>     moon.[49]
> His broken stele will be so engraved in people's memory in
>     the ensuing millennium,
> That the world will never know of Tuan Wen-ch'ang's
>     [account].

Poems like this are a reminder that Han Yü's "Huai-hsi Inscription" shines as a work of literature despite its many departures
from historical facts.[50] Yet little effort has been made to reconcile
the two accounts. It makes little sense to say that Han Yü deliberately distorted history either to gain the favor of P'ei Tu or for the
sake of literary showmanship. There is in fact a purpose behind the
apparent discrepancy between historical facts and the literary representation of these facts, and the key to that purpose emerges

from Han Yü's "Memorial to the Throne on the Presentation of the Memorial Inscription on the Pacification of the Huai-hsi Rebellion" (818).[51]

Your subject so-and-so speaks.

On the fourteenth of the first month [in 818], I received the edict in which you took note of the supplication of the officials to have the achievement in the recovery of Huai-hsi inscribed on stone so that it might be made known to the world and serve as a model for the future. Your Majesty was kind to me and allowed me to realize my wishes; you commissioned me to write the text of the inscription on the pacification of the Huai-hsi rebellion....

I humbly think that ever since antiquity, whenever a saintly and sage king achieved an outstanding deed, a special virtue, or a peerless feat, there has invariably been a scholar who was exceptionally talented, widely informed, and eloquent, born at the right time to hold the writing tablet and brush to record it. Each of these works had its own order, form, and sequence. And they filled heaven and earth magnificently and grandly with the splendor of the emperors and kings.

In the *Shu ching*, there are the two "Canons" of Yao and Shun, the "Yü-kung" of Hsia, the "P'an-keng" of Yin, and the five "Announcements" of Chou. In the *Shih ching*, the "Hsüan-niao" and "Ch'ang-fa" celebrate the imperial clan of Yin, and the "Ch'ing-miao," "Ch'en-kung," "Major Odes," and "Minor Odes" sing of the king of Chou. Their expression is worthy of the topic. And they are called "classics" for having contained at once goodness and splendor. They have been included in the curriculum of the imperial academies, and teachers and students have been enlisted for their study. From the beginning to the present, nobody has ever dared to criticize these works.

However, had it happened that the wrong man had been chosen to write such works, and had he written them in an obscure style and diction, then, who would care to read them even if the works contained such splendid subject matter? The deeds would have sunk into oblivion together with the writings, and good and evil would have been confused and would have merged into one.

Clearly Han Yü regarded the Huai-hsi expedition as comparable in magnitude to the great events celebrated in the *Shih ching* and the *Shu ching*, and his own principle of *tz'u-shih hsiang-ch'eng* dictated that he treat the Huai-hsi expedition with comparable grandeur. His references to the "Canons" of Yao and Shun, the "P'an-keng," and the "Announcements" in the *Shu ching* and to the hymns and odes such as "Hsüan-niao" and "Ch'ing-miao" in the *Shih ching* have a double significance. On the literary level, these references make explicit the sources of Han Yü's literary inspiration and the models that his "Huai-hsi Inscription" emulated in style and diction. On the conceptual level, they provide a key to the structural principle behind Han Yü's work.

According to Ts'ai Yung (A.D. 133–92), the great Han dynasty master of inscription writing, "the *Ch'un-ch'iu* held that in bronze inscriptions [the record should concentrate on] the virtue of the Son of Heaven and the commands he issued, the timely advice of the feudal lords and their achievements, and the military actions of the grandees."[52] In view of the fact that Han Yü adhered to the diction and style of the Confucian classics even to the extent of violating current usage,[53] it is possible that he went further and adopted the principle behind ancient Confucian inscriptions for the "Huai-hsi Inscription." If this is true, then the many inaccuracies in the "Huai-hsi Inscription" assume a meaningful pattern. Han Yü's concentration on the "virtue" of the T'ang emperors (especially at the beginning of the inscription) and on the commands that Hsien-tsung issued corresponds exactly with the *Ch'un-ch'iu*'s first requirement for an ancient inscription. Similarly, his emphasis on the role of P'ei Tu involves no distortion of fact but is another aspect of the same tradition: an inscription should record the "timely advice of the feudal lords and their achievements," P'ei Tu being the T'ang counterpart of an ancient feudal lord. The same applies to Li Su, who, as the T'ang counterpart of an ancient grandee, is remembered in the "Huai-hsi Inscription" for the military actions in which he engaged.

Thus, stylistically and conceptually, the apparent discrepancy between the historical facts and the "Huai-hsi Inscription" is part of a rational program conceived by Han Yü to elevate the language and ideals of his works to the level of a Confucian classic. Neither the departures from history nor the presence of archaic usages is randomly conceived. These apparent eccentricities are in fact intimately related to Han Yü's ideal of *ku-wen* style, and they reflect his unceasing efforts to revive the *ku-wen* tradition. In the "Huai-hsi Inscription," it is interesting to see which specific methods and techniques Han Yü used to accomplish his virtuoso recreation of a classical bronze inscription (*ming*).

*Memorial Inscription on the Pacification of the Huai-hsi Rebellion*

August Heaven, deeming the sovereigns of the House of T'ang its worthy sons and cognizant of the unflagging obedience and reverence paid to it by them, who, all sagelike and godlike, succeeded one after another for eons, has entrusted them with all that it covers; all within the domain enclosed by the Four Seas and coextensive with the Nine Provinces, regardless of distance, have invariably paid homage and offered allegiance to them. The emperors Kao-tsu and T'ai-tsung succeeded in extirpating the rebels and in making order prevail. The emperors Kao-tsung, Chung-tsung, and Jui-tsung gave the people repose and nurtured the country's growth. When it came to Hsüan-tsung, he reaped the harvest of all these labors, and the [T'ang] reached its acme of prosperity and wealth. As the population increased and the domain became vast, evil sprouted at this stage.[54] The emperors Su-tsung, Tai-tsung, Te-tsung, and Shun-tsung applied themselves assiduously to government affairs, but they tolerated the sprouts of evil. After the eradication of the chief malefactors [An Lu-shan and Shih Ssu-ming], not all weeds were uprooted.[55] Ministers and generals indulged in relaxation; they grew accustomed to the status quo and took everything for granted.

When His Majesty Jui-sheng wen-wu [that is, Emperor Hsien-tsung] accepted homage from his multitudinous officials, he wished to exact tributes in accordance with the records [i.e., he wished to make the provinces obedient]. He said, "Alas! Heaven having entrusted the entire empire to our House, sovereignty has now passed to me; should I be unable to attend to my duties, how am I to present myself at the sacrifices to Heaven and at the imperial Ancestral Temple?"

The many officials, shaken and terrified, hurried and ran to carry out their respective duties. In the following year, Hsia was pacified.[56] And in the year following, Shu was pacified.[57] And in the year following, Chiang-tung was pacified. And in the year following, Tse and Lu were pacified. Then Yi and Ting were brought under control.[58] Similarly, neither Wei, Po, Pei, Shan, nor Hsiang stood against the imperial will.[59]

The emperor said, "We shall not resort to our armed forces endlessly. We shall give our people some rest."

In the ninth year [of the Yüan-ho era, 814], the general of Ts'ai died. The people of Ts'ai set up his son [Wu] Yüan-chi [as their governor] and petitioned for the emperor's sanction.[60] Their request was not granted. Then they burned Wu-yang, invaded Yeh and Hsiang-ch'eng, jolted the Eastern Capital, and unleashed their troops to plunder the surrounding regions. The emperor sought counsel from his court. With the exception of one or two officials, all said, "For fifty years, the commanders of Ts'ai have not been appointed by the court. Its governorship has passed successively to four of their own generals from three different families.[61] Its roots are firmly planted, its arms and weapons strong, and its soldiers hardy. Its position is without challenge. If we try to win it over through appeasement, then it will behave agreeably and cause no trouble." The dignitaries sounded confident, and everybody sang the same tune. They were unanimous in their opinion and unswerving in their conviction.

The emperor said, "Heaven and our ancestors entrusted the world to us with a view to situations like this. How dare I not do my best? Moreover, as there are still one or two ministers who are of my mind, I am not completely without support."[62]

He said, "[Li] Kuang-yen, you shall be the commander of Ch'en and Hsü. You are to command all the forces in the three armies of Ho-tung, Wei-po, and Ho-yang."

He said, "[Wu] Ch'ung-yin, you used to govern Ho-yang and Huai.[63] Now I assign you Ju-[chou] in addition. You are to command all the forces in the seven armies of Shuo-fang, Yi-ch'eng, Shan, Yi, Feng-hsiang, Yen, and Ch'ing."

He said, "[Han] Hung, you shall take twelve thousand soldiers and go with your son Kung-wu to attack the enemy."[64]

He said, "[Li] Wen-t'ung, you shall defend Shou and command all the forces in the four armies of Hsüan-wu, Huai-nan, Hsüan-hsi, and Che-hsi that are now stationed at Shou."

He said, "[Li] Tao-ku, you shall be inspector general of O-yüeh."[65]

He said, "[Li] Su, you shall command T'ang, Teng, and Sui and lead their armies to battle."[66]

He said, "[P'ei] Tu, you, as chief censor, shall go and review the armed forces."

He said, "[P'ei] Tu, you are the only one who is of one mind with me. You shall be my chief minister and mete out rewards to those who carry out their orders and punishments to those who do not."[67]

He said, "[Han] Hung, you shall be commander-in-chief of all the armies."[68]

He said, "[Liang] Shou-ch'ien, you have served by my side and are my intimate courtier. You shall go and inspect the armed forces."[69]

He said, "[P'ei] Tu, you shall go and give the warriors their clothes and food. Do not let them suffer from cold or hunger. Once the war is over, look after the livelihood of the people of Ts'ai. I bestow on you the insignia of an axe, a T'ung-t'ien girdle, and three hundred guards. You may choose your own retinue from my courtiers. Make their talent and competence your criteria of choice, and have no scruples about their high ranks. On the day keng-shen [in 815], I shall come personally to see you off at the city gate."[70]

He said, "Censors, I pity the warriors and officials for the hardship of their battle; from now on, let there be no music except for the sacrifices to Heaven and the sacrifices at our Ancestral Temple."

[Li Kuang-]yen, [Wu Ch'ung-]yin, and [Han Kung-]wu joined forces and attacked the enemy from the north. After sixteen battles, they occupied twenty-three stockades, fortresses, and country towns and forced forty thousand civilians and soldiers to surrender.

[Li] Tao-ku attacked from the southeast. He [and his troops] fought eight battles, and forced thirteen thousand men to surrender. He further penetrated to Shen-chou and breached its outer wall.

[Li] Wen-t'ung fought in the east. After more than ten encounters, he forced twelve thousand men to surrender.

[Li] Su penetrated the enemy's territory from the west. When he captured rebel generals, he invariably set them free and did not kill them. By means of this strategy [of employing the surrendered generals], he always won victories.[71]

In the eighth month of the twelfth year of the Yüan-ho era [817], Chief Minister [P'ei] Tu arrived in the field.[72] The commander-in-chief, [Han] Hung, pressed the fighting harder, and [Li Kuang-] yen, [Wu Ch'ung-]yin, and [Han Kung-]wu exerted themselves even more in their joint attack.

For his part, [Wu] Yüan-chi gathered all his forces together at Hui-ch'ü to prepare against the forthcoming attack of the imperial armies.

On the day jen-shen in the tenth month [of 817], [Li] Su, using a surrendered general and taking advantage of a snowstorm, set out from Wen-ch'eng and rode a hundred and twenty li at full speed. They arrived at Ts'ai that very night. They broke down the city gate and captured [Wu] Yüan-chi. They also took prisoners of [Wu] Yüan-chi's men and soldiers.

On the day hsin-ssu [in 817], Chief Minister [P'ei] Tu entered Ts'ai and announced an amnesty in the name of the emperor. After Huai-hsi was pacified, there were great feasts, and awards were meted out to those who earned merit.

On the day the imperial army was due to leave, they gave their food to the people of Ts'ai. Of the thirty-five thousand soldiers of Ts'ai that surrendered, nine out of ten preferred to return to farming rather than to continue to be soldiers. They were all released. [Wu] Yüan-chi was beheaded in the capital.

Appointments according to merit were made [as follows].[73] [Han] Hung was made a *shih-chung* (gentleman-in-waiting). [Li] Su was to be *tso-p'u-yeh* [deputy minister of the left] and to govern the Eastern Circuit of Shan-nan.[74] [Li Kuang-]yen and [Wu Ch'ung-]yin were both made *ssu-k'ung*, [Han] Kung-wu was to govern Fu-chou, Fang-chou, Tan-chou, and Yen-chou in the capacity of *san-ch'i ch'ang-shih*. [Li] Tao-ku was promoted to *ta-fu* [grandee]. And [Li] Wen-t'ung was made *san-ch'i ch'ang-shih*. Chief Minister [P'ei] Tu was enfeoffed duke of Chin while still on his way back to the capital and promoted to the rank of *chin-tzu kuang-lu ta-fu* while retaining his position as chief minister. His deputy [Ma] Tsung was made minister of public works and was appointed governor of Ts'ai.

Once the report on the expedition was completed, the officials petitioned to have His Majesty's achievement recorded on a stele. The emperor commissioned his subject [Han] Yü. And I, His Majesty's subject [Han] Yü, making obeisance [to His Majesty] again and again, present the following [*ming*].

T'ang received its mandate from Heaven and made the ten
    thousand states its subjects.
Who would have expected that the nearby states would
    descend to banditry and grow insubordinate?
During the emperor Hsüan-tsung's reign, the country, after
    glorious prosperity, began to decline.
The generals north of the river became arrogant and those
    south of the river rose up in their wake.[75]
The four sage ancestors [of the present emperor] would not
    tolerate such behavior; they frequently sent armies on
    expeditions.[76]
When their expeditions were not successful, they increased
    the troops with garrison soldiers.
Men tilled but could not enjoy the food; women wove but
    could not wear the clothes.
All [the produce of the land] was loaded into carts and sent
    to the soldiers as provisions.
The provincial governors would not come to pay their
    respects at court, and the emperors were unable to make
    their tours of the domain.

The sundry officials were lax in their duties, and the old
    usages were not carried out.
When the reigning emperor [Hsien-tsung] succeeded to the
    throne, he looked about him and sighed:
"Civil and military officials, which of you are solicitous for
    our House?"
After he quelled Wu and Shu, he reconquered the region
    east of the [T'ai-hang] Mountain.
The general of Wei first offered allegiance and the six
    prefectures surrendered.[77]
Huai and Ts'ai refused to submit, deeming themselves
    strong.
They marshalled their troops and raised a clamor; they
    would fain have continued in their old practice.[78]
When the order of expedition was issued, they formed an
    alliance with their miscreant neighbors.[79]
They secretly sent an assassin to harm His Majesty's chief
    minister.[80]
Although the battles were not successful, the assassination
    shook the capital.
The courtiers presented their opinions to the emperor and
    suggested winning the enemy with favors.
The emperor heeded not such counsel but consulted the
    spirits.[81]
His chief minister was of one mind with His Majesty and
    held that the enemy should be exterminated as Heaven
    decreed.
He then issued edicts to [Li Kuang-]yen, [Wu Ch'ung-]yin,
    [Li] Su, [Han Kung-]wu, [Li Tao-]ku, and [Li Wen-]
    t'ung,
Placing them all under the command of [Han] Hung, though
    each was assigned a different task.
The attack was conducted from three sides; and the enemy
    consisted of fifty thousand soldiers.
When the main force attacked in the north, the number of
    soldiers was doubled.
During the battle at Shih-ch'ü, our warriors fought none
    too bravely.
But once Ling-yün was cut off, the Ts'ai soldiers were
    greatly harassed.[82]
With the victory at Shao-ling, Yen-ch'eng came to
    surrender.[83]

When summer passed into autumn, the armies settled in the
military colonies and remained inactive.
The campaign was brought to a halt, and there were no
timely military achievements.
The emperor felt pity for the men at war; he ordered his
chief minister to go and oversee the situation.
Then the soldiers were well fed, and they broke out in song;
the horses moved restlessly by the troughs.
When they tried their force at Hsin-ch'eng, the rebels were
routed.
They collected all their remaining resources and gathered
themselves together to guard against us.
The western army broke in; there was nothing that could
withstand it.
The rebellious city of Ts'ai controlled a territory extending
over a thousand *li*;
Once the imperial army conquered it, none of its people
failed to submit.
The emperor had some gracious announcements, which
Chief Minister [P'ei] Tu proclaimed.[84]
The death penalty was for the leaders only; the followers
were all to be released.
[Hearing that], the soldiers of Ts'ai threw away their armor
and began to shout and dance.
The women of Ts'ai greeted each other at their doors,
laughing and chatting.
When the people of Ts'ai reported their hunger, shiploads of
grain were transported there to feed them.
When the people of Ts'ai reported that they were cold, silk
and cloth were bestowed upon them.
The people of Ts'ai used to be under restraint: they were not
allowed to interact socially.
Now they enjoy each other's company, and the village gates
are open at night.
The people of Ts'ai used to be driven to the battlefield and
were slaughtered if they retreated.
Now they rise when the day is bright and enjoy their food
freely and unhindered.
We choose the right men for them to attend to their other
wants.
We select officials for them and give them cattle; we instruct
them but levy no tax.

The people of Ts'ai say that they were misguided.
Now they are awakened to the right understanding, and
they feel ashamed of their former behavior.
The people of Ts'ai acknowledge the Son of Heaven as
perspicacious and sagelike.
He exterminates only the clans of those who are
insubordinate but spares the lives of the obedient ones.
If you do not believe my word, take a look at the example
of Ts'ai.
Whoever disobeys, the axe will sever his throat.[85]
Rebels have their predestined terms; they were mutually
dependent.
They could not withstand our superior force, and they
found themselves hopelessly weak.
Better run and tell this to your elders, to your fathers, and to
your brothers; ask them to hurry here and join us in our
peaceful life.
When Huai and Ts'ai stirred up disorder, the Son of Heaven
organized an expedition against them.
After the expedition, the people were hungry, and the Son
of Heaven revived them.
When the expedition against Ts'ai was first suggested, the
dignitaries and officials would not endorse it.
During the four years of the expedition, all men high and
low questioned its wisdom.[86]
The only one who did not regret and did not question was
our perspicacious Son of Heaven.
The successful completion of this expedition against Ts'ai
was brought about because of his determined decisions.
Once Huai and Ts'ai were brought to order, all the
barbarians from the four quarters came [to pay homage].
Then the *Ming-t'ang* door was opened so that our Emperor
may sit there and rule the world.[87]

Here, then, are two parts of the "Huai-hsi Inscription": a narrative prose preface in three units and a verse section, the *ming*
proper. The opening sentence of the prose preface is a powerful
expression of Han Yü's overall vision of the moral and political
significance of the event. Politically, this sentence asserts the unchal-
lengeable sovereignty of the T'ang emperors and thereby forestalls
any future need to justify action against insubordinates. Morally, it
reinforces political authority with the ideas of the heavenly man-

date. The language of the first narrative unit is an imitation of the language of the *Shih ching* hymns and odes.[88] Predicated on the principle *tz'u-shih hsiang-ch'eng*, this language glorifies the origins and the successive rulers of the T'ang imperial house.

Once the principle of imperial rule is thus simply and universally established, Han Yü does not describe in detail the events of the intervening years between Kao-tsu and Hsien-tsung. It is a matter of course that the T'ang emperors, being "worthy sons" of Heaven, should have the authority and the duty to bring the "Nine Provinces, regardless of distance" into perfect peace and order. The subsequent enumeration of the imperial line of succession and the brief mention of sundry achievements and failures of these emperors fulfills one of the conventional requirements in inscription writing, namely, genealogy. The narrative then swiftly passes on to its second unit—the commands issued by Hsien-tsung.

The technique of dramatization that Han Yü adopts in the second narrative unit is designed not so much to record historical facts as to accentuate the sweeping force of Hsien-tsung's "determined decisions."[89] The shift in style here from that of the *Shih ching* hymns and odes to that of the "P'an-keng" in the *Shu ching* creates an effective contrast between the historical past and the dramatic present.[90] The first "Alas!" of Hsien-tsung's commands and Han Yü's narrative creates the illusion of the Huai-hsi expedition actually taking shape with each issuance of imperial commands. The forcefulness of Hsien-tsung's will is greatly enhanced by such dramatic phrases as "shaken and terrified," "hurried and ran." Once the command to attack is issued and the impetus of pending action defined, the focus shifts from Hsien-tsung's omnipotence to his all-embracing "virtue." The tone of his voice, in accordance with his new role, changes from that of a commander-in-chief to that of a magnanimous sovereign. He begins to issue orders to P'ei Tu, first to oversee the welfare of the imperial armies and then to be mindful of the livelihood of the conquered people of Ts'ai. The third narrative unit opens with the carrying out of the imperial commands on the battlefield. It properly ends with the glorification of the ultimate victory and a list of titles and awards meted out to the officials and generals who had distinguished themselves.

The verse section (*ming*) that follows recalls the same events in rhymed four-word verse. The descriptions in this section duplicate the content of the prose preface, but they differ from the preface in two respects. Whereas the prose preface elucidates the factual events, the *ming* sings the glory of the achievements these events yield. Whereas the prose preface provides a realistic background for the joy that ensued from the victorious expedition, the *ming* encapsulates that emotion in the most classical and therefore the most appropriate and worthy manner of expression.

Han Yü's "Huai-hsi Inscription" is a work of multiple dimensions. As history, it has been severely criticized and discredited; as literature, it is unique in terms of artistic merit and in terms of the *ku-wen* ideals it strives to realize. Li Shang-yin (813–58), a disciple of the Han Yü school in the early years of his literary apprenticeship and a gifted poet and stylist in his own right, put his finger on the excellence of the "Huai-hsi Inscription" in "The Stele Inscription by Han Yü":

> His Honor withdrew to his little study and observed the rite
>   of fasting.
> How freely his huge brush, soaked with ink, moved!
> He adapted and he modified the works of the "Canon of
>   Yao" and the "Canon of Shun";
> He blotted and he altered the "Ch'ing-miao" and "Sheng-
>   min" [hymns].
> When the work was done and the writings transmitted onto
>   paper, it shattered all [conventional conceptions of] form
>   and style.
>                    . . .
> Its literary expressions were extraordinary, and its meaning
>   profound; very few people understood them.[91]

Li Shang-yin may not have been conscious of Han Yü's unifying principle, but his lines remain the most pertinent and the most cogent comment on the nature and the significance of Han Yü's achievement in the "Huai-hsi Inscription." Li emphasizes Han Yü's unconventional and creative adaptation, an aspect arrived at by a steady and craftsmanlike approach to the literary task at hand. In a well-balanced appreciation of Han Yü's greatness, Li's remarks on the welding of the extraordinary and the profound in the "Huai-hsi Inscription" demonstrate a knowledge of Han Yü's literary program and a recognition of his singular literary achievement.

## The Principle of Uniqueness (3): Creativity and Stylistic Transformation

The first two stages of Han Yü's literary development were marked by the establishment of his theories and the evolution of his stylistic practice in conformance with these theories. The "Examination Letter" and the "Li Yüan Valediction" illustrate Han Yü's earliest attempts at reforming prose style and his approach to the classical ideal of originality and uniqueness through the doctrines of "learning from the ancients" and "expurgating all clichés." Stylistic analysis of these works demonstrates the general awkwardness and immaturity of Han Yü's expression of his ideas and emotions, as well as the brilliance and ingenuity of his mixed use of traditional literary forms. Analysis of the "Huai-hsi Inscription" reveals Han Yü's classicism at its height and shows the shift in emphasis in his style from imitation and ingenuity to craftsmanship and artifice, from expurgation of clichés to expression worthy of the topic. This shift marks the second stage of Han Yü's literary development and represents significant progress in his artistic control over the material and method of his work.

The portrait of the artist that emerges from this study is that of a perfect "Mr. Academy," like the pedantic figure Han Yu himself portrayed in his "Explications of the Method of Learning."[92] He presented himself as a stalwart Confucianist, unbending in his insistence on classicism in literature, extremely scrupulous about the relationship between style and concepts, and stoically indifferent to his personal destiny in an unsympathetic world. This is undoubtedly the way Han Yü wished the world to see and remember him; and this indeed is the light in which he has been seen and remembered through the centuries. All of his creative works and all of his activities to promote ku-wen have been interpreted by posterity in these terms.

But Han Yü did sometimes stray beyond the limits of classicism and Confucianism to seek literary inspiration from less orthodox sources. Analysis of the "Examination Letter" suggests such a testing of the boundaries of orthodoxy. The modern scholar Ch'en Yin-k'o has demonstrated Han Yü's extensive borrowing from the "tales of marvels" and other literary forms popular in his time.[93]

Kuo Hsi-liang, discussing the linguistic aspect of Han Yü's writings, points out that the style of his works is characterized as much by its abundant use of contemporary colloquial expressions as by its resurrection of classical prose.[94] Jao Tsung-yi has discovered evidence that Han Yü was not as hostile to Buddhism as he was reputed to be.[95] Although a sworn enemy of Buddhism, he did not hesitate to appropriate the subjects, forms, and stylistic devices of Buddhist literature for his own use. These unorthodox features would seem difficult to reconcile with Han Yü's program of classical revival in literature, but this seeming paradox can be resolved by examining the final stage of his literary development, illustrated by his "Stele Inscription on the Lo-ch'ih Shrine in Liu-chou" (823, hereafter the "Lo-ch'ih Inscription").[96]

The Lo-ch'ih Shrine was built in honor of the late prefect Liu [Tsung-yüan]. When Liu was prefect [of Liu-chou][97] he did not hold its people in contempt but led them with rites and laws. In three years, the people there were all working very hard. [And they said,] "Although this land of ours is remote from the capital, nonetheless we are His Majesty's people. Now that Heaven has granted us this kindly lord, if we do not conform to his civilizing influence, we are truly unworthy to be called human beings."

And so the people, young and old, admonished one another never to disobey their lord's order. Whenever they did anything in the village or at home, they invariably asked themselves, "Would our lord, when informed of our action, disapprove of it?" In this manner, they always thought [about Liu's preferences] before they started to do anything.

When a date was set for some public duty to be performed, the people urged one another to rush to it; and the duty was always completed on time, never too late or too early. As a consequence, the livelihood of the people was in good order, and they owed no back taxes to the government. Those who had fled to other places now returned from all quarters. Men enjoyed their lives, and their enterprises thrived. New houses were built, and at the river-crossings [pu], there were new boats.[98] Ponds and gardens were kept clean and trim. Pigs, cows, ducks, and chickens were big and fat; they multiplied and prospered. Sons respected their father's words; wives followed their husband's will. In weddings and funerals, the appropriate conduct was observed. In public, people showed respect to each other's age. At home, they showed kindness and filial piety as becoming to parents and children.

Formerly the people had been so impoverished that they had to offer the male and female members of their household as security for loans. If they could not redeem the members after a long time, then the members were forfeited into slavery. When his lordship arrived, he had the borrowed capital defrayed by the service rendered [by the pledged members] as was the custom of the place and had them all returned to their original households.[99] He renovated the Confucian Temple[100] and repaired city walls and roads to make them orderly looking; and planted well-known trees along them. The people of Liu-chou were all pleased and happy.

Once he was drinking with his subordinate military officers Wei Chung, Hsieh Ning, and Ou-yang Yi in a postal pavilion. He said to them, "I have been forsaken by my time, so I take my residence here and make friends with you. Next year I am going to die. After I die, I shall become a god. Three years after my death, please have a shrine built to offer sacrifices to me."[101] At the predicted time, he died.

In the third year, on the day *hsin-mao* in the first month of autumn [822],[102] [the spirit of] his lordship descended into the back hall of the prefectural building. Ou-yang Yi and others saw it and bowed to it. That evening, he visited Yi in a dream and told him, "Have my dwelling installed at Lo-ch'ih." On the day *ching-ch'en* of that month,[103] the shrine was completed and a great sacrifice was held. A visitor by the name of Li Yi was drunk, and he behaved insolently in the shrine hall. He was taken ill. He was escorted out of the shrine and promptly died.

In the spring of the following year, Wei Chung and Ou-yang Yi sent Hsieh Ning to the capital to ask me to record these incidents and have them inscribed on stone. I say that his lordship Liu, being able to extend his beneficence to the people during his life and to enjoy sacrifices in that land because of his influence over the people's welfare after his death, can indeed be regarded as divine. I therefore composed a hymn to welcome his spirit at the sacrifice and to say farewell when it departs. It is a hymn to be given to the people of Liu-chou so that they may sing it during the sacrifice and have it inscribed on stone.

His lordship Liu was a native of Ho-tung. His given name was Tsung-yüan, and his second name was Tzu-hou. He was talented, and he was skilled in the art of letters. He once held office in the court and gained renown. Later he was dismissed and was never reinstated.[104]

The text of my hymn reads:

The lichee fruits are vermilion, and the bananas are yellow;
The meats and vegetables are presented in his lordship's hall.
The ship of his lordship has two flags;[105]
It crosses to the middle of the stream and is stalled by the
    wind.
We wait for our lord, but he does not come! Who can
    understand our sorrow?
Riding high on a steed, his lordship enters the shrine.
He comforts us, the people; he smiles and does not frown.
In the hills of E and on the waters of Liu,[106]
The cinnamon trees are round and plump, and the white
    stones stand forth.
The lord goes on an excursion in the morning, and he comes
    back in the evening;
He sings with the monkey in the spring and flies with the
    crane in the autumn.
The people of the northern country found fault with our
    lord;
May we never be separated from our lord for thousands of
    years.
May he bless us and grant us longevity;
May he banish the evil spirits and drive them to the shady
    side of the hill.
May there be no flooding in the lowland and no drought in
    the high ground;
May the crops be abundant, and the snakes keep company
    with their own kind.
May we people always requite his favor and never be lax in
    our duty;
May the memory [of our lord] be cherished from generation
    to generation.

The "Lo-ch'ih Inscription" tells the story of Liu Tsung-yüan's
apotheosis. The narrative begins with his prefectship at Liu-chou
and reaches a climax in the course of two dramatic episodes. The
first episode describes a drinking party at which Liu Tsung-yüan
predicts his own deification after death; in the second, Liu Tsung-
yüan, already dead and a deity, descends to his shrine on the day of
its dedication and displays his supernatural power by visiting a
drunken and insolent visitor with sudden death. After this climax,
the action of the story tapers off with Han Yü's personal comments

on the event and ends with a hymn in the *Ch'u tz'u* style to the new patron god of Liu-chou, Liu Tsung-yüan. Critics in the past have differed widely in their opinions of the merits and meaning of the work. Liu Hsü (887–946), Han Yü's biographer in the *Chiu T'ang shu* (Old T'ang history, completed 945), for instance, regarded the supernatural episode in this work as groundless fiction and dismissed the entire work as one of Han Yü's most absurd writings. In his "Appraisal," he said, "When the southern people foolishly believed that Liu Tsung-yüan had become the patron god of Lo-ch'ih, [Han] Yü substantiated their belief by writing the 'Inscription' for the shrine.... [It is among] his most wrongheaded writings."[107]

Sung Ch'i (998–1061), Han Yü's biographer in the *Hsin T'ang shu* (New T'ang history, completed 1060), held the opposite view. Speaking from a new critical standpoint that had emerged with the resurgence of the Confucian revival movement early in the Sung dynasty, he saw Han Yü as an advocate of the time-honored orthodoxy of the *tao* of Confucianism, and his works "as a rule" as the "fruits of the most pure and the most orthodox tradition."[108] In the eleventh century, the *Hsin T'ang shu's* evaluation of Han Yü superseded that of the *Chiu T'ang shu* and became the official verdict, generally accepted by later critics, on his achievements. This interpretation of Han Yü's literary achievement artificially limits the frame of reference of his individual works. In the case of the "Lo-ch'ih Inscription," the nature of this bias is evident in the following passage from the "Records of the Renovation of the Lo-ch'ih Shrine" (1644) by Wang Ming yüeh (1609–67).

I say that matters concerning spirits and miracles are the favorite subjects of women and children, but no Confucian will chatter about them. His Lordship Liu [Tsung-yüan] was skilled in the art of letters and was able to use literature as a medium to convey the quintessence of heaven and earth. His understanding was profound, and he gave it many forms of expression. He undertook a complete renovation of the Temple of Confucius [at Liu-chou]. Hence the local people were given a place to pay their respects [to the Master]. Moreover, the fact that he was able to make his policies prevail and that the people benefited from them makes him a man whose life approximated the *tao*.
    Supernatural events and miracles do not repeat themselves, and

in the long run they are forgotten. But the *tao* does not perish even in tens of millennia. This is why His Honor Tai [Chi] wished to renovate this shrine: it is precisely to propagate the *tao* [as manifested in the life and deeds of Liu Tsung-yüan at Liu-chou]. His Lordship Liu, driven by *ch'iung* ["extremity"], came upon the *tao* and progressed with it. Because of his meeting with the *tao*, his name has become immortal between heaven and earth. In the case of an educated man, unless he is tempered by *ch'iung*, he cannot have lasting achievements.[109]

This assessment is a typical example of the Neo-Confucian rationalization of the Lo-ch'ih myth, which was developed and perpetuated by critics from Sung times onward.[110] Unmindful or ignorant of the judgment of the *Chiu T'ang shu*, the critics applied their own rationalizations retroactively to Han Yü and admired his "Lo-ch'ih Inscription" as the first historical document on the institution of the shrine and the first literary attempt to glorify the Confucian *tao* as reflected in the benign prefectship of Liu Tsung-yüan.

Though not primarily conceived as literary criticism, this version of the Lo-ch'ih shrine myth seriously distorted critical judgment of the subject matter and style of the "Lo-ch'ih Inscription." For instance, instead of attributing the foundation of the shrine to the superstitions of the southern people, it presented the shrine as an official means of "propagating the *tao*." This shift quite casually eliminated a basic incongruity between the form and the content of the work, the incongruity that had incurred the disapproval of the *Chiu T'ang shu* biographer.

The *Chiu T'ang shu* clearly disparaged the "Lo-ch'ih Inscription" not merely because Han Yü, a self-advertised orthodox Confucian, had given full rein to personal whim and had written on the unseemly subject of ghosts and supernatural deeds, but because as a self-consciously classical stylist, he had misused the *pei* (stele inscription) form—a medium traditionally reserved for recording historical facts—in order to give a spurious appearance of historical truth to his fictitious tale.[111] This was the gravamen of Liu Hsü's charge that Han Yü had helped "substantiate" the local inhabitants' superstitions. The incongruity of form and content was the basis for Liu's charge of "wrongheadedness."

In the Neo-Confucian interpretation of the subject, however, this incongruity no longer exists. Once the frame of reference has been changed to that of the Confucian *tao* and the style has been declared to be in the purest and most orthodox classical tradition, the perception of the subject matter and of the stylistic aspect of the work changes accordingly. From the newly rationalized point of view, Han Yü's use of the *pei* form, far from suggesting anything "wrongheaded," appears instead to be the most decorous way to express the Confucian *tao* as reflected in the fate and achievements of a Confucian magistrate.

This Neo-Confucian interpretation persisted, with minor variations, into modern times. Lin Shu (1852–1924), a sensitive and perceptive critic of the late Ch'ing *ku-wen* school, was deeply influenced by the Neo-Confucian bias in his analysis of the "Lo-ch'ih Inscription." At one point in his stylistic appraisal of the work, he underscored Han Yü's "tasteful" choice of diction, applauding the use of such words as *chiang* ("to descend") and *kuan* ("to house") in the episode that describes the visitation of Liu Tsung-yüan's spirit and the use of *chi ssu* ("promptly died") in Han Yü's description of the sudden death of the drunkard as "classic and refined . . . forestalling any criticism of frivolity from the reader." He also singled out Han Yü's artistic control in the latter episode for special comment: "This passage is poised between the real and the unreal, but makes no commitment one way or the other. If treated by a conventional hand, the supernatural element in the tale would certainly have been emphasized. One false step, and the purity of form and style would have been lost."[112] Lin Shu probably had the *Tso chuan* in mind when he referred to Han Yü's "classic and refined" style,[113] and his comment on Han Yü's "poised" treatment of the supernatural is clearly intended to identify the "Lo-ch'ih Inscription" with the classical historical tradition of the *Tso chuan* and the *Shih chi*, which show no compunction about incorporating supernatural materials into their narrative.

Lin Shu's appraisal of Han Yü's style was remarkably perceptive; it was probably the first assessment to turn away from ideology and base its critical comments on purely literary and stylistic considerations. Yet his identification of the style of the "Lo-ch'ih Inscription" with that of the *Tso chuan* and the *Shih chi* is not entirely convincing. First, the diction he labeled "classic and refined" and the treatment of the supernatural that he denoted as poised are not enough to support his argument since such diction had already become common in the preceding centuries. The Chin dynasty writers of supernatural tales, for instance, had frequently used such modes of expression without being particularly sensitive to its "classic and refined" character. Second, in spite of its apparently literary focus, Lin Shu's criticism still embodies the Neo-Confucian view that the "purity of form and style" of the "Lo-ch'ih Inscription" is a necessary condition of an intrinsically pure subject matter. This perspective inevitably limits his approach to the subject and manner of the work, and his ultimate conclusion sounds like a distant echo of the "Appraisal" in the *Hsin T'ang shu*:

Han Yü probed deep into the roots and origins [of great writings], attained outstanding achievements there, and established a separate school of teaching. . . .
    In the Chen-yüan era [785–805] and the Yüan-ho era [806–820], Han Yü led the literati with his studies of the Six Classics. He stemmed the flow of worthless [heterodox] streams of thought and turned back from the jaded to the ore of simplicity. He chiseled out the false and replaced it with the pure. He regarded his own talent as the equal of Ssu-ma Ch'ien's and Yang Hsiung's and did not deign to speak of those [who had written since] Pan Ku's [A.D. 32–92] time. What he achieved as a rule was the fruit of the most pure and the most orthodox [tradition]. He expelled the clichés, galloped unbridled on an independent path, and gave full rein to his vast spirit. In short, he did not come into conflict with the practice of the sages. He compared his own *tao* with that of Mencius and deemed the *tao* of Hsün-tzu [fl. 298–238 B.C.] and Yang Hsiung not pure enough. How true! . . . He was indeed a gentleman of principle who never deviated from the *tao*.[114]

The "Lo-ch'ih Inscription" differs in all respects from the sort of literature described above and from Lin Shu's interpretation of it. The subject matter, style, theoretical justification, and motivation of this work can better be understood in the context of other literary traditions developed since the *Tso chuan*, of Han Yü's own late view of style, and of his personal relationship with Liu Tsung-yüan.

The following five excerpts from collections of Chin dynasty supernatural tales contain certain features resembling aspects of the "Lo-ch'ih Inscription" (the passages in question are italicized).

[1] The immortal Ma-ku *descended* to the house of Ts'ai Ching at Tung-yang. Her fingernails were four inches long. [Ts'ai] Ching thought to himself, "These are indeed exquisite hands. I would love to have them scratch my back for me." Ma-ku was greatly infuriated. *Suddenly* Ching *was seen* tumbling to the ground. Blood flowed from both his eyes.[115]

[2] During the T'ai-yüan era [376–97] of the Chin dynasty, Kao Heng of Lo-yang was prefect of Wei-chün.... [One day] his grandson Ya-chih was heard calling out from a stable, "A god *has descended* here. He calls himself the White-Headed Old Man."[116]

[3] Liu Chi, a Han dynasty magistrate of Yang-hsien, once said, "*After I die, I will become a god.*" One evening he got drunk and died without cause. There was a thunderstorm, and his coffin disappeared in the storm.... When the local people went to look for it, they found the coffin already buried under a mound. They changed the name of that hill to Chün-shan and set up a shrine there to offer sacrifices [to his spirit].[117]

[4] There was a man named Chiang Tzu-wen.... He was much given to wine and women.... Yet he frequently asserted that his bones were black and that *he would become a god after he died.*[118]

[5] During the Hsien-ning era [A.D. 275–79] of the Chin dynasty, the master of ceremonies Han Po's son, the Kuei-chi prefect's son, and the imperial household minister's son took an excursion together to the shrine of Chiang [Chiang Tzu-wen of the preceding tale] in the mountains.

Inside the shrine were several statues of women. The features of these statues were quite delicate. The three men were all drunk. They pointed at the statues playfully, and each in his imagination selected one as his wife.

That night all three of them had the same dream. They dreamed that his lordship Chiang sent a messenger to them with the following message: "My daughters are all very ugly. It has been a great honor to them that they should have attracted your fancy. On such-and-such a day, please come to take them...."

They confirmed their extraordinary dreams with one another and were greatly alarmed. They prepared the three sacrificial animals and went to the shrine again to apologize for their offense, and at the same time to beg for mercy.

Again [that night] they had a similar dream in which the lord Chiang *descended* personally and said to them, "Since you gentlemen have taken a fancy to my daughters, you must be eager to be together with them. The appointed day is drawing near; how can you get out of it now?" Shortly afterward they all died.[119]

In the first, second, and fifth excerpts, *chiang* ("descend") is used as part of the common vocabulary of a conventional supernatural tale. In the first, *hu chien* ("suddenly seen") is used in a structure that loosely corresponds to that of *chi ssu* ("promptly died") in Han Yü's "Lo-ch'ih Inscription." Here the technique is one not of "poise" but of compression, achieving the stylistic effect of abruptness and violence. This brevity does not fit Lin Shu's description of Han Yü's abstention from confirmation of the supernatural. The same interpretation applies to the use of the phrase "shortly afterward they all died" in the fifth excerpt. Again, abruptness rather than classical restraint is desired.

Thematic and structural parallels between the Chin tales and the "Lo-ch'ih Inscription" reinforce these lexical parallels. In the third, fourth, and fifth tales, the theme of a man's foreknowledge of his own death and later deification recalls the theme of the first dramatic episode in the "Lo-ch'ih Inscription"; the motifs of the close relationship between wine drinking and death appear in all three passages, and the verbal echo "After I die, I will become a god" is an especially conspicuous link between Han Yü's work and its Chin antecedents. Further parallels include the institution of a shrine, the theme of a god's retaliation on insolent men, and the literary device of a dream in the fifth tale, all of which recall the second dramatic episode of the "Lo-ch'ih Inscription."

Such parallels invite several conclusions. The link between the *Tso chuan* and the *Shih chi* and the "Lo-ch'ih Inscription" is indirect, broken by the intervention of the tradition of the supernatural tale, so that Lin Shu's interpretation of the "classic and refined" antecedents of Han Yü's diction and style is not entirely accurate. In terms of subject matter, style, and literary technique, the "Lo-ch'ih Inscription" is akin more to the Chin dynasty supernatural tales than to the historical writings of the *Tso chuan* and the *Shih chi*. This second point raises the problem of the theoretical justification of Han Yü's work. If the "Lo-ch'ih Inscription" was written essentially as a fictional work, then how can the apparent discrepancies between its form and matter be resolved, and how can Han Yü's Confucian standing be reconciled with his un-Confucian interest in the supernatural? The answer to these questions emerges at least in part from an examination of Han Yü's later discussions of style.

In analyzing Han Yü's works from an ideological point of view, a view that he himself suggests in several passages, the ideological purity of subject matter becomes the basis for judging his style. His artistic efforts are assumed to have been intended solely to defend his values when necessary, to exalt them when he was so moved, and to recreate them when they were not readily accessible to the eye. Toward the end of his life, however, especially during the years immediately preceding and following his second banishment to the extreme south in 819,[120] Han Yü seems to have attained a new perspective on style: he discovered that the moral significance of the subject matter is determined not by its intrinsic orthodoxy or unorthodoxy but rather by the way in which it is perceived. Since there is always more than one way to perceive a subject, the logical corollary is that there is also more than one way to express these different perceptions. The battle of ideas, at the level of literary expression and from the vantage point of style, can simply imply a battle of wording. The conscious choice of one type of diction to the exclusion of others constitutes the material difference between one school of thought and another as well as between one manner of expression and another. This awareness of style as ultimately being purely a matter of conceiving the appropriate type of diction is reflected in Han Yü's dictum of 821: "Writing becomes fluent when the diction is apt, each style being proper to its own function."[121]

The concept that the use of a different type of diction can transform the nature, and therefore the moral or ideological frame of reference, of the subject matter is an infinitely more sophisticated view of *kung* ("artistry") than that expressed in the earlier principle *tz'u-shih hsiang-ch'eng*. The transforming power of a tradition-conscious diction is most apparent when it is applied to works treating unorthodox subjects. In this new concept of *kung*, the subject matter, even if "wrongheaded" or un-Confucian, no longer autonomously dictates its own meaning and frame of reference; now it is the style, the author's conscious choice of one type of diction to the exclusion of others, that defines its meaning.

Therefore, when Han Yü chooses certain key words and phrases from the supernatural tale genre, he is warning the reader that what he is recording in the "Lo-ch'ih Inscription" is a popular belief, something essentially fictional and not factual. His adaptation of the *pei* form does not contradict its traditional usage: in exposing the fictional nature of his subject, Han Yü *is* fulfilling the traditional function of a *pei*, namely, to record facts. However, what is recognized as fact no longer resides with the subject; it is revealed in the way in which the subject matter is interpreted and the manner in which the interpretation is expressed. This technique of transforming the moral and ideological framework of a piece by the conscious choice of a specific kind of diction appears in a number of Han Yü's late works. The "Biography of the Brush" (809) and the "Address to the Crocodiles" (820) are two notable instances.[122] These two works recall Han Yü's earlier attempts to achieve the "extraordinary" but are clearly distinguishable from the early works because of their sophisticated handling of form and style.

In the end, it is still extremely difficult to discern Han Yü's motive in writing the "Lo-ch'ih Inscription" in such an unorthodox fashion. The tone of the work is complex, perhaps humorous, perhaps reverential. Interpretation of this tone depends in large measure on understanding the nature of the personal relationship between Han and Liu.

Biographers and critics of Han Yü and Liu Tsung-yüan in the present century have approached the question of the relationship between the two T'ang *ku-wen* masters from various viewpoints. Some, like Lo Lien-t'ien, are interested in the question primarily for reasons of biographical information.[123] Others, like Hou Wai-lu and Ch'ien Mu, are interested in it because it indirectly reflects on Han's and Liu's political and intellectual convictions, which seem to them to be antithetical.[124] The consensus is that Han and Liu were antagonistic throughout their lives as a consequence of the wrong Han Yü suspected Liu Tsung-yüan had done him in 803.[125] It has been pointed out that these two men belonged to different political cliques. Han Yü had been friendly with Chü Wen-chen and his associates,[126] whereas Liu Tsung-yüan was an active member of the radical reformist camp of Wang Shu-wen and is held responsible for the first setback in Han Yü's political career. In literature, the genuine admiration of each for the other's talent was not always accompanied by mutual approval: Liu, for example, once severely criticized Han for his wanton cynicism about the precarious position of official historian.[127] Han Yü, in turn, is said never to have lost his early hostility to Liu Tsung-yüan; and in the three works that he wrote on Liu's death, he made two critical allusions to Liu's moral weakness.[128] This view was perpetuated as late as 1963 by Ch'ien Mu and 1977 by Lo Lien-t'ien in his book on Han Yü's life and works. Both Ch'ien and Lo perceived the antithetical views of Han and Liu on Buddhism and the mandate of Heaven as manifestations of their intellectual rivalry and of a basic personality conflict.

This consensus, however, sidesteps a central contradiction in the situation: if Han Yü indeed remained resentful of Liu Tsung-yüan's role in his first exile in 803, how are we to account for the three memorial pieces that Han Yü wrote on Liu Tsung-yüan? If we compare Han Yü's "Elegy [on the Death] of Liu Tzu-hou [Tsung-yüan]" (820) to that by Liu Tsung-yüan's close friend Liu Yü-hsi, a difference is immediately noticeable in their responses to Liu Tsung-yüan's demotion and exile.[129] Liu Yü-hsi's "Elegy," a reiteration of loud laments, has no indignation in it, even though, as a fellow political victim, Liu might be expected to be sensitive to the injustice of Liu Tsung-yüan's defeat. The indignation is in Han Yü's "Elegy." "All creatures loathe to be useful materials. To be shaped into a sacrificial vessel, carved and decorated with green and yellow patterns, is the undoing of a tree"—this is the sound of intransigent protest. "[We], who are not adept at hewing and carving, work with bloodied hands and sweaty faces, while [you], the skilled carpenter, [can only] look on, with your hands in your sleeves"—these are hardly the words of a lifelong political adversary.[130]

*Elegy [on the Death] of Liu Tzu-hou*

On such and such a day, month, and year, I, Han Yü, respectfully make, with this clear wine and assorted foods, an oblation to the spirit of my late friend Liu Tzu-hou.

Alas, alas! Tzu-hou, that you should have to come to this! But then, all men have died since of old, and wherefore should I grieve?

Man's life on earth is like a dream that finally comes to its awakening. Of what significance is gain or loss therein?

While the dream lasts, there are joys and there are sorrows; but on awakening, is there anything in it worth recollecting?

All creatures loathe to be useful materials. To be shaped into a
sacrificial vessel, carved and decorated with green and yellow patterns, is the undoing of a tree.

You left the world in the prime of your life, Heaven releasing
you from the fetters. You used to pour out your words, all pendants
of exquisite jade.

The rich and honored of this world being all incompetent, who
will record their deeds when they are dead? But your achievements
were eminent and supreme.

[We], who are not adept at hewing and carving, work with
bloodied hands and sweaty faces, while [you], the skilled carpenter,
[can only] look on, with your hands in your sleeves.

Since your literary talent was not employed, ordinary people
like us had to attend to the imperial edicts.

In your judgment of men, you thought you were unsurpassed.
Yet, once dismissed, you were never reinstated, while others, the
churls, soared sky-high.

Alas, alas, Tzu-hou, now you are gone from us. Your parting
voice sounds, oh, so clear and distinct.

You requested that your friends look after your children. Unworthy though I am, I was among those included in your dying
wishes.

Social relations nowadays depend so much on power and position. How can I be sure that my own fate will permit me to carry
out your charge?

It is not that I am qualified to know you best; it is that you have
chosen to command me. Since ghosts and spirits may well exist,
how dare I be remiss and fail you?

Mindful that you are gone, never to return again, I offer this sacrifice before your coffin and bid you eternal farewell.

Alas, alas! May you be pleased with these offerings!

From the other side of the relationship, given the uncompromising character of Liu Tsung-yüan, how are we to account for his
continued correspondence and repeated attempts to involve Han
Yü in debates over intellectual issues and current affairs? How on
his deathbed could Liu Tsung-yüan have entrusted his two sons to
Han Yü's care, a trust openly acknowledged and accepted not only
in Han Yü's "Elegy" but also in his "Epitaph for Liu Tzu-hou"
(820)?

Tsung-yüan was his given name and Tzu-hou was his courtesy
name. His seventh-generation ancestor Liu Ch'ing [517–67] served

as a chamberlain under the T'o-pa house of [Western] Wei and was made a nobleman with the title of duke of Chi-yin. His great-great-grand-uncle Liu Shih [d. 659], a chief minister of the T'ang dynasty, lost his life during Emperor Kao-tsung's reign, together with Ch'u Sui-liang [596–658] and Han Yüan [606–59], for opposition to Empress Wu. His father, Liu Chen [740–93], gave up the post of academician in the Court of Imperial Sacrifices to become a mere sub-prefect in Chiang-nan in order to care for his mother. Later Chen lost his position as a censor because he failed to ingratiate himself with a powerful personage [Tou Ts'an, 733–92] of the day; when this powerful personage died, he was restored to his position. He was known for his integrity, and his friends were all men of renown of the day.

Tzu-hou was keen in mind from boyhood and comprehended everything with ease. While his father was still living, he was already an accomplished man in spite of his youth. He succeeded in taking the chin-shih degree, showing striking promise. People said, "The Liu family has a worthy son indeed!" Later, having passed the po-hsüeh hung-tz'u examination, he was appointed a corrector in [the library of] the Hall of Assembled Worthies. A man of intellectual acumen and moral integrity, he referred freely in his discourses to the ancients as well as to contemporaries and quoted the Classics, the histories, and the philosophers. His erudition and eloquence usually overwhelmed the gathering. His fame became widespread, and his friendship was much coveted. Dignitaries and high officials vied with one another to become his patrons, and they joined voices to recommend and to praise him.

In the nineteenth year of the Chen-yüan era [803], he was promoted from personnel officer of Lan t'ien to the position of supervisory censor. When Emperor Shun-tsung ascended the throne [in 805], he was made an under-secretary in the Ministry of Rites. When the chief minister fell into disgrace, he was dispatched to be a provincial prefect after the usage of the time. Before he reached his destination, however, he was further demoted to be an administrator of [Yung-]chou. Living in banishment, he worked more diligently than ever; he devoted himself to reading and cultivated the art of prose as well as poetry. Thus accumulating and extending [his knowledge and skill], his depth and breadth became limitless. And he would lose himself among the mountains and streams. During the Yüan-ho era [in 815], he was routinely recalled to the capital, only to be dispatched again, like the others, to be a provincial prefect. This time Tzu-hou was assigned to Liu-chou.

When he arrived at Liu-chou, he said with a sigh, "Is this region really unworthy of one's administrative talent?" Taking the local customs into full consideration, he drew up a list of admonitions and prohibitions, and the people abided by them. According to local custom, men and women could be held as security for loans. In case of failure to repay in time, when interest accumulated to the same amount as the principal, the person held as security was forfeited as a slave. Tzu-hou devised a way to have all the slaves redeemed and returned home. For those who were too poor to pay their debts, he ordered their masters to keep an account of their services rendered. When their services sufficed to pay off their debts, he made their masters release them. The provincial inspector ordered that this rule be applied to other prefectures. In one year, nearly a thousand slaves were liberated and returned to their homes.

All the *chin-shih* degree holders south of Mt. Heng and the Hsiang River regarded Tzu-hou as their teacher. Those who received personal instruction from him in the writing of prose and poetry all showed notable accomplishment.

At the time [Tzu-hou] was recalled to the capital for reassignment, Liu Meng-te of Chung-shan, whose given name was Yü-hsi, also due for provincial reassignment, was dispatched to be prefect of Po-chou. Tzu-hou wept and said, "Po-chou is hardly fit for human habitation and Meng-te's mother is still living. I cannot bear to see Meng-te forced to this extremity; nor can I find the words to inform his parent. In any case, it would be unthinkable for the mother to go with the son." He was going to petition the court and offer to exchange his post at Liu-chou for Po-chou, even at the risk of incurring once more the displeasure of the court and possibly the death penalty. It happened that someone brought Meng-te's case to the attention of His Majesty, and Meng-te was made prefect of Lien-chou instead.

Alas, only when a man is in extremity are the qualities of integrity and righteousness revealed. Nowadays people profess their admiration for each other on the streets and entertain each other and make merry with wining and dining. With forced smiles and prattle, they flatter each other. Clasping hands, they bare their hearts to testify to their friendship. Calling upon Heaven, with tears streaming down, they swear never to betray each other in life or in death. It all looks so genuine. And yet the moment a point of self-interest arises, be it as tiny as a hair, they will avert their eyes and act as though they had never known one another. Should someone fall into a pit, they not only will not lift a hand to rescue him but will push him farther down and drop stones on him. This we see everywhere. Even birds and beasts and barbarians cannot bear to do such things, yet these men think themselves "smart." They should learn a lesson from Tzu-hou's conduct and feel a modicum of shame. In his younger years, Tzu-hou was eager to cut a figure for himself and was negligent about his own safety. Presuming that he could establish a career immediately, he became involved in a scandal and was disgraced. Once he was disgraced, none among his acquaintances had the power or influence to bring about his reinstatement. Thus he died finally in extremity in a remote land, with his talent unemployed and his principles unrealized. But alas, had Tzu-hou been able to conduct himself while serving in the Chancellery in the same way as he did later when he served as an administrator and prefect, he would not have been dismissed. Even when he was repudiated, had there been some powerful personage to give him preferment, Tzu-hou would surely again have held proper appointments indefinitely. On the other hand, if Tzu-hou had not suffered banishment for such a long time, or if his situation had been less extreme, he might still have surpassed others in certain things, but surely his application to the art of letters would not have been as thorough, and his literary achievement would not have been assured a place in posterity, as it undoubtedly is now. Tzu-hou might have had his wish fulfilled and become a high minister for a time. Whether it would be a gain or a loss to exchange what was for what might have been should be evident, at least to some people.

Tzu-hou died on the eighth day of the eleventh month in the fourteenth year of Yüan-ho [November 28, 819] at the age of 47 [sui]. On the tenth day of the seventh month in the fifteenth year [August 22, 820], his body was brought back to Wan-nien to be buried in his family cemetery. Tzu-hou had two sons: the elder, named Chou-liu, was just about to be four; the younger, named Chou-ch'i, was born after Tzu-hou's death. He had two daughters, both young. P'ei Hsing-li [d. 820] of Ho-tung, the provincial inspector, paid for all the funeral expenses, enabling Tzu-hou's body to be brought home for burial. Hsing-li is a high-minded and honorable man. He was a good friend of Tzu-hou's, and Tzu-hou was devoted to him. And he proved to be very helpful. Tzu-hou's maternal cousin Lu Tsun arranged the burial of Tzu-hou at Wan-nien. Tsun, a native of Cho-chou, is a very prudent man and never tires of learning. After Tzu-hou was banished, Tsun went to live with him and did not leave him until he died. Now that Tzu-hou is buried, he will attend to the family's livelihood. He may be said to be a man of constancy.

The epitaph reads:

Here is the abode of Tzu-hou,
Secure and restful.
May it bring blessings on his heirs.

In examining the lives of Han Yü and Liu Tsung-yüan and the contacts between them, I have come to a reassessment of two key moments in their lives. The first is the year 803–4, when both were serving in the censorate at court and Liu Tsung-yüan was suspected of saying something about Han Yü that caused the latter's exile to Yang-shan. The second was the year 814, when Han Yü had finally attained prominence in court and Liu Tsung-yüan, after some ten years of exile, was summoned back to Ch'ang-an for review and reassignment. From a clearer knowledge of these two episodes, a better understanding of the relationship between the two men emerges, an understanding that makes it possible for us to see why Han Yü tried to bring Liu Tsung-yüan back to the court in 814, why Liu, when dying in 819, entrusted his sons to Han Yü, and why Han Yü, after the death of Liu, wrote three memorial pieces on Liu.

To place the events of 803–4 in context, it is first necessary to trace the social background of the immediate ancestors of Han Yü and Liu Tsung-yüan. Han Yü came from a family that had become relatively undistinguished in the preceding two or three generations. His grandfather had served as a magistrate in the provinces.[131] His father's highest position was that of a secretary of the ninth grade in one of the ministries. There is no record that his grandfather or his father was involved in court intrigues or high-level factional struggles. One of his uncles, Han Yün-ch'ing, had served as a censor and attained the position of chamberlain (*lang-chung*) in the Ministry of Rites. The uncle was known for his literary talent and as a practitioner of *ku-wen* who moved in the social circle of such celebrated *ku-wen* writers as Li Hua and Hsiao Ying-shih. Han Yü's eldest brother, Han Hui, studied *ku-wen* with Li Hua and Hsiao Ying-shih and was an intellectual of some repute. Han Hui went to Ch'ang-an in 774 and became friends with Liu Tsung-yüan's father, Liu Chen, in 774–75. Han Yü, age seven, accompanied him. In 777–78, Han Hui became implicated in the celebrated Yüan Tsai case and was demoted to Shao-chou (present-day Kwangtung), where he died in 780. Han Yü went to Shao-chou with Han Hui and, after the death of his brother, traveled with his sister-in-law; he did not go to Ch'ang-an again till 786, when he was ready to take the *chin-shih* examination. Han Yü took the *chin-shih* examination in Ch'ang-an three times (788, 789, and 791) and failed each time. On the fourth attempt, he succeeded (792). Then, in the years following, he unsuccessfully tried the *po-hsüeh hung-tz'u* placement examination three times (793, 794, and 795).[132] So he left Ch'ang-an and accepted employment in 796 on the staff of the military governor Tung Chin at Pien-chou (present-day Honan).

In the winter of 800, Han Yü went to Ch'ang-an to try his luck again at the placement examination. This time he passed and was appointed *ssu-men po-shih* (seventh-grade rank);[133] in 803, he became a supervisory censor (eighth-grade rank). In that year, according to some critics, his outspoken memorial to the throne on the subject of land rents and taxes in the capital area during a severe drought and widespread famine offended Li Shih, the metropolitan governor of the capital area. As a consequence, he was expelled to Yang-shan in Lien-chou (present-day Kwangtung).[134] Han Yü's career before banishment had not been brilliant; he had obtained a post in the central government only after great effort and would have had every reason to nurse a lasting grudge against a colleague who had brought about his dismissal.

Liu Tsung-yüan, in sharp contrast to Han Yü, was the scion of many generations of famous ministers and generals. His great-uncle, Liu Hun, was under-secretary of the Ministry of Military Affairs (*ping-pu shih-lang*) in Ch'ang-an in 787, at the very time that Liu Tsung-yüan was about to move to the metropolis. When Liu Tsung-yüan was preparing for the *chin-shih* degree examination in 789–93, his father created a scandal in Ch'ang-an by clashing with the powerful and corrupt prime minister Tou Ts'an. Liu's father was demoted, exiled, and then reinstated. Liu Tsung-yüan's immediate family background therefore contrasted markedly with Han Yü's. Further in the background is Liu Tsung-yüan's great-great-grand-uncle, Liu Shih, a prime minister during Emperor Kao-tsung's reign, who was executed by the Empress Wu for his devotion to the T'ang house.[135] Such a family history made Liu Tsung-yüan a member of the upper-class elite; his reception in

Ch'ang-an was altogether different from that of the orphaned and provincial Han Yü.

When Liu Tsung-yüan arrived in the capital in 788 at the age of 16 (two years after Han Yü), he was welcomed in the highest circles. The memory of his reception in Ch'ang-an was still vivid when, 30 years later, Han Yü wrote his epitaph for Liu Tsung-yüan: "His erudition and eloquence usually overwhelmed the gathering. His fame became widespread, and his friendship was much coveted. Dignitaries and high officials vied with one another to become his patrons, and they joined voices to recommend and to praise him." This adulation could not be further removed from the indifference that Han Yü faced in the same city, and it could not help but make a deep impression on the latter, causing admiration or envy or both.

In the years 788–93, Liu Tsung-yüan rapidly made his way up the ladder of court service. In 793, he passed the *chin-shih* examination at age 21 (Han Yü had received the degree the year before at age 25); at 24, Liu married the daughter of Yang P'ing, a metropolitan governor of the capital area; at 26, he passed the placement examination and was appointed secretary in the Chi-hsien Hall (Han Yü did not pass that examination until three years later, in 800, at age 33). In 803, when Han Yü was finally appointed a supervisory censor, Liu Tsung-yüan was promoted from assistant magistrate of Lan-t'ien to supervisory censor. Now that they had duties in common, they were brought together for the first time (so far as we know). There is no record as to whether they competed or collaborated, but there is evidence that during 803–5 they shared a common platform on many important issues. Examination of such evidence reveals that they had a common response to weighty issues and events.

First, Han Yü and Liu Tsung-yüan agreed on the duty of a censorial official. Each in his own way had praised the courage of Yang Ch'eng, the famous scholar and intellectual, who, while a censor, had long kept silent before finally denouncing the then-powerful official P'ei Yen-ling.[136] Second, as young men, Han Yü and Liu Tsung-yüan, witnesses to the lawless behavior of local military governors, had both deplored the sufferings this lawlessness imposed on the people; when in office, they had supported the policy of reducing the power of military governors. Evidence for their stance can be gleaned from Han Yü's "Postscript to the Biography of Chang Chung-ch'eng," in particular his description in it of Chang's heroic defense of his city against the riotous "bandits" (lawless followers of the military governors); from Liu Tsung-yüan's depiction of Tuan Hsiu-shih's fearless arrest and punishment of the lawless followers of another powerful military governor;[137] and from their celebrations of the pacification of the Huai-hsi rebellion —Han Yü's historical "Memorial Inscription on the Pacification of the Huai-hsi Rebellion," and Liu's stately "Odes on the Pacification of the Huai-hsi Rebellion."

Third, while they were supervisory censors in the capital in 803, both criticized the corrupt government of Li Shih, the metropolitan governor of the capital area. Han Yü's outspoken memorial against Li Shih, compounded by his criticism of the corrupt purchasing practices of palace commissioners in the market, was said to have been the cause of his exile to Yang-shan.[138] Two years later, Liu Tsung-yüan, by then a member of the Wang Shu-wen party, also took issue with these corrupt commissioners. The 805 reforms, as we shall see below, effected what Han Yü and his memorial had failed to accomplish.

Han Yü's and Liu Tsung-yüan's similar criticisms of the control of the military by local military governors and eunuchs and of the corruption of the court commissioners and Li Shih are usually discussed in biographical and critical studies of these authors as if they had no bearing on the relationship between the two. This omission explains the legend of their lifelong animosity. Recent critics have failed to consider their similar responses to contemporary political corruption, responses that are evident in written record. Instead, they make Liu Tsung-yüan's possible role in Han Yü's 803 exile the only salient feature of the relationship between the two authors.

The reforms initiated by the Wang Shu-wen party during the few months in 805 when it was in power militate against viewing the party as the collection of villains that contemporary history described. Two of their reforms deserve attention. Immediately on taking power, the Wang Shu-wen party denounced and banished Li Shih, waived land rent and taxes to relieve the distress of the population in the capital area, and abolished the notorious purchasing practices of the palace commissioners. They took military power from the hands of the eunuchs and military governors and transferred it to the control of professional soldiers with established reputations and tested loyalty to the emperor. Because of such actions, the party fell within the year. The new emperor, Hsien-tsung, sentenced its leaders to death and exiled the other members, who were never to be reinstated to service in the capital.[139]

One can well imagine the impact of the radical reforms and the subsequent fate of the party's members on the then-exiled Han Yü. Certainly, whatever suspicions he may once have held of Liu Tsung-yüan's role in his own dismissal were wiped out by the reforms made during the brief reign of Emperor Shun-tsung and by the subsequent reprisals. To argue that Han Yü never forgave Liu Tsung-yüan for his suspected role in the 803 exile and continued to have doubts about Liu Tsung-yüan's integrity and moral courage would be absurd. It would be reasonable to assume that after 805 a sense of comradeship developed between the two, fortified on the personal level by a mutual sympathy and a common identification of mission, and on the political level by a common conviction of the necessity to act, irrespective of personal consequences. After a thousand years of misrepresentation, it would be worthwhile to re-examine the relationship between these two giants of T'ang literary and intellectual history.

Given the apparent readiness of these two men to perform their public duties whatever the consequences, any consideration of their relationship that implies petty self-interest on either side, in the form of an unfounded grudge or of purposeful misconduct, is deeply flawed. The obvious moral fraternity of Han and Liu render these other theoretical considerations inconsequential. In fact, it is quite understandable that Han Yü and Liu Tsung-yüan maintained a lifelong interest in each other's ideas and activities, remaining well informed about each other's ideas on history, the mandate of Heaven, literature, and ideologies and feeling totally free to express their frequently clashing opinions on any of these subjects. Friends traveling between provincial posts and Ch'ang-an served as couriers to keep them in touch.[140] Through their correspondence, Han Yü and Liu Tsung-yüan argued back and forth on such topics as the righteousness of family vendettas, Buddhism, the fate of a historian, and the role of a teacher. Liu Tsung-yüan was among the first to read Han Yü's "Biography of the Brush" and was the first person to defend it against unfavorable criticism.[141] They enjoyed each other's literary games and took pleasure in exercising their enormous talents on literary forms previously thought unbecoming to intellectuals. Serious writers and thinkers though they were, they had no qualms about using fictional biographies or any other form to make moral or political statements. They both valued friendship greatly; they never hesitated to help a friend in trouble. In 814, Liu Tsung-yüan experienced a sudden outburst of creative energy. Over half of his best-known works were written in that year, for example, the "Discourse on Heaven," "Disquisition on Feudalism," and "Three Admonitions," as well as his biographical sketches of common men. That same year, he also wrote several poems on the topic of loyal statesmen and generals who sacrificed their lives for the state, a topic that he did not treat before or after this cluster of poems.[142] Obviously, something was stirring inside Liu Tsung-yüan—was it a spark of hope that he would be reinstated? All things considered, his hope was not too farfetched: his father's case provided a precedent for reinstatement after exile. Recently the situation in Ch'ang-an had become more favorable, and many of his sponsors and friends were back in power in 814. Besides, his father-in-law had been reinstated, and his former sponsors, Hsiao Mien and Hsü Meng-jung, were also back at the capital,[143] as was Han Yü, an official historian and friend. It is conceivable that all these men made a concerted effort to bring Liu back to serve in the central government. Han Yü's "Epitaph for Liu Tzu-hou" contains a long passage on the contemporary scene: "But alas, had Tzu-hou been able to conduct himself while serving in the Chancellery in the same way as he did later when he served as an administrator and prefect, he would not have been dismissed. *Even when he was repudiated, had there been some powerful personage to give him preferment,* Tzu-hou would surely again have held proper appointments indefinitely." (Italics added.)

Because Han Yü later did promote Liu Tsung-yüan's intimate friends and political associates Liu Yü-hsi and Han T'ai,[144] it is possible to see that Han Yü in 814, backed by people like his own patron, P'ei Tu, and through Liu Tsung-yüan's own connections, did everything he could to provide Liu Tsung-yüan with the necessary preferment mentioned in the epitaph. How else are we to understand the passage in which Han Yü wishes that "Tzu-hou would surely again hold proper appointments indefinitely"? Judging from a preceding passage in the same epitaph on the betrayal of friendship, it is most likely that Han Yü had done all he could for Liu Tsung-yüan and earned with his demonstrated loyalty the right to condemn Liu's false friends in his epitaph. It would have been a rather strange thing to do otherwise.

With this background in mind, let us examine three possible interpretations of the "Lo-ch'ih Inscription." The first is reminiscent of the *Chiu T'ang shu*'s opinion that the "Lo-ch'ih Inscription" is a literary joke, an ostentatious, absurd exhibition of Han Yü's literary virtuosity and a reflection of his undying infatuation with the ingenious and the extraordinary in literary writing. Considering Liu Tsung-yüan's status and the positive aspects of the relationship between the two men,[145] this is not very convincing. The second interpretation goes a step further and sees the work not only as a literary joke reflecting Han Yü's vices but also as a practical joke on Liu Tsung-yüan, who had had a fancy for fictional writings. Given that the two men's mutual regard was strongest in the sphere of literature, it is not impossible that Han Yü should have written the "Lo-ch'ih Inscription" with tongue in cheek, not really intending it to "substantiate the false belief of the southern people," but to play a good-natured joke on a friend who had had a highly developed taste for such writings and was eminent enough (even in death) to make the game worth the effort. The third, most plausible, answer is that the "Lo-ch'ih Inscription" expressed feelings more complex and an intention more worthy than those suggested above. It must not be forgotten that Liu Tsung-yüan was one of the few contemporary writers who showed a genuine appreciation of Han Yü's literary gifts: it was he who defended the conceptual originality and literary brilliance of the "Biography of the Brush" when it was under attack.[146] It is not unlikely that, when Han Yü was offered the subject matter of the "Lo-ch'ih Inscription," he remembered that defense and thus was prompted to accept. The "Lo-ch'ih Inscription," immortalizing Liu's (other-worldly) virtue in a form that could not have been done for his achievements in this world, is couched in the same mock-historical style Han Yü had used in the "Biography of the Brush." The technical reprise was undoubtedly a personal salute to Liu Tsung-yüan; its underlying affection and apparent humor, Han Yü was confident, would have been appreciated by Liu had he been alive.

When all is said and done, the "Lo-ch'ih Inscription" is a work with many levels of meaning. As a supernatural tale, it stands on its own with its element of the marvelous and its unity and completeness of plot. As an inscription, its historicity is justified (at least from Han Yü's point of view) by its conscious adaptation of the Chin dynasty antecedents and by Han Yü's most recent views on style. As an illustration of Han Yü's lifelong quest, it demonstrates how Han Yü could resurrect a relatively classical form of the supernatural tale as an alternative to the gaudy specimens of his own time.

This examination of Han Yü's *ku-wen* theory and some of the methods by which he translated his theory into practice makes it clear that he distinguished himself as a purist in theory and in style. He defined the normative use of the term *ku* ("ancient") by identifying it with orthodox Confucianism; by discriminating against Taoism and Buddhism, he made Confucian orthodoxy the only didactic tradition of antiquity worth reviving. Under the influence of Han Yü, *ku-wen* literature became an antithesis not only to parallel prose but also to the Buddhist and Taoist literature popular at his time.

Scholars and historians have repeatedly stressed that the *ku-wen* movement neither began nor ended with Han Yü. Yet it was in Han Yü that the movement found its most intense expression. He may not have been the original thinker and writer that his Sung dynasty admirers considered him to be; yet no other *ku-wen* master struggled so valiantly for originality, experimented so widely, and suffered so intensely for it. He may not have been, for that matter, the ideal Confucian that he professed to be; yet his un-Confucian moments contained such clairvoyance and were imbued with such a sense of self-irony that, in those moments, Han Yü was not so much yielding to aberration as playing with it, not so much bowing to his own weaknesses and foibles as showing them off with relish and gusto.

In summary, four salient features of his achievements in *ku-wen* deserve emphasis. First, throughout his literary career, Han Yü advocated that literature should be didactic and that a writer, to be truly great, must submit to a threefold discipline: a writer must read the Classics extensively, learn to discriminate between the true and the false, and be in constant communion with classical masterpieces.

Second, Han Yü's preeminence as a writer in his time does not lie in the fact that he was a great polemicist able to influence the world with his unpopular Confucianism; rather it lies in the genius that created an inventive and powerful prose style quite different from that of his opponents and produced a body of literature in that style whose excellence compelled the admiration even of those who did not subscribe to its message.

Third, this style was very flexible and encompassed elements of very different genres. The unifying principle in Han Yü's prose is essentially the principle of stylistic transformation. Works that seem to contradict his Confucian stand can be made consistent in light of this principle. The "Lo-ch'ih Inscription" is a concrete illustration of the way in which Han Yü could adapt an un-Confucian subject to his Confucian outlook by his manipulations of stylistic elements.

Fourth, Han Yü's theory of literature evolved along consistent lines. Han Yü's succession of stylistic doctrines—the "extraordinary," "learning from the ancients," "expression worthy of the topic," and "writing becomes fluent when the diction is apt"—reflects no real changes in his literary ideals. In their chronological order, they are evidence of a growing sophistication in his conception and control of the art of writing. The chronology of these doctrines, largely neglected by critics, is of prime importance to an understanding of Han Yü's development as a literary theorist and his progress as a *ku-wen* stylist.

Han Yü conceived his *ku-wen* theory creatively and not dogmatically. Its creative potential should be measured not by what it failed to be, but by what it tried to be—above all, by Han Yü's numerous imaginative attempts to annex literary domains that until his advent had lain outside the Confucian realm.

## 2

# LIU TSUNG-YÜAN

# The Individual in History

IN A.D. 805 the emperor Shun-tsung, patron of the reform party to which Liu Tsung-yüan belonged, abdicated and died only months after ascending the throne. The chief reformers were sentenced to death, and their followers were banished to minor posts in distant regions. Liu Tsung-yüan, age 33 *sui* and at the beginning of his political career, suddenly found himself relegated to Yung-chou (in modern southwestern Hunan).[1] He never regained his position at court. A spark of hope kindled by a routine recall to Ch'ang-an in 815 was quickly snuffed out when Liu was again ordered south, this time to Liu-chou (in modern Kwangsi), a prefecture even more remote from the capital than Yung-chou.[2] There he remained, a conscientious functionary, until his death on the eighth day of the eleventh lunar month of 819.

## The Impact of Political Exile

Many students of the scholar-official tradition in China have noted that the Chinese intelligentsia were at heart servants of the state: "Only the agony and distress of a ruined or frustrated official career, as in the case of Liu Tsung-yüan, could drive the T'ang intelligentsia into serious literary pursuits."[3] Indeed, the ten years in exile at Yung-chou (805–15) are generally acknowledged to have been the most productive years in Liu Tsung-yüan's career as a writer.[4] Statements in Liu's own writings lend support to such a view. In a letter of 809 to Wu Wu-ling (ca. 785–835), for example, Liu said:

> I have been writing for a long time, but I made little of it and never applied myself to it. I looked on it as a special skill like toss-pot or chess. Hence when I was in Ch'ang-an [before 805], I never used it to angle for fame. My idea then was to apply [my talent] to practical affairs, making it my goal to assist the current government and to attend to the well-being of the people. After I became a transgressor, and as soon as I stopped trembling in fear, I found myself idle and unoccupied. So I simply resumed writing. When you cannot demonstrate the way of assisting the current government and attending to the well-being of the people in the present, it is only right that you preserve it for posterity. Statements unaccompanied by literary skill become muddled.[5] That being so, I suppose literary skill should not be disparaged.[6]

Undoubtedly, this leisure from court politics allowed Liu Tsung-yüan to devote himself to serious literary work. At Yungchou, he wrote 18 disquisitions that set forth his political ideas; he also wrote 82 poems, 8 *fu* ("rhymeprose"), and 9 pieces in the style of the *Li-sao* poems to vent his frustration and bitterness.[7] In addition, the compulsory idleness provided him with the necessary setting for writing on subjects other than politics and personal discontent. His involvement with the daily life of the local people, for example, inspired 11 biographical sketches and 11 fables, many of which are moral allegories with philosophical dimensions. His excursions in the countryside produced nine unconventional and distinctive "records of excursions" (*yu-chi*), which earned a respectable position in the history of Chinese literature for this marginal literary form.[8] Moreover, the scattered statements on literature that he made during this period, in prefaces (*hsü*) and valedictions (*sung-hsü*), and in letters to friends (*shu*), contributed significantly to the broadening of the horizon of *ku-wen*.[9] Taken together, the corpus of works Liu Tsung-yüan produced at Yungchou demonstrates the range and the profundity of feelings that a traditional Chinese intellectual was able to attain in adverse circumstances.

After leaving Yung-chou, Liu Tsung-yüan seems to have deliberately chosen obscurity. Liu's reaction to his two periods of exile differed considerably. During the first exile, his political ambitions were frustrated, and he wrote a great deal. During the second exile, when his political future had become quite hopeless, he neglected literary pursuits and showed less discontent. In his four years as prefect of Liu-chou (816–19), aside from writings of an administrative nature, Liu wrote very little: only 33 poems, no *fu*, no *sao*-style works, no disquisitions, and no fables or biographical sketches except for one about a fearless local 12-year-old boy.[10] He seems to have put an end to his inquiries into the world, into its history of injustice and evil, and to have ceased to blame himself for having failed to write a purer chapter in that history. At Liu-chou, a certain lucidity characterized his life and his ultimate perception of nature and of the human world. Both allegory and critical contentiousness disappeared from his writings.[11] Many of the ideas that he had discussed in his writings during the Yung-chou period but had not acted on because of his continuing hope of recall to Ch'ang-an were finally translated into deeds. Having abandoned the prospect of ever returning to the capital, he embraced instead the role of prefect at Liu-chou.

His life and deeds at Liu-chou, in that sense, reflected much of what he had written about the nature of *tao* and the role of the individual in history while assistant magistrate at Yung-chou. For example, his insistence in the earlier years on a narrowly political characterization of *tao*—which at first he had seen in terms of sociopolitical reality (*shih*) and the roles (*wei*) that men play within that reality—matured into a philosophical understanding of the inherent principle of things (*li*).[12] The concept of the natural and spontaneous (*tzu-jan*), as contrasted with both the supernatural and the manmade, which he had once invoked to interpret Heaven (*t'ien*) as the origin of political authority and institutions, now suffused his outlook on *tao* and informed his way of life.[13] Although Liu Tsung-yüan never fully developed the philosophical implications of *tao* as seen from the perspective of *tzu-jan* in his writings, the logical conclusion of that position was certainly familiar to him from the writings of his intimate friend and fellow exile Liu Yü-hsi (772–842).[14] And it is possible to detect in some of his fables (as in the "Three Admonitions" discussed below) the implication that, once moral and political considerations are excluded, the events of one's life as seen from the pure perspective of *tzu-jan* are nothing more than the configurations of *shih* and *wei* as governed by a kind of mathematical determinism (*shu*).[15] The last years of Liu Tsung-yüan's life were characterized by his detachment from court politics. His accomplishments at Liu-chou no longer suggest the radical reformer and brilliant writer. At Liu-chou, Liu Tsung-yüan fulfilled his role as prefect simply by performing the duties that pertained to his office. He planted trees and dug wells; he reformed the local custom of selling children into slavery; he wrote stele inscriptions for the temple of Confucius as well as for an unknown girl from the local community.[16] He took the well-being of the people of Liu-chou to heart and worked assiduously to improve their lives. Liu's activities at Liu-chou were in complete contrast to those in Yung-chou. This seems to have been Liu Tsung-yüan's way of realizing his earlier aspiration to the *tao* of the sages; in this process he made that *tao* a reality in the lives of many other people. To the politically minded, this period of Liu's life marks his failure as a servant of the state. To literary critics and historians, this period is a blank page in the book of Liu's achievements. But to the local people of Liu-chou at the time, Liu Tsung-yüan was first and foremost their virtuous magistrate and after his death a benevolent divine influence.[17] "If his virtue is established among men, after his death they will seek out his descendants and serve them";[18] Liu Tsung-yüan made this statement in defense of his theory of the institution of feudalism, but it can also serve as a commentary on the meaning of his last years.

This study begins with a brief consideration of Liu Tsung-yüan's theory of literature and continues with an analysis of his concept of nature (*tzu-jan*), which was basic both to his thought and to his literary practice. The study distinguishes three aspects of nature in his poetry and informal prose—the lyrical (particularly in his descriptive lyrical prose), the rational (in his animal fables), and the moral (in his moral biographies). Even as his work evolved from the lyrical to the rational and finally to the moral view of nature, Liu Tsung-yüan was always preoccupied with the individual's place in history and time.

## Liu Tsung-yüan on *Tao* and *Wen*

Liu Tsung-yüan, like the other *ku-wen* masters, was not a systematic literary theorist in the modern sense.[19] His understanding of literature, like that of Han Yü before him and of Ou-yang Hsiu and Su Shih afterward, fluctuated considerably with his changing views of the world and of his own role in the world. In Liu Tsung-yüan's case, he made his best-known statements on literature and writing in the same years (805–15) in which he wrote his famous essays "Disquisition on Feudalism" and "Discourse on Heaven," as well as the now-popular group of fables and biographical sketches. The works of that period exhibit a critical and iconoclastic spirit, but his concern with literature and writing (*wen*), and with the relationship between *tao* and *wen*, occupies a rather marginal place in the corpus. When Liu Tsung-yüan discusses *tao* in these works, it is usually the *tao* of political rule. When *tao* is brought together with literature and writing, two basic themes appear: *wen yi ming tao* ("literature is meant to clarify the *tao*") and *wen yu erh tao* ("literature serves two basic functions"). The relationship between *tao* and *wen* is central to *ku-wen* theory, and since these two theses occupy a central position in Liu Tsung-yüan's artistic theory, they make a convenient focus for discussing his opinions on literature.

*Wen yi ming tao and Liu Tsung-yüan's Theory of Tao*

One inference frequently drawn from the phrase *wen yi ming tao* is that Liu Tsung-yüan shares a common position with other *ku-wen* theorists such as Han Yü in affirming that *tao*, as exemplified by the way of the ancient kings, is manifested in the writings of the ancient sages; hence, to revive the *tao* in the present, one must emulate (*hsüeh*) the words and deeds of the sages. This is not quite the case. Liu Tsung-yüan differs significantly from the other theorists both in his conception of the *tao* and in his conception of the historical role of the sages. Whereas Han Yü emphasizes the idea of orthodoxy and recognizes as sages only those who advocated the orthodox Confucian *tao*, Liu Tsung-yüan understands *tao* in historical and relativistic terms and ascribes little sanctity to the sages in general. In a letter to Ts'ui An, Liu said, "The sayings of the sages are meant to clarify the *tao*." [20] This line has been quoted to support the argument that Liu Tsung-yüan believes that *tao* is manifested in the sayings of the sages. But the point of this statement is that Liu Tsung-yüan does not believe that a sage has a monopoly on the *tao*. The key word in *wen yi ming tao* is not *tao* but *ming*. *Ming* is sometimes translated as "to illuminate," but in Liu Tsung-yüan's usage it is probably better rendered as "to clarify" or "to make clear and manifest." The procedure of *ming*, in Liu's words, is "to analyze in accordance with the inherent principle of things" (*yi li hsi chih*), and the objective of *ming* is "to determine rightness and wrongness" (*ting ch'i shih fei*).[21] His position on the role of the sages in history is stated explicitly in the "Disquisition on Feudalism" (814):

> The way of [governing] the world is to stabilize the principle behind peaceful political order, and then to find the right persons to place correctly in service. . . . Feudalism came about as a result of men's doings. How can one attribute its development to the sages' instituting it? I firmly hold that feudalism did not come into existence because the sages intended it to; it came into existence because the circumstances called for it.[22]

*Tao*, by the same token, was not an invention of the sages; the sayings of the sages serve merely to "clarify" the *tao*. And this clarification of the *tao* is not the prerogative of the sage alone; it can be the goal of every serious writer. In a letter of 813 to Wei Chung-li, Liu says, "At first, when I was young and immature, I concentrated my effort in writing on verbal skill. Only when I grew older did I realize that the aim of writing is to clarify the *tao*."[23]

In the letter to Wu Wu-ling cited earlier, Liu Tsung-yüan points out specifically that when the purpose of a piece of writing is to clarify the *tao*, then brilliance of style should not be a consideration. In fact, works that are stylistically dazzling but deficient in substance are dangerous:

> When a person does a piece of writing, devoting all his effort to embellishment of its literary brilliance, paying no attention to substance, what is more, he introduces the scandalous and the bizarre into the work, expanding [the appeal of his writing] with that which is exotic and incredible, thus enticing the young with a glowing facade and leading them in the end to what is farfetched; this is like covering a pit with a piece of brocade. Unless [the pit] is clearly exposed, many will topple into it. Hence I post signs to alert those who seek the proper way [in such writings].[24]

Liu Tsung-yüan is skeptical about attempts to "clarify the *tao*" through imitation of the sages. His distinction between *tao* and the sayings of the sages is implicit in his discussion of emulation (*hsüeh*). In his view, emulation is not a matter of duplicating the sages' words and deeds:

> One can emulate Confucius but cannot [by so doing] act like Confucius. Once the emulation is perfect, a person would himself become a Confucius. However, if he tries to perform Confucius's deeds before attaining perfection, he is like Duke Hsiang of Sung, who, wishing to be hegemon of the states, lost his country and was finally killed by an arrow.[25]

Emulation must be measured against a person's *ming* ("critical intelligence") and *chih* ("aspirations"):

> There are those who are untiring in their learning and yet lose their way and become perplexed in their aspirations. This is because their critical intelligence is not yet perfected. There are those who illuminate everything with their all-encompassing perception and yet have no control over their own innate character and slip completely away from their principles. This is because their aspirations are not yet perfected.[26]

Liu Tsung-yüan is quite emphatic about the inherent perils of misguided efforts at emulating the sages: "When one's words overreach one's virtue, and when one's writings fail to express fully one's aspirations, there is nothing but trouble in store."[27]

Liu Tsung-yüan's understanding of *tao* is at once historical and relativistic. *Tao* is defined by sociopolitical reality (*shih*) and by the power and influence invested in that reality; and it takes into consideration the diverse roles (*wei*) a person plays in differing circumstances. Hence, in Liu Tsung-yüan's theory, *tao* is multiple. In addition to the way of governing the world (*t'ien-hsia chih tao*), he speaks of the way in which sages bring life to the people (*sheng-jen chih tao*), the way of that which is constant in the world of human affairs (*ching* or *ch'ang*), and the way of the expedient and the efficient (*ch'üan*).[28] With regard to the practice of *tao*, he differentiates between the way of the superior man (*chün-tzu chih tao*) and the way of the man of great accomplishments (*ta-jen chih tao*).[29] In Liu Tsung-yüan's writings, his method of "clarifying the *tao*" is an extremely critical one—as exemplified in many disquisitions and discourses such as "On [King Ch'eng's] Enfeoffment of His Younger Brother with a Leaf of the T'ung Tree," "A Rebuttal of the Argument in Favor of Penalizing Those Involved in Vendettas," "Explicating the *Annals of Yen-tzu*," and "Explicating the

*Analects.*"[30] He also often dwells on the importance of steering a proper and balanced course (*chung tao*) when putting the way that one has envisioned into practice.[31] His critical approach to *tao* and to the role of the sages in history puts him in an unusual position in the *ku-wen* tradition, one quite distinct from the orthodox and didactic position occupied by his contemporary Han Yü and later by Ou-yang Hsiu. He brings a refreshing liberalism to the otherwise overly moralistic *ku-wen* outlook, broadening the intellectual horizon of *ku-wen* theory and enriching *ku-wen* literature.

## Wen yu erh tao and Liu Tsung-yüan's Theory of Wen

The second theme, *wen yu erh tao* ("literature serves two basic functions"), occurs in Liu's postscript to the collected works of Yang Ling.[32] The word *tao* in *wen yu erh tao* means path, direction, or function and has little to do with the *tao* of *wen yi ming tao*, which means essentially the way of political government. *Wen yu erh tao* deals primarily with the question of the relationship between literary form and function.

In Liu's view, the two functions are, in historical writings, to praise or blame (*tz'u ling pao pien*) and, in poetry, to serve a didactic or satiric function (*tao yang feng yü*). The prototypes of the first category of *wen* are the announcements and counsels in the *Shu ching*, the appendixes to the *Yi ching* (Book of changes), and the implicit criticisms in the *Ch'un-ch'iu*. The prototypes of the second category are the "ballads of the time of Yü and Hsia and the songs and odes of Yin and Chou." The formal principles for the two categories are also quite different. For the first, the principle is that of "words being correct and the principle of political order being fully represented"; for the second, the principle is that of "language being expressive and the ideas good." Stylistically, literature in the first category excels in being "lofty and rigorous, spacious and solid"; in the second category, "parallel and ordered, fresh and unconventional." Since the objective, form, function, and stylistic orientation of the two categories of writing are different, Liu Tsung-yüan believes that "those who wield a brush ordinarily excel in the one or the other type of writing; rarely does one encounter a writer who excels in both. . . . The difficulty that lies in excelling in both is indeed excessive."[33]

Because of his political exile early in his career, Liu Tsung-yüan was not in a position to write much that conforms easily to either of the two categories of *wen* in question. His "Odes on the Pacification of the Huai-hsi Rebellion" are probably the only pieces that approximate the ideal in the second category.[34] The scope of *wen* implied in *wen yi ming tao* is much broader than that of the *wen* in *wen yu erh tao*, which applies only when the writer is serving in the ideal position of court historian or imperially commissioned secretary and poet. Because Liu Tsung-yüan had little opportunity to write in such a capacity, the waste of the exquisite scenery of remote places like Yung-chou, which he laments, becomes an obvious analogy with the waste of his own talent. Yet his lasting eminence in the realm of letters was confidently predicted by Han Yü as early as 820 in the "Epitaph for Liu Tzu-hou."

Liu Tsung-yüan wrote indirectly on world affairs and on his own role in history in his more personal poems, his landscape prose, and his fables and biographical sketches. These works are expressive of the mind of an individual and of his values in the realm of nature rather than of those of an adviser in the imperial court. There are always moments in life when the need for inner refuge becomes predominant, and Liu expressed this need in a poem.

> Since my banishment I have long been wasting away;
> Not until now have I had occasion for cheerfulness.
> What gladdens my heart does not remain for long;
> The thought that I am away [from home] comes to court
>     my cares.
> Looking northward, I am separated from my dear ones;
> Looking southward, I live intermingling with the
>     barbarians.
> Enough of that, I shall say no more,
> I shall simply take refuge in the fleeting moment.[35]

The aesthetic distance provided by the dominant theme of "taking refuge" (*chi*) enables Liu Tsung-yüan to reflect on the inherent principles in the many facets of nature and the self: the lyricism in scenic nature, the amoral operation of rational *li*, and the ultimate good immanent in the phenomenon of life and growth in all creatures. Through his contemplation of the many principles of nature, Liu Tsung-yüan matured in his philosophical thinking and in his way of living. These aspects of his thought became an integral part of *ku-wen* literature.

## Nature in Liu Tsung-yüan's Writings

If history supplies the definitive statement on the life of an intellectual as a political being, nature provides the stage for him to act out the drama of self-questing and self-definition as a human being. In the course of his political career, the traditional Chinese intellectual discovered the laws governing the world of human affairs, and to the extent he was able to apply those laws, he found fulfillment of his political ideals. As long as there was harmony between the political life of the self and the political order that supported the fulfillment of the self, he enjoyed a sense of well-being and felt that he was in tune with the way of the universe. Falling out of that order was therefore inconceivable to the Chinese intellectual because it meant not only a negation of his personal success and fulfillment but also a negation of the universal order on which success and fulfillment were predicated. The quest for reintegration with his lost success was frequently pursued in nature, outside of the world that rejected him. And, more often than not, such a quest involved an inquiry into the phenomena of change in the fortunes of man and, by extension, into the principle governing change in all of nature. Change, when it first appears in the consciousness of the questing individual, impinges on his perception of reality; it challenges his mode of life, which, until the moment of his failure, he assumed to be lasting. Depending on his conclusions about the nature of change and of reality, he adapts to, remains aloof from, or departs from the old world order that structured his earlier mode of success.

Ch'ü Yüan, for instance, did not in his quest find change to be the immanent law of his reality. To him, ideals were more real. Nature was merely appearance. The qualities of nature inherent to men deceived them with their games of paradox and of mutability and consequently corrupted the trusting and persecuted the pure. The natural landscape, mirroring the inconstancy and duplicity to be found in the nature of man, was a source of perpetual disappointment and suffering for Ch'ü Yüan. Unable to revise his vision of reality, he ultimately took his life in protest against the ubiquitous deceptions of nature, defying the demands of change, which he perceived to promise nothing but caprice in return for the purity of his ideals.[36] Chuang-tzu, in a different time and under different circumstances, found it both real and natural for all beings to exist and to behave as they did. To him, nature seemed to be explicable basically in terms of differences. Change was a theory that allowed man to comprehend the fundamental principle of how things came to differ. Chuang-tzu's theory accounts not only for artificial differences in human success and failure but also for natural differences among forms of life, deformity and death not excepted. Chuang-tzu accounts for the nature of man, in its private and political manifestations alike, by assuming that man's "nature"—that which makes him behave as he does—is not only what he is born with but also his appropriate form of behavior. That form, in the works of Chuang-tzu, is described in terms of the scale of things: the *p'eng* bird flies 90,000 miles up in the air, whereas the sparrow hops from one branch of a tree to another; the owl feeds on the decaying body of a rat, whereas the eagle would not think of doing so.[37] In Chuang-tzu's theory of nature (*tzu-jan*), to force oneself to behave in a manner different from what is innately appropriate is painful; it is unnecessary to strive to transcend the scale of things. Only when a person does not strive to accomplish either the painful or the unnecessary does he approximate the state of his nature.

Whereas Ch'ü Yüan idealizes the natural landscape in his poetry and uses it as a symbol of the perverted ways of man, Chuang-tzu turns to animal behavior to illustrate his concept of *tzu-jan* and to satirize man's unnatural aspiration to become ideal within the natural scale of things. These two different modes of perception and depiction of nature and of man are further developed in Liu Tsung-yüan's writing into a threefold perception of the reality of nature, a perception that is expressed by three different aspects of nature and three different literary modes: nature as landscape and the lyrical mode; nature as animal behavior and the rational mode; and nature as living and growth and the moral mode. An understanding of these three modes, and of the evolution of Liu Tsung-yüan's thought from one mode to another, will greatly elucidate our analysis of his *ku-wen* style and his literary career.

*Nature as Landscape and the Lyrical Mode*

Liu Tsung-yüan, like the poets Ch'ü Yüan, T'ao Ch'ien, and Hsieh Ling-yün (385–433), came to nature through political misfortune.[38] For all its unspoiled scenery, Yung-chou seemed at first a most uncongenial place.[39] Liu was still young and had embarked, it seemed only yesterday, on a brilliant career at court. His heart was still in Ch'ang-an, preoccupied with the turn of events that had brought him to his current disgrace. Recrimination and self-reproach ate deeply into him. In rage and remorse, he berated his political enemies and blamed himself.[40] To relieve his frantic mind, Liu turned to drinking, to the oblivion of sleep, and finally, quite by accident, to the natural landscape. His first encounter with the beauty of nature aroused a sympathetic response. The seclusion of the natural setting of Yung-chou, the pent-up energy and the beauty of its unusual formations of rocks and streams, seemed to correspond precisely to his own talents and abilities—all wasted, unwanted. A gnawing consciousness of loneliness began to replace his anger and depression.

Slowly, slowly, the sky cleared after the rain;
Alone, I followed the bends of the limpid brook.
I plumbed the deserted spring with my staff,
And put my belt around the fresh bamboos.
What are the sighs and deep thoughts all about?
Is not loneliness what I really want?
It is fortunate that here all the bustle is stilled;
As I whistle and sing, the heat subsides.[41]

From his many visits to the scenic sights of Yung-chou, Liu Tsung-yüan left a sizable body of essays and poems that are vividly descriptive not only of what he saw but also of the feelings and thoughts that informed his heart. The most famous essays from this group are the "Eight Records of [Scenic Visits at] Yung-chou."[42]

The "Eight Records" describe two sequences of visits by Liu Tsung-yüan to the hills and waters of Yung-chou. The first sequence was inspired by a fortuitous trip to the West Mountains in the ninth lunar month of 809, during the fourth year of Liu's ten-year stay at Yung-chou. The initial excursion was followed by three subsequent visits to nearby lakes and hills in the following month of the same year. The second sequence began with a trip in 812 to an inlet on the property of a certain Yüan family, followed by visits to the Rocky Trough and the Rocky Gorge nearby. Between the two sequences, Liu made a single visit to the Mountain of Little Stone Walls in 811. Liu's response to the natural landscape of Yung-chou is anything but indiscriminate. The "Record of [a Visit to] Yüan Family Inlet" (812), for example, begins:

> Going southwest for ten *li* by water along Jan Brook, there are five enjoyable views in the landscape, none of which, however, can match the beauty of the Flatiron Pool. Going west by land from the mouth of Jan Brook, there are eight or nine enjoyable views in the landscape, none of which, however, is the match of the West Mountains. Going southwest by water from Morning Sun Crag to the Fu River, there are three enjoyable views, none of which, however, can match the Yüan Family Inlet. These are all remarkable sites in Yung-chou, secluded and delightful.[43]

This demonstration of his critical and discerning taste suggests that, after some seven years at Yung-chou, Liu Tsung-yüan had finally developed a certain appreciation for his surroundings and was less tortured by the misfortunes that he had formerly tried to forget in drinking and sleep. The sense of kinship with Yung-chou's isolated natural beauty that he expresses, not without some mocking humor, in the "Record of the Mountain of Little Stone Walls" (814) reveals a mind that is more at peace with itself.

> Alas, for a long time I have been wondering whether there is indeed a creator of the world. Now [on seeing the Mountain of Little Stone Walls], I really do think that there is one. But it seems strange that he did not create this hill in the central states instead of in this barbaric region, where his art will find no purveyor for hundreds and thousands of years. This, indeed, is laboring to no purpose. A divine being ought not to have done anything like that. But then, is one to say that the creator does not exist? Some say the sights are there to comfort talented men in disgrace. Some say that his creative energies went exclusively into the making of these objects rather than into the making of great men, and as a result, there are more rocks and stones in southern Ch'u than there are men. I do not believe either explanation.[44]

The lyricism, innovative form, and technique of Liu Tsung-yüan's "Eight Records" have been thoroughly studied.[45] Their evocation of the emotional sympathy between the isolated beauty of the scenery and the wasted talents of the visitor has been noted many times. William Nienhauser, for instance, has written: "It is not difficult to follow Liu's grandest metaphor, that of spots of natural beauty isolated and neglected by their creator representing a good man who has been isolated and neglected by his friends and monarch. This meaning... underlies the entire group of essays." [46] Nostalgia, loneliness, and self-pity are conspicuous motifs in the landscape essays written at Yung-chou, but fortunately these are not the only sentiments that informed Liu's writings of this period. His brilliant critical intellect was also at work (although not always on noble and praiseworthy subjects—as we shall see, he used this intellect to dissect and condemn his political opponents in the animal fables). A set of poems and a prose preface, written concurrently with the "Eight Records," dwell on the theme of "foolishness" (*yü*) and express not Liu Tsung-yüan's love for scenic nature but his obsession with the change in his fortunes and his own role in his disgrace. [47]

In the "Eight Records," Liu Tsung-yüan refers three times to a certain Jan Brook at Yung-chou. In several of the poems that he wrote concurrently with the "Eight Records," Jan Brook appears as Foolish Brook. In the preface to these poems, written in 810, we are given a privileged look into the inquisitive, questing self behind the lyricism and visual beauty of his scenic "records"—a self engaged in an obsessive inquiry into the phenomena of change, the underlying principle of these phenomena, and the author's role in relation to that principle.

*Preface to the "Foolish Brook Poems"*

To the north of the Kuan River, there is a brook. It flows eastward into the Hsiao River. Some say that a Mr. Jan once lived there and hence named it Jan Brook. Some say that the water in the brook can be used for dye [*jan*] and that it was named "Dye Brook" because of this property. I have transgressed through my foolishness [*yü*] and consequently have been banished to the bank of the Hsiao River. I am fond of this brook. I went upstream [one day] for two or three *li* and came upon an especially exquisite place, and I made my home there. In ancient times, there was a Valley of the Foolish Old Man. [48] Now, having made the brook the site of my home, I could not decide on a name for it. Everyday, people passing by argued continually over its name, so that the name could not remain unchanged. Therefore I changed its name to Foolish Brook. Along Foolish Brook I purchased a small hill and called it Foolish Hill. Sixty paces to the northeast of Foolish Hill, there is a spring. I purchased it for my dwelling place and called it Foolish Spring. The spring has six mouths out of which water gushes up from under the hill. Flowing together, [the water from the six openings] meanders southward to form Foolish Ditch. I had earth carried there and stones piled up to dam the water where the passage is narrow, and thereby made Foolish Pond. East of Foolish Pond, I built Foolish Hall, and south of the hall, I built Foolish Pavilion. In the pond is Foolish Island. Beautiful trees and rare stones are placed there. They are all remarkable sights in this landscape, but because of me, they suffer the mortification of carrying the name "foolish." Water is a substance in which the wise man takes delight. Why must this brook alone suffer the mortifying name "foolish"?

Its water level is so low that it cannot be used for irrigation. Moreover, its currents are too rapid, and there are too many islets and rocks in it, so that large boats cannot enter it. Besides, it is too secluded and too recessed, too shallow and too narrow; no dragon would ever deign to live in it because there is not enough water with which to make clouds and rain. It has nothing to offer to the world. In that respect it is exactly like me. This being the case, it might as well tolerate the humiliation of being called "foolish."

Ning-wu Tzu acted as if he were foolish when his country was in disorder.[49] He was a wise man, but he acted in [an apparently] foolish way. Master Yen [Hui] never disagreed [with any of Confucius's teachings] as if he were a foolish man.[50] He was someone who was intelligent but appeared to be foolish. In my case, I live under an orderly government, but I have gone against the inherent principle [li] of things and mishandled state affairs. Hence no one who has acted foolishly is as foolish as I am. This being so, then no one in the world can rival my claim to this brook. I have the sole right to name it "foolish."

The brook has nothing to offer to the world, but it serves well as a mirror to all creation.[51] It is limpid, lustrous, graceful, and pure. It jingles like the ancient bells and musical stones. It delights the foolish one so much that he, laughing merrily, is totally infatuated with it and cannot bear to leave.

Although I am out of tune with the times, yet I still take considerable comfort in writing. I can immerse the myriad creatures [in my works] and capture all their forms and poses, letting nothing escape. I sing about Foolish Brook with my foolish verses; they go surprisingly well together in their common obscurity. Overtaking the undifferentiated state of the primordial world, and submerging myself in its insentience, vacuous and inane, I will thus be recognized by no one. Therefore, I have written eight foolish poems and have recorded them on rocks by Foolish Brook.[52]

Liu Tsung-yüan's self-mocking identification with foolishness at the end of the preface, together with the long introduction that leads up to it, can be considered a studied literary device by means of which he understood and revealed the cause of the demise of his political career. This method of revelation—the confession of foolishness—is a thought-provoking one. Foolishness (*yü*) is the reverse of intelligence (*ming*). Ming, as Liu defined it in his theoretical writings, is a process of critical reasoning by means of which one judges the rightness and wrongness of things (*ting ch'i shih fei*). Now that Liu's life had already been irreparably spoiled, *ming*, theoretically speaking, was of no further use to him in clarifying the cause of his fall. This situation calls for the limpidity of Foolish Brook to mirror (not to clarify), and the Foolish Brook poems to record (not to determine the right and wrong of), the point at which his life has gone astray.

The reflection of Liu Tsung-yüan's self in the mirror of Foolish Brook was not the only image he saw there. It also reflected the images of those who were "cunning at heart." In the poem "Taking Recluse Hsieh to Foolish Pond at Daybreak" (810), Liu Tsung-yüan sings:

After washing my hair, I changed to a light kerchief;
In the morning breeze, the dew by the poolside looked
    clear.
In harmony with my otherworldly feelings,
I had the honor of the company of a recluse.
Morning clouds dispersed and the winding mountain
    [emerged];
The sky was high, and several wild geese cried [flying by].
Let the cunning at heart stay with those in power;
I shall follow the style of primitive man.[53]

In another poem, "Living by [Foolish] Brook" (810), the images of the official cap-pin and robe-girdle are symbols of ambition, Liu's own included.

For a long time I was tied to the cap-pin and robe-girdle;
It was by a stroke of good luck that I was banished to this
    barbaric southern land.
I live, unoccupied, with farmers as neighbors;
Every now and then, I am a guest of the mountains and
    woods.
The morning ploughs turn over grass that is still wet with
    dew;
The evening boats make splashing sounds against the rocks
    in the brook.
Coming and going, I meet not a soul;
Singing my long drawn-out songs under the blue skies of
    the south.[54]

The blue skies and the songs are reflected images of loneliness and
sadness, of the incorruptibility of Liu Tsung-yüan's unyielding
spirit, and also of his ceaseless yearning to be recalled to Ch'ang-an.
Political ambition reappears in yet another poem, simply entitled "Jan Brook"—Liu Tsung-yüan's sobriquet at Yung-chou.

In my youth I paraded my strength and hoped for a court
    position;
I promised myself to the state and no longer worked for my
    own interest.
Once I tumbled down with the wind and tide, I was cast out
    ten thousand *li*.
My ambition distintegrated, and nothing is left of me except
    a prisoner in bonds.
A prisoner to the end of my life, there is nothing for me to
    do;
I shall find a place to live by Jan Brook in the western part
    of Hsiang.[55]
I shall imitate the Marquis of Shou-chang, Fan Ching,[56]
Who planted varnish trees in his southern garden and waited
    to make lacquer vessels.[57]

Loneliness, frustration, resentment against the machinations of
those "cunning at heart," and lost hopes for reinstatement in the
capital are feelings and thoughts that have no place in purely descriptive landscape essays, but they find candid expression nonetheless in the "Foolish Brook Poems." Neither landscape essays nor
lyrical poems can comfortably accommodate ambition and greed—

agents of political misfortune and the primary cause of Liu Tsung-yüan's disgrace; such passions appear in another literary context, that of fictitious dialogues.

Liu Tsung-yüan invented two dialogues, modeled on "The Fisherman" (*Yü fu*) in the *Ch'u tz'u*, as meditations on the workings of political ambition and greed in life and on the premise of man's ability—through his foolishness or wisdom—to control his own fate. The "Dialogue at the Foolish Brook" (810) is couched in the form of a conversation between Liu Tsung-yüan and the spirit of Foolish Brook, who appears in a dream to challenge Liu's behavior.[58] The "Hypothetical Dialogue Between a Fisherman and the Count of Chih" (810) studies the interplay of ambition, greed, and misfortune by punning on *yü* ("fisherman") and *yü* ("foolish") and on Chih-po (count of Chih) and *chih po* ("wise elder").[59] In these dialogues, beyond the moral issue of whether it is right or wrong to follow the lead of one's ambition and greed, there is also the beginning of a philosophical inquiry into the question of whether ambition and greed are part of the *nature* (*hsing*) of man or whether they simply impair man's ability to discern (*ming*) the factors in his circumstances that determine his well-being or misfortune.

According to the *Shih chi*, the downfall of the count of Chih in 453 B.C. was the result of his insatiable ambition for territorial conquest.[60] In Liu Tsung-yüan's "Hypothetical Dialogue," the early historical account provides the point of departure for the fisherman's advice, which might have saved the count from defeat.

On his way to invade the state of Chao, the count of Chih encounters a fisherman and asks him what he is doing. The fisherman answers by describing his experience with fishing. He began by catching small fish in ponds, then he caught bigger fish in rivers, and finally he caught whales in the ocean. In each case, the reason the fish were there to be caught and he was there to catch them was simply that neither had ever thought of doing anything different. The fisherman ends his story by reminding the count how the most famous fisherman of all, Lü Shang, gave up fishing when he finally "caught" King Wen of Chou while fishing on the southern bank of the River Wei.[61]

Liu Tsung-yüan's fisherman then compares the count of Chih's territorial expansionism to bigger fish catching and eating smaller fish and being caught in turn by the fisherman. He points out that in his experience the greater size of the fish that eat other fish does not in any way alter their ultimate fate. The largest are caught and killed just like the small ones. Hence, if the count continues to follow the example of the fish, he will eventually end like the largest whale: "with his head severed at Hantan [the capital of the state of Chao, which the count is on his way to conquer], his hair torn off at An-i [another place in Chao], his chest spread open at Shangtang [in Chao], his tail broken off at Chung-shan [a place near Chao], and his guts spilling into the marshes to become food for the families of the Three States [Chao, Han, and Wei, which in history eventually destroyed Chih Po and divided his land]."[62] The dialogue concludes with a suggestion from the fisherman that all the count's power will not make him a King Wen and that he must not expect to outdo King Wen by not listening to his fisherman. Of course, Liu's count of Chih does not listen and goes off to his defeat, just as he did in history.

The fisherman's argument is straightforward, and so is the end of the story. In all reason, neither the historical nor the fictional count of Chih should have persisted in his greedy ways; but he did. On the other hand, the fisherman, if he had been truly farsighted and wise, probably should have known that the count could not be persuaded and therefore should not have risked his life in trying to advise him, but he did. The ambiguity remains, then, as to which of the two is the really foolish one. Liu Tsung-yüan offers no answer because either answer would be correct.

Evidently, Liu Tsung-yüan was able at this juncture to imagine arguments and counterarguments as to why certain foolish things had been done in history and in life, but he could not thereby undo the foolishness in his own past or avert the recurrence of foolishness in his future. Wisdom and foolishness coexist in history and in life, and the absurdity of their coexistence, which cannot be exorcized at will by reflective thought, began to stir Liu Tsung-yüan's imagination.

The "Dialogue at Foolish Brook" reiterates the theme of foolishness and explores with similar irony the logic of foolish behavior, this time not of a historical personage but of Liu Tsung-yüan himself. The spirit of Foolish Brook challenges Liu Tsung-yüan's name for the brook. To the spirit, there is an obvious discrepancy between the beauty and utility of the brook's water and its name. Liu draws an analogy between the brook's situation and his own and points out that, in spite of his personal integrity, he has not been able to maintain his rightful position at court. The fact that neither of them is in any way impure and yet neither is sought out by the powerful and the wise is reason enough for the name. The fact that neither of them is able to change his way or nature merely underscores the helpless foolishness of each participant in the dialogue.

The moral of the "Dialogue at Foolish Brook" is as obvious as the moral of the "Hypothetical Dialogue": had Liu Tsung-yüan wished to avoid disaster, he should not have behaved foolishly, like the count of Chih, in pursuit of his ambition. But, as in the earlier dialogue, the clear logic of the answer cannot reverse the consequences of his actions. The repeated confrontation in Liu Tsung-yüan's thinking between rationality and life in absurd settings begins to take on the character of a philosophical impasse. When a resolution is nowhere in sight, the potential wit and humor in the situation become the dramatic reality.

The question of whether man is by nature foolish and thus necessarily blind to the course that leads to disaster or whether he is blinded by circumstance occupies Liu Tsung-yüan in other compositions of the Yung-chou period. The animal fables, for instance, can be read as dramatizations of this basic question.

## Nature as Animal Behavior and the Rational Mode

Altogether Liu Tsung-yüan wrote 11 pieces based on animal themes. The tradition of employing animal behavior to satirize human behavior is an ancient one in China, traditionally associated with the *Chuang-tzu*. But Liu Tsung-yüan did not write simple animal fables; some of these tales served as vehicles for personal attacks. The "Curses on the Corpse Worms" (814), for instance, is a virulent attack on his political enemies, revealing more of Liu Tsung-yüan's intense hatred for the targets than of his objective observation of human behavior. The "Story of the Fu-pan" (814), however, is a more gentle moral satire, mocking man's instinct for accumulation.[63]

The *fu-pan* in Liu's story is a small insect that can carry enormous loads for its size. Whenever it finds something to carry, it puts the load on its head and crawls off with it. If someone takes pity on it and tries to help by taking the load off its head, as soon as the *fu-pan* catches its breath, it resumes the load. The *fu-pan* is also fond of climbing. It will climb and climb until it reaches such a perilous height that it falls to its death. Liu Tsung-yüan used the *fu-pan* as a model for greedy and stupid creatures. The *fu-pan* story is a simple moral satire with no basic ambiguity, and the moral is easy to accept: man should not accumulate so much and climb so high as to cause his own destruction. Little is written into the story to lead our inquiry in other directions—for instance, what existence would be like for the *fu-pan* had it not been cursed with its morbid need to overburden itself. The story seems to say that it is in the nature of the *fu-pan* to overload itself, and it is in the nature of the *fu-pan* to die because of it. The *fu-pan*'s nature and its mode of existence are one, unmediated by moral or religious influences.

This relationship between nature and mode of existence becomes more problematic in some of Liu Tsung-yüan's other fables, for example, the famous "Three Admonitions" (814).[64] The "Three Admonitions" are of special interest here because they mark a turning point in Liu Tsung-yüan's thinking. The parallels in their structural pattern strongly suggest that Liu Tsung-yüan had finally realized that the law of nature (*tzu-jan*) stands completely aloof from human conceptions of right and wrong. The question then becomes, If right and wrong are not part of the inherent principle (*li*) of nature, what then is the basis of human action?

Each of the "Three Admonitions" deals with a victim of circumstances, and each ends in the death of the victim. Thematically and formally speaking, they are three studies of the same phenomenon; namely, the natural principle inherent in the behavioral patterns of all creatures and the moral implication of this principle for man. The development of the plot in each story is dependent on the interaction between the changing circumstances and the nature (sometimes also changed by nonnatural considerations) of the characters involved. For example, in the story "The Deer of Lin-chiang" (814), which we will examine first below, the unchanged nature of the dogs, combined with the changed nature of the deer, brings about the unhappy ending. There are three parties involved in the fable: the man who captures the deer and arbitrarily trains his dogs to be friendly to the deer against the dogs' nature; the deer, which is raised in ignorance of the nature of the dogs; and the dogs, those of the master's that are forced to behave against their nature and the dogs in the street with no such inhibitions. The moral of the tale, as we shall see, depends on *how* we analyze the question of nature and ethics.

A man of Lin-chiang captured a young deer while hunting and took it home to keep. His dogs all came out, their tails wagging, their mouths dripping. The man was angry [at the dogs] and worried [about the deer]. From that day on, he carried the deer to the dogs so that they could get used to it. While showing the deer to them, he would order the dogs to stay still. Gradually, he made the dogs play with the deer. As time went on, the dogs behaved as the man wished them to. So the deer grew up, forgetting that it was a deer and thinking that dogs were its good friends. It would butt them and lie down with them, becoming more and more intimate. And the dogs, out of fear of their master, accepted the deer's behavior. From time to time, however, the dogs would lick their chops. One day three years later, the deer went out of the [master's] house. Seeing many unfamiliar dogs in the street, it ran over to play with them. When those dogs saw the deer, they were at once overjoyed and enraged. Together they killed the deer and ate it, strewing its remains all over the street. The deer died without ever understanding what had happened.[65]

The usual interpretation of this story is that the deer symbolizes Liu Tsung-yüan before his exile—innocent, trusting, having to pay, so to speak, with his life for having kept the wrong kind of company in Ch'ang-an.[66] However, such an interpretation leaves out two-thirds of the story. A reading of the story as a fable, rather than as an autobiographical episode, reveals a different picture.

The deer and the dogs need not be identified with historical people. The simple knowledge that deer are not by natural inclination trusting of dogs is more crucial to an understanding of the story than any possible historical associations. Like any deer in nature, the Lin-chiang deer would have run away at the sight of a dog. In the story, its natural character has been modified by the master's training so that it accepts all dogs as friends. In the same light, the natural impulse of dogs to attack deer is easily recognized. If we do not let the partiality of the master in the story for his pet deer blind us (a partiality that most readers would be inclined to share), we can accept the behavior of the "unfamiliar dogs" as quite natural. If it must be decided who is to be blamed for what happens to the deer, the choice is between taking the position of the master in the story or taking the position of nature. Ambivalence enters into the meaning of the fable at this point. From the perspective of nature, the role of each of the three characters looks altogether different. For instance, the deer in nature is not necessarily a symbol of innocence. In nature, innocence means vulnerability and usually promises an early death in the natural struggle for survival. Here, the cultivated foolishness of this deer is an unnatural phenomenon that causes its own tragic end. Nor can the behavior of the master provide the moral frame of reference since his intervention is also a cause of the deer's tragedy. He trained his deer not to fear dogs, but he did not train it never to leave the premises. He trained his own dogs, but he should have known that he could not train all the dogs of Lin-chiang. He did not foresee that his benevolence could function only within a specific combination of circumstances: the confines of his house, the obedience of his dogs, and the distorted nature of the deer. His personal love for the deer created a precarious state of existence for all concerned.

The same situation of cultivated innocence and therefore foolishness is examined from another perspective in "The Rats of a Certain Family at Yung-chou" (814). This time, the victim is a less sympathetic character.

There was a man of Yung-chou who was extraordinarily afraid of taboos and unpropitious days. Since he had been born in the year of the rat, he regarded rats as divine. Because of his love for rats, he kept neither cats nor dogs and forbade his servants to attack any rat. He let the rats do anything they wished, without interference, in his barns, granaries, and kitchens. As a consequence, the rats told one another about it, and all of them came to this man's house and ate their fill without retribution. There was not a single utensil in the man's chambers that was unbroken, not a single garment on the rack that was untorn. Most of the food and drink were leftovers of the rats. In the daytime, swarms of rats sauntered alongside men. At night, they stole, they bit, and they staged violent fights. They were so noisy that no one could sleep. But the man never tired of all this.

Several years later, the man moved to another prefecture to live. When someone else came to live in the house, the rats went on behaving as before. This man said, "These are sinister and evil crea-

tures, more violent than bandits. How could things have come to this?"
He obtained five or six cats, closed the doors, removed the tiles, and poured water into the rat holes. He brought several servants in to catch them wherever they appeared. There were piles of dead rats dumped in secluded corners. The stench lasted for several months. Alas, the rats thought they could eat their fill without retribution. How could that last?[67]

Here is the same pattern as in "The Deer of Lin-chiang." There are three parties in the fable: the man, who for his own reasons protects the rats in his house; the rats, who, like the deer, do not realize the nature and limits of their protection and do what they are allowed to do under the impression that such is their natural mode of existence; and the cats and servants, who are called in after the first man's departure to get rid of the rats. Of course, we do not feel as sympathetic toward the rats as we do toward the deer, and we are not quite sorry when the cats and servants exterminate them. Liu Tsung-yüan seems to have anticipated our human bias when he wrote the prefatory remarks to the "Three Admonitions":

I have always had a dislike for people who have no understanding of how to develop and apply their own endowment and merely rely on external aid to reach their goals. They either rely on [borrowed] influence to confront those who are not of their kind [as the deer does]; or they exhibit their skills to annoy those who are more powerful [like the donkey in the third fable below]; or they take advantage of the times and give full play to their tyranny [like the rats]. Thus they eventually meet with disaster.[68]

If we insist on the obvious historical subtext and interpret the deer in the first fable as Liu Tsung-yüan, the rats in the second as his enemies, and the donkey in the third as the braggarts and incompetents that Liu hated,[69] then we are not only disregarding much that is in the fables, we are also overlooking the central concern of all three, which Liu Tsung-yüan emphasized in his prefatory remarks; that is, a concern with those who "have no understanding of how to develop and apply their own endowment" (*pu-chih t'ui chi chih pen*). From the perspective of the principle of nature-in-the-self (*chi chih pen*), the basic problem with the deer, and the cause of its tragedy, is not its innocence or the benevolence of its master: the deer has no understanding of its own fundamental nature. Blinded by the influence of its master, it can no longer distinguish right from wrong in its own mode of existence, and consequently, it invites its own disastrous fate.

The fate of the rats does not come about because rats are obnoxious and destructive and therefore are deservedly eaten and killed. The rats, like the deer, are blinded to their own fundamental nature by the master's unnatural protection, and their unnatural behavior results in their destruction.

The moral of the stories is clear: one who has no understanding of his own fundamental nature will sooner or later come to grief, regardless of his moral character (good deer or bad rat). Briefly stated, misfortune is the consequence of acting on false premises. The two fables leave open the question of responsibility—after all, both deer and rats are misled by someone else, and so perhaps they cannot be blamed for their folly. "The Donkey of Kueichou" (814) eliminates this possibility.

There were no donkeys in Kueichou till some busybody brought one in by boat. Once he got it there, he could find no use for it, so he set it free at the foot of a mountain. A tiger saw it. Seeing that it was such a colossal animal, the tiger took the donkey to be a god. Taking cover in the woods, the tiger peeked out at the donkey, coming gradually closer; but, holding the donkey in respect, the tiger never attempted to make its acquaintance.

One day, the donkey let out a bray. The tiger was so frightened that it ran far, far away, thinking that it was going to be eaten. It was extremely frightened. But as it came back again and again to look at the donkey, it perceived that the latter had no particular ability. Moreover, the tiger had become accustomed to the braying. So the tiger came closer yet to the side of the donkey; but still it never dared to attack.

Gradually it came even closer and got more and more familiar. It swung about the donkey, leaning toward it, bumping it and provoking it till the donkey was beside itself with rage and kicked out at the tiger. The tiger thereupon happily concluded, "So this is all it can do!" Then, with a great roar, the tiger pounced on the donkey. It severed its throat, ate all its meat, and went away.

Alas, the sheer size of the donkey seemed to suggest virtue, and the sheer volume of its voice seemed to suggest ability. Had it not [been tempted to] show off what its skill consisted of, the tiger, for all its ferocity, would have felt uncertain and fearful and would never have dared to seize it. What a pity matters ended as they did![70]

In this fable, there is no master to influence the behavior of either the donkey or the tiger. Human agency is reduced to a minimum. The donkey, then, should have had some innate ability to defend itself. Things, however, do not turn out that way. The tiger, although it is not shown to be more intelligent, is by its natural endowment the stronger beast. Therefore, the situation, when stripped of all moral considerations and external influences, becomes a mere contest of brute force.

These three fables bring Liu Tsung-yüan to a moral and philosophical impasse. The fables of the deer and the rats imply that neither a moral character nor a patron's influence can guarantee security and success. The laws of nature will continue to operate, as exemplified in the fable of the donkey, irrespective of the morality of the individual, in the absence of any protector. What is common to all three fables, over and above the foolishness of the donkey, the villainy of the rats, and the naïveté of the deer, is the ultimate dominance of nature over human bias and the futility of man's desire to control his own fate. One question still remains: If morality is only a human fabrication, if everything that happens in life is simply a matter of nature taking its course (for example, cats eating rats), and if the inherent principle of things (*li*) presupposes no moral judgment of the self, then on what basis can Liu Tsung-yüan formulate a critical criterion for the rightness or wrongness of his own situation at Liu-chou and on what premise can he act? Shall he become a wiser deer and avoid the dogs in town? Shall he become a wiser donkey and conceal his talents in order to live out his allotted term of life? Or shall he, *can* he, emulate the tiger and dogs and triumph over the donkeys and deer of the world? Would circumstances make such a course possible? Liu Tsung-yüan, as he reasoned through the alternatives, began to see that nature (*tzu-jan*) and its inherent principle could offer him no more consolation or guidance than the scenic landscape at Yung-chou. The mode of existence that brutal nature promised was too disagreeable.

*Nature as Living and Growth and the Moral Mode*

Once Liu Tsung-yüan had comprehended the basic amorality of nature in the world of human affairs, he began to see that it did not really answer his need for a rational principle of action for the self. He questioned whether there was really no premise on which a man could act and live without subjecting himself to the seemingly inevitable contest of brute forces in his life. In the biographical sketches of the Yung-chou period—the last group of works to be studied here—Liu Tsung-yüan finally found in the lives of the common people of Yung-chou the means by which he could live with, and at the same time transcend, the limitations of his environment and of his own nature.

Altogether, Liu Tsung-yüan wrote 10 or 11 biographical sketches while at Yung-chou.[71] Three of these sketches provide the material for a discussion of Liu's understanding of human morality: the biography of Sung Ch'ing, a druggist (814); the biography of Camel Kuo, the arborist (805); and the biography of the snake-catcher (814). Each of the three biographies shows that a man's life can be good despite the temptations of greed and despite the powerful forces of injustice, failure, and death.

Sung Ch'ing was a man of the drug market, in the western part of Ch'ang-an. He stocked good medicines. People coming from distant mountains and marshes always went to Mr. Sung Ch'ing, and Ch'ing always received them well. When the doctors in Ch'ang-an got their medicines from Ch'ing, they sold their prescriptions easily. Hence they all praised him. People with various illnesses and sores all gladly sought medicines from Ch'ing, hoping that they would get well more quickly; and Ch'ing was always happy to respond [to their requests]. Although some brought no money with them, he still gave them good medicines. The credit notes would pile up as high as a mountain, but he never went out to collect. He would even accept credit notes from people coming from afar whom he did not know. At the end of the year, when he concluded that there was no chance of his being paid, he would burn the notes and never mention them again.

The people in the market thought him strange. They would all laugh at him and say, "Ch'ing is silly." Or they said, "Isn't Ch'ing truly a man of the *tao!*" On hearing this, Ch'ing said, "I am only seeking enough profit to provide for the livelihood of my wife and children. I am not a man of the *tao*. However, those who say that I am silly are also wrong."

Ch'ing had been in the business of selling medicine for forty years and had burned the credit notes of well over a hundred people. Some of them later became high officials, and some became governors of several prefectures with ample salaries. The gift bearers they sent to Ch'ing would line up at his door. Although there were hundreds and thousands of others who could not pay in time and died with their debts outstanding, this did not affect Ch'ing's prosperity.

Ch'ing was farsighted about his source of profit, hence his profit was enormous. How could he be compared to petty merchants, who, when they are not paid, get angry and curse and become hostile? How nearsighted they are in their pursuit of profit. Their silliness is quite evident to me. Ch'ing earned great profits in this way. He was never silly but followed his own way without fail. In the end he became rich.

As the people who sought his help grew more numerous with time, the magnanimity of his response to them grew. Some of them were later dismissed from their posts and cast out, and some went under and became helpless. They were treated with indifference by their own relatives. Ch'ing, however, did not treat them disrespectfully but gave them good medicine as before. As soon as these people regained power, they repaid Ch'ing all the more generously. Such was his farsightedness about profit.

I have observed that when people make friends nowadays, they adhere to them in prosperity and discard them in adversity. Few are able to do as Ch'ing did. When speaking about such people, one merely calls their friendship "friendship of the marketplace." Alas! Ch'ing was [merely] a merchant; but today, [even] among friends, is there anyone who can look for long-range profit as Ch'ing did? If there were some who resembled [Ch'ing], then many of the impoverished and harassed, the helpless and humiliated of the world, might be spared death. How can one do without such "friendship of the marketplace"?

Some say, "Ch'ing was not a man of the marketplace." Mr. Liu says, "Ch'ing lived in the marketplace but did not follow the customary way of the marketplace. On the other hand, those who reside at court, in government offices, in schools and local communities, and call themselves literati–officials, contrary to what one expects, strive to practice the way of the marketplace. How sad! That being so, Ch'ing was different not only from the men of the marketplace!"[72]

Sung Ch'ing's approach to profit eliminates greed as a governing law in his action and frees his life from the consequences of greedy behavior. It enables him not only to provide for the livelihood of his own family but also to assist many others who would otherwise die for lack of medicine. Camel Kuo of the next sketch points to another way of cultivating a livelihood.

No one knew Camel Kuo's original name. He had a prominent bump [on his back] and walked stoopingly like a camel; and so the people in his village nicknamed him Camel. When Camel heard that, he said, "Very well, it is indeed an appropriate name for me." Thereupon he discarded his own name and also called himself Camel.

His village was called the Village of Joy in Abundances, located to the west of Ch'ang-an. Camel planted trees for a living. All the great families and wealthy people in Ch'ang-an, whether [their interest] was in landscape gardening or in the fruit business, vied with each other to invite him to their house to live. They saw that all the trees that Camel had planted or moved [continued to] live and in addition grew large and luxuriant. They bore fruit early and multiplied well. Other cultivators could never do likewise, no matter how they spied on him and imitated him. Someone asked him [how he did it]. He answered, "It is not that I, Camel, can make a tree live long and thrive. All I can do is comply with the nature [t'ien] of the tree so that it can fully develop its innate character [hsing].

"The innate character of a tree to be planted is such that its roots must be spread out; the fill must be banked up level; the soil must be the original [in which the tree was seeded], and it must be tamped down until it is compact. Once the tree is planted, I do not touch it and do not fuss about it; once I leave, I do not look back. I plant it with the care I would use for a child. When I leave it, I leave it as if I were abandoning it. Then, what is in its nature [t'ien] will remain whole, and what is in its innate character [hsing] will be realized. Thus, I merely take care that I do not hinder its growth; it is not that I can cause it to grow large and luxuriant. I merely take care that I do not suppress or waste its substance; it is not that I can make it bear fruit early and multiply.

"Other arborists do their job differently. [When they plant a tree,] the roots are cramped and the soil is changed. When they bank up the earth around it, they make it either too deep or too shallow. If they happen to avoid these errors, then they love it with too much care, worry about it too solicitously—visiting it in the morning, stroking it in the evening, and, having already left, again looking back at it. In extreme cases they will scratch its bark to test whether it is alive or dead, rock the tree to see if the roots are sparse or thick. As a consequence, the innate character of the tree ebbs away day by day. Although they call this loving the tree, it is in fact harming it; although they call it worrying about the tree, it is in fact harassing it. Hence they are not as good as I am. What special abilities do I possess?"

The listener said, "Would it be possible to translate your way [of growing trees] into a principle of government?"

Camel said, "I know only about planting trees; principles [of government] are not my business. However, from living in my village, I see that the leaders like to complicate their orders as if they had great concern for the people, but the outcome is disaster. Morning and evening, petty officials come and shout, 'The magistrate orders you to hurry up and plough, to exert yourselves and sow. Oversee your harvest; reel and spin your silk thread early; weave it into cloth betimes. Nurture your young children; raise your chickens and hogs.' They beat the drum for the villagers to gather; they knock the wooden clappers to summon them. We little folk, even if we go without our meals, cannot find time enough to cater to the wishes of the petty officials; how are we to increase our livelihood and enjoy what comes naturally to us? That is why the people are discontent and remiss. In this respect, [government] does bear some resemblance to my profession."

The listener exclaimed, "Isn't that splendid! I asked how to care for trees and got the method of caring for the people instead. I shall pass this on as an admonition for government officials." [73]

According to Camel Kuo, love and care without understanding of the innate character (*hsing*) of a tree serve only to kill it. And he demonstrates quite effectively that one does not become an arborist simply by joining the profession. "The Biography of Camel Kuo" brings two new concepts, *t'ien* and *hsing*, to bear on the way in which trees live and grow—two ideas not present in Liu Tsung-yüan's discussion of nature as *tzu-jan*. Liu here seems to be moving away from his conception of nature as *tzu-jan*, which explains only how things come to be in terms of external circumstances. Concurrently, he is moving toward a fresh and fundamentally different conception of nature as the way in which things live and grow.

"The Story of the Snake-catcher" is in this sense an affirmation of the necessary moral good of living and growing, as opposed to the impersonal law of *tzu-jan*, which equates good and evil, right and wrong, life and death, with its uniform and a-human concept of *li*.

In the wilderness of Yung-chou, there grows an unusual kind of snake that has a black body with white stripes. It kills plants at a touch, and no man can survive its bite. But once it is caught and preserved for food, it can cure leprosy, arthritis, and various pestilential diseases; it can revive withered flesh and kill all three types of corpse worms. In the beginning, the court physician collected them by imperial ordinance. The quota was two per year; and when levies were imposed, anyone who had been able to catch [a snake] could submit it in lieu of land tax. The people of Yung-chou fought for the chance.

There is a man from a certain family named Chiang that has had the monopoly [of snake-catching] for three generations now. When asked about his occupation, he said, "My grandfather died doing this work; my father died doing it. Now I have been on the job for twelve years and have come very close to death myself several times." As he spoke, he looked very sad.

I felt sorry for him, so I said, "Are you bitter about it? I will tell the people in charge and change your assignment back to tax-paying; how about that?"

Mr. Chiang was deeply distressed, and with tears falling copiously, he said, "Will you, sir, take pity on me and let me live? The misfortunes that come with this job are never so grievous as the misfortune of restoration of my taxes would be. But for this job, I would have been in the worst straits long ago. It has been sixty years now since my family came to live in this village, over three generations ago. The livelihood of our neighbors has grown more difficult by the day. They have exhausted everything that their land produces, used up all the earnings of their houses, cried out for help, and moved away. Staggering and falling with hunger and thirst, they have braved the wind and the rain, the cold and the heat, breathed poisonous vapors, and frequently died falling on top of one another. Of those who lived in my grandfather's time, fewer than one in ten are left in their houses. Of those who lived in my father's time, fewer than two or three in ten are left in each family. Of those who have been living with me for the last twelve years, not four or five in ten are left in each family. They either died or ran away. But I alone have survived because I catch snakes. When the ruthless tax collectors come to our village, they yell and scream from east to west, dart from south to north, making such a frightful din that even the chickens and dogs have no peace. I carefully get up to look into my jar. If my snakes are still there, I relax and lie down to sleep again. I feed them carefully and present them at the proper time. Then I go home and eat with great relish all that the land produces until I have lived out my span. This way, I risk death only twice a year. I enjoy the rest of the time heartily. So I am not at all like my village neighbors, who suffer from one day to the next. Even if I were to die on my job today, it still would be later than the deaths of most of my neighbors. How dare I be bitter about my job?" Hearing this made me even sadder. Confucius said, "Harsh government is fiercer than tigers."[74] I once wondered about the truth of that, but judging from Chiang's case, it is true still. Alas! Who could have thought that the poison of tax collection is worse than that of a snake? Because of this, I have written this story for the use of those who observe human ways.[75]

The snake-catcher's balanced perception of the perils and profits of his work enables him to face the danger of death without fear. As a consequence of his fearlessness, he is able to enjoy his unthreatened moments in peace, and he accepts his hazardous calling with equanimity and even a bit of enthusiasm.

Man, like a tree, is born to live; that is the *t'ien* in him. His *hsing* is to grow. Both his *t'ien* and his *hsing* demand that he be allowed to live and grow peacefully, within the limits of his environment. Liu Tsung-yüan's administrative record at Liu-chou demonstrates how the lesson of the "Biography of Camel Kuo" and the philosophy of life expressed in the "Snake-catcher" can be put into practice. During the last four years of his life, Liu wrote little and complained even less. He attended to the well-being of his people and took care that they were not unduly hindered from leading their day-to-day lives in peace.

First in his writings and then in practice, Liu Tsung-yüan, in his exile at Yung-chou and Liu-chou, demonstrated the ways in which a traditional Chinese intellectual perceived and practiced the *tao*. His view of human nature and of human life in his final years comes very close to Mencius's theory that men are by nature good, the subtle difference being that Liu further refines the philosophical perception of man's nature by portraying it as being endowed with the faculty of *ming*. He thus introduces into the discussion of the moral choice between good and evil a notion of freedom that transcends the limitations of Mencius's earlier definition of the natural goodness of man. Two and a half centuries later, the philosopher-artist and *ku-wen* stylist Su Shih, who was also deeply interested in the phenomena of change in history, in the notion of man's moral freedom (which he translates in his aesthetic context as *yi*), and in their implications for the forms of life man leads, noticed this similarity between Mencius's theory and Liu Tsung-yüan's perception:

> On the whole, Master Liu's theory treats rites and music as empty forms and heaven and man as mutually without sympathy and understanding. . . .
> From T'ang times to the present, men have eulogized the patriarchs, but none of them was so comprehensive, so lucid, so precise, or so correct as Tzu-hou. When one explores the fundamentals of his thoughts, they agree with those of Meng K'o.[76]

Su Shih captured the pivotal point in the development of Liu Tsung-yüan's thought and ethics and the special position that Liu Tsung-yüan came to occupy in the history of *ku-wen* literature in T'ang and Sung times—namely, as a radical thinker who reasoned his way back to one of the earliest springs of the Confucian school of thought not by conforming to the ancients but by thinking independently and critically.

## The Achievements of Han Yü and Liu Tsung-yüan

In studying Liu Tsung-yüan's *ku-wen* theory and practice, one cannot avoid noticing that Liu advances in his writings ideas that are significantly different from those of Han Yü, with regard to both the meaning of *tao* and the function of *wen*. When one thinks of the height of achievement in T'ang *ku-wen* writing, one usually thinks of Liu Tsung-yüan and Han Yü together, as if they were literary twins. But in discussions of the more specific questions of *ku-wen* theories and *ku-wen* ideology, Liu Tsung-yüan has been, more often than not, considered the lesser theorist, even though his prose style is frequently regarded as finer and richer than Han Yü's.

We can trace the beginning of this evaluation of Han Yü's and Liu Tsung-yüan's theories of *tao* and practices of *wen* to Ou-yang Hsiu in the Sung dynasty. It was Ou-yang Hsiu, as we shall see in the following chapter, who rediscovered Han Yü 200 years after the latter's death, rescued him from oblivion, and established his theory of *tao* and *wen* in the mainstream of the Sung *ku-wen* movement. By contrast, Liu Tsung-yüan, politically suspect in his own time, remained politically suspect for Ou-yang Hsiu and other orthodox Confucians in later ages. His critical approach to the question of *tao*, moreover, stigmatized him as an intellectual radical. For these reasons, praises for his literary achievements were comparatively faint, often carrying elegiac overtones and accompanied by vague laments for his political misfortunes. In the Ch'ing dynasty, several scholars reexamined the historical records of Liu Tsung-yüan and his political reform clique,[77] but it was not until the 1970's that his career and works were given a full defense by Chang Shih-chao.

Today evaluations of Liu Tsung-yüan's works and thought are more positive.[78] Intellectual historians and literary critics are beginning to look beyond the Sung bias and to search among the writings of the ancient thinkers for the original inspiration behind Liu Tsung-yüan's and Han Yü's reinterpretation of *tao* and *wen*. Because of the work of recent scholars, it has become increasingly clear that the *tao* discussed by Han Yü and Liu Tsung-yüan was originally a general term used by the ancient thinkers to describe the various positions of their philosophical inquiry.[79] Among the subjects of inquiry were "nature" and "man" and the principles behind their manifestations; "nature" and "man" in historical perspective and the principles behind their interactions; "change" from the perspective of nature and from the perspective of history; and the concept of predestination (*ming*). The Confucian *tao* in ancient times was but one way (*tao*) among many of approaching these issues.[80]

In their writings, Han Yü and Liu Tsung-yüan revived the many arguments that had once supported the conflicting positions of the ancient schools on *tao*. In so doing, they also revived the language in which these arguments had originally been cast. Some modern scholars and critics sympathize with Han Yü's position and therefore endorse his reconstruction of the ancient *tao* and the ancient language (*ku-wen*) as one that came down to him from Confucius and Mencius. Others defend the historical rationalism of Liu Tsung-yüan and compare him to Hsün-tzu and Ssu-ma Ch'ien.[81] Indeed, Han Yü and Liu Tsung-yüan themselves debated, with as much heat and vehemence as the ancient masters, the questions of *tao*, the innate nature of man (*hsing*), the concept of *t'ien*, the concept of *tzu-jan*, and the role of history. They differed in their attitudes toward *ming*, in their evaluation of the meaning of antiquity for the present, and in their understanding of the function of literature and the purpose of learning (*hsüeh*).[82]

In these chapters on Han Yü and Liu Tsung-yüan, I have analyzed in some detail the similarities and differences in their political, intellectual, and literary concerns. These similarities and differences have created an uncertainty in the minds of some modern critics as to which of the two is the more representative of the T'ang *ku-wen* spirit.[83] But in general they are considered complementary, and scholars from Shao Po (d. 1158) in the Sung to Kuo Shao-yü in the present century have sought to explain their dissimilarities by tracing Han Yü's literary inspiration to the Classics and Liu Tsung-yüan's to the histories.[84] This interpretation not only delineates which of the ancient traditions was represented by Han, and which by Liu, but also explains Han Yü's lifelong predilection for idolizing the ancients, his insistence on defining the absolute in terms of the purity and superiority of the ancients, and Liu Tsung-yüan's refusal to recognize any absolute and his insistence on man's freedom to question the rightness and wrongness of his actions. In this respect, Han Yü's doctrine of a single superior *ku-wen* style and Liu Tsung-yüan's thesis that there is no one correct style, only appropriate or inappropriate use of a given style, can be understood as a reflection, on the literary level, of the same basic difference in their intellectual orientation.

In contrast to Han Yü, Liu Tsung-yüan did not write philosophical treatises; there is no "On the True Way" or "On the True Nature of Man" among his works. He eschewed the name and the role of a teacher, and he had no set curriculum for the cultivation of a *ku-wen* style, such as Han Yü prescribed in his letter to Li Yi. If asked, Liu Tsung-yüan might be willing to discuss the usage of grammatical particles in a given work or to outline the stylistic characteristics of the Six Classics, the *Ch'u tz'u*, the *Shih chi*, and other writings by ancient masters that any writer should appreciate and internalize.[85] But according to Liu, except for a specific purpose, no one style of writing or school of thought could be said to be better than another. Liu Tsung-yüan never used an expository form to explain the *tao*. In his theory and practice, he consistently held to the belief that all explanations and interpretations are human constructs and must be partial and limited. He did not believe in an absolute *tao* transcending humanity. Thus, he considered the idea of *tao* in terms of the ways of man and of other forms of life such as insects and animals; his reflections invariably assumed a mode of expression that was somehow distanced from direct exposition. This distancing from prescriptive speech can be observed in his animal fables and in his novelistic approach to the lives of the common people in his biographical sketches. Literary forms in these works serve the function of moral and intellectual perspectives.

According to Liu Tsung-yüan, life is more complex than philosophy and morality. Feelings and phenomena that are contradictory in philosophical and moral terms regularly coexist in life, are accepted in history, and appear in literature. Whatever philosophy could not resolve and politics could not accommodate was by T'ang times assimilated more and more into the realm of literature. The evolution of *ku-wen* literature was one result of this tendency. Literati in the T'ang were no longer content to write only for the state. Their preparations for the civil examinations and government office had expanded from specialization in one or more of the Classics to poetry and narrative prose. And the latter discipline brought to its culmination a literary tradition of "personal" prose that paralleled the histories and state papers. A personal perspective on the worlds of nature and of man, which before the T'ang had customarily been confined to poetry, was extended to prose in the writings of Han Yü and Liu Tsung-yüan.

Han Yü advised purity, authenticity, and originality in his famous program for aspiring writers; Liu Tsung-yüan encouraged objectivity, diversity, and critical, individualistic thinking. The similarity in their literary training and background has often led critics to equate their common allusions to certain texts with a common objective and an identical school of thought. It is not unusual even today to find Liu Tsung-yüan discussed in the context of the T'ang Confucian revival because, like Han Yü, he recommended study of the Six Classics to candidates for the civil examinations and an official career.

However one perceives the different outlooks of Han Yü and Liu Tsung-yüan on antiquity and on literature, it is incontestable that they shared a common core of concern with the ancient masters and contributed definitively to the crystallization of *ku-wen* writing as a prose tradition in Chinese literature. However, because they merely revived these old concerns and did not perceptibly go beyond the intellectual horizons of the ancient philosophers, they have never been considered as philosophers.[86] Rather, they have essentially been viewed as writers, intellectuals who chose to be professional men of letters.

The next two chapters follow the development and achievements of the *ku-wen* movement into the early Sung period. In studying the thought and works of Ou-yang Hsiu and Su Shih, I examine the elements that unite all four masters in a single tradition as well as identify the elements that make the Sung tradition distinctly different from that of the T'ang.

# 3

## OU-YANG HSIU

## The Return to Universality

### The Development of *Ku-wen* from the T'ang to the Sung

The *ku-wen* movement is usually regarded as an unbroken tradition from the T'ang to the Sung, and the prose of the whole period is seen more or less as a homogeneous whole. Seen from a broad enough perspective, the development of *ku-wen* does seem to lend support to this view. Han Yü protested against ornateness and excessive use of allusion in writing, objected to the Buddhist and Taoist ideology in the literature of his time, and proposed, as an alternative, a return to the Six Classics, which to his mind embodied the dual virtues of elevated style and orthodoxy. Two centuries later, at the beginning of the Sung dynasty, Han Yü's *ku-wen* program was reactivated by writers like Liu K'ai (947–1000) and Mu Hsiu (979–1032). The enemies by then were the so-called current style of parallel prose (*shih-wen*) and the *Hsi-k'un* style of poetry, both of which, like the parallel prose of an earlier time, were elegant in expression but devoid of moral message. A half-century later, Ou-yang Hsiu (1007–72) developed his theory of universality (*ch'ang*) and simplicity (*yi*). When he was the chief examiner in 1057, he made *ku-wen* the required essay style for the civil service examination. In the Ming, another factor consolidated this view of a homogeneous T'ang-Sung *ku-wen* style. Ming writers felt a need for models of prose composition. Anthologies were made in response to that need, and the phrase "eight masters of the T'ang and Sung" (T'ang-Sung *pa ta-chia*), first used by Mao K'un (1512–1601) in the title of his anthology, has been popular ever since as a codified evaluation of T'ang and Sung prose.[1]

This standard view, however, subsumes individual writers under the general rubric of "*ku-wen* masters" and obscures their distinctive excellence. Sung writers, in fact, as we shall see in this chapter and the next, adopted a style quite distinct from that of their T'ang predecessor Han Yü because they had a different literary ideal—an ideal based on a reinterpretation of the program of "returning to the Six Classics" and of "literature as a vehicle for truth."

For Han Yü, the meaning and value of the Six Classics lay in the fact that they were Confucian and that they were absolutely without precedent. To emulate the ancients who wrote them was to be as creative as they were; in stylistic terms this meant replacing the clichés and allusions of parallel prose with one's own expressions and exchanging its balanced and polished syntax for one considerably more dynamic and free. Although a deep current of Confucian orthodoxy ran through Han Yü's thought, his style was highly unorthodox and not infrequently verged on "extraordinariness" (*ch'i*)—a term used by later critics. Equally characteristic of Han Yü's writing was "loftiness" (*kao*), an attribute of both the style and the moral viewpoint of the Six Classics that he emulated in his own writing. This view of the Six Classics as the model for *ku-wen* writing was shared by two of Han's contemporaries, Li Ao (772–841) and Huang-fu Shih (fl. 810). Li Ao, better known for his treatise on the theory of a two-tiered human nature (the amoral *hsing* and the moral *ch'ing*), entitled "The Recovery of the Nature," studied the Classics because, like Han Yü, he venerated the deeds and the way of the ancient saints and sages and admired the originality in their thoughts and words. Huang-fu Shih, a disciple of Han Yü's and an able practitioner of the extraordinary and lofty *ku-wen* style, perpetuated that particular vein in Han Yü's theory of *ku-wen*.[2]

But for the Sung writers, the Six Classics embodied not so much the unique and the exclusive as the common and the universal (*ch'ang*)—that which has application everywhere and at all times.

They believed that in the very beginning the cosmos was filled with "vital energy" or "material force" (*ch'i*), which is an undifferentiated, elemental, and indissoluble substance, and that the basic principle (*li*) inheres in all existence, both as form and as change. In order for literature to function as a vehicle of truth, it must render a true description of this elemental reality. The most appropriate style, then, is common and universal, representing the world as it is.

The unique and the uncommon that Han Yü advocated as the stylistic qualities that distinguished the Six Classics had thus been transformed by early Sung times into their antitheses. This transformation from the unique to the universal is illustrated in the writings of two outstanding Sung *ku-wen* writers, Ou-yang Hsiu and his disciple Su Shih. It can be discerned in Ou-yang Hsiu's emphasis on the credible (*hsin*) and the real (*shih*), and in his theory of the universal and the simple, as well as in Su Shih's numerical definition of *li* and his representation of change in continuity as a manifestation of *li* in visible form, the themes of his two "Rhymeprose on the Red Cliff" (1082). Su Shih's playful projection of the concept of change in numerical terms (the two-oneness of change and continuity in the riddle of one crane and two Taoists in the second "Rhymeprose") would certainly have been perceived as highly irregular in Han Yü's time. If Han Yü had indulged in such metamorphosis play, it would have been denounced as another example of his notorious addiction to the extraordinary by people like Liu Hsü, his *Chiu T'ang shu* biographer.

Shortly after Han Yü's death, *ku-wen* as a prose style began to lose its grip on the imagination of writers. The twin qualities of "extraordinariness" and "loftiness," conceived by Han Yü as essential to superior writing, soon degenerated into literary mannerisms as the search for the unusual or the bizarre became divorced from the moral commitment that had inspired Han Yü. After his generation of *ku-wen* writers—Li Ao, Huang-p'u Shih, P'ei Tu (765–839), and Li Te-yü (787–849?)—poets and prose writers began to turn away from the orthodox, didactic trend of the school of Han Yü and his followers. Li Shang-yin (813–58), for instance, was a noted parallel-prose stylist; Tu Mu (803–52), a poet and military strategist, emphasized the practical use of prose over Confucian didacticism; P'i Jih-hsiu (834?–83?), a minor poet, continued to write on the Confucian moral and literary traditions but was not known for the excellence of his prose style.[3] By the early eleventh century, *ku-wen* writings had grown so self-consciously abstruse that they often deserved the charge "no longer suitable for use."[4]

In the meantime, the literary mainstream had shifted to *shih-wen*. Yang Yi (947–1020) was the master of this style. Evolved during the Five Dynasties (907–60), between the T'ang and the Sung, *shih-wen* can be seen stylistically as a Sung version of parallel prose. The term *shih-wen* denotes at once a poetic style and a prose style. In prose, it refers particularly to the "four-six style" of parallel prose in the late T'ang, which had come to be accepted as standard in court documents. In poetry, *shih-wen* refers to a highly personal, ornate, and allusive style of poetry that had been perfected by Li Shang-yin and, as superficially imitated by early Sung poets, came to be known as the "Hsi-k'un style." This mannered style of poetry, even more than the prose, is said to have emphasized "preciosity, overrefined technique, elaborate allusions, and stereotyped themes."[5] Charges of sentimentality and lack of moral content similar to those raised against parallel prose by T'ang *ku-wen* advocates were leveled at *shih-wen*.

A number of writers tried to formulate a simpler and more flexible concept of *ku-wen* style as an answer to *shih-wen*. Despite the extent to which it had degenerated by the eleventh century, Han Yü had, after all, solidly demonstrated *ku-wen*'s worth as a vehicle for meaningful discussion of ideas, especially of the Confucian *tao*. And so it was to *ku-wen* that early Sung writers turned as a possible alternative to the overly mannered *shih-wen*. Ou-yang Hsiu, for instance, in describing his own situation, wrote:

> At that time [early eleventh century], scholars studied only the works of Yang [Yi] and Liu [Yün, 971–1031], whose practice was known as *shih-wen*. The competent ones obtained degrees by it; they achieved fame and won praise in the world. No one ever spoke of Han [Yü's] prose. I, too, was at that time preparing for the *chin-shih* examination and devoted myself to poetry and rhymeprose according to the regulations of the Board of Rites.... Although I wondered then ... why no one followed [Han Yü's] *tao*, I, too, lacked the time to study it. But all along I had been thinking to myself: at present I am only trying to pass the *chin-shih* examination and earn an official salary to support my mother; once this is accomplished, I

will devote my entire effort to that style and thereby fulfill my long-cherished ambition.[6]

In the state in which *ku-wen* then stood, it could scarcely have served to counteract the artificiality of *shih-wen*. Even before Ou-yang Hsiu, Liu K'ai and Wang Yü-ch'eng (954–1001) had attempted a redefinition and revitalization of *ku-wen*. Liu K'ai, a self-appointed apostle of Han Yü and Liu Tsung-yüan,[7] noted in one of his letters how he viewed the question of *ku-wen*:

> You asked me what is *ku-wen*. That which I call *ku-wen* is not something that aims to be so harsh or painstakingly difficult that no one can read it; rather, that which I call *ku-wen* aims to follow the principle of the ancients, to elevate one's mind and to formulate one's expression in accordance with changing circumstances, just as the ancients did.... To want to practice the way of the ancients but write in the style of people today is like someone who tries to travel on the sea by riding on the back of a steed; how can that be done? If that cannot be done, then I will follow the practice of *ku-wen*.[8]

Liu K'ai's position here was not unlike that of Han Yü in the "Letter to Li Yi."

Wang Yü-ch'eng, an advocate not only of T'ang *ku-wen* by Han Yü and Liu Tsung-yüan but also of T'ang poetry by Li Po, Tu Fu, and Po Chü-yi, was particularly emphatic in his view that literary style should be simple and natural.

> Literary works profess to transmit the *tao* and to explain the writer's mind. The ancient sages wrote because they could not otherwise achieve these ends.... [That being so,] would they deliberately have made the sentences difficult to read or their meaning difficult to understand?... In recent ages, only Han Li-pu [Han Yü] practiced *ku-wen*. When I look at Li-pu's writings, it never strikes me that his phrases are difficult to read or his meaning difficult to understand. He said in praise of the writings of [his contemporary] Fan Tsung-shih that they were always original and that they never adopted a single word or phrase from former writers.[9] He also praised the manner in which [another contemporary] Hsüeh Feng wrote, [for Feng] adhered always to the first principle of differing from the common. But Fan's and Hsüeh's works are no longer in circulation, whereas the writings of Li-pu endure alongside the Six Classics. This is how Li-pu taught untiringly, using the two of them [Fan and Hsüeh] as examples to encourage other students. For Li-pu

said, "I do not imitate that which is modern, I do not imitate that
which is ancient; I do not imitate that which is difficult, I do not
imitate that which is easy; I do not imitate that which is common, I
do not imitate that which is rare; I imitate only that which is
right."[10]

Liu K'ai and Wang Yü-ch'eng both argued that the style of the
Six Classics was simple and that *ku-wen* must change with time and
usage. These ideas—simplicity and flexibility—set the Sung *ku-
wen* revival on a path different from that of its T'ang predecessors.
Simplicity facilitates the achievement of universality in a work, and
flexibility introduces a comprehensive and tolerant approach to the
subject. The orthodox T'ang *ku-wen* advocates had held that the
Confucian *tao* was superior to all others and that, by virtue of that
fact, *ku-wen* writings were purer and more profound than all
others. But Liu K'ai and Wang Yü-ch'eng, while still exalting the
Six Classics, both realized that insisting on such a theory of *ku-wen*
without the intellectual range and creativity of a Han Yü was tan-
tamount to advocating empty pomp and obscurity. This, too, is
how Ou-yang Hsiu, the first successful Sung *ku-wen* stylist, assessed
the situation when, some 30 years after Liu K'ai and Wang Yü-
ch'eng, he set himself the task of remaking *ku-wen* into an effective
literary force.

## From the Unique to the Universal

Ou-yang Hsiu, the central figure among the prose masters of the
T'ang and the Sung, appeared on the scene slightly later than the
Sung *ku-wen* pioneers Liu K'ai, Wang Yü-ch'eng, and Mu Hsiu;
and he was the senior by half a generation of the historian Ssu-ma
Kuang (1019–86) and the legal reformer Wang An-shih (1021–86)
—both of whom were also notable *ku-wen* stylists. In intellectual
history, he followed the liberal thinkers Hu Yüan (993–1059) and
Sun Fu (992–1057) and preceded the first Neo-Confucianists Chou
Tun-yi (1017–73), Shao Yung (1011–77), and Chang Tsai (1020–
77) by more than a decade.

His public life was a stormy one. At the beginning of his political career, he was a protégé of the great liberal reformer Fan
Chung-yen (989–1052); later, he worked closely with the more
conservative Han Ch'i (1008–75) and Fu Pi (1004–83). All of his
life he was involved in the conflict of rival factions at the court; he

was close to the throne and thus in a perpetually precarious position. Although rigidly uncompromising in his youth, with age Ou-yang Hsiu grew more supple. Dedicated to utilizing talent in public administration, he recommended the incompatible Wang An-shih and Ssu-ma Kuang with fine impartiality. He was twice banished: first to Yi-ling (in modern Hupei) in 1036, when Fan Chung-yen's faction fell from power, and again to Ch'u-chou (in modern Anhwei) in 1045, as the result of an unsavory scandal involving allegations of incest with a niece. After he was recalled to the capital in 1054, he continued to participate in party politics at the court.

Like Han Yü and Liu Tsung-yüan, Ou-yang Hsiu wrote many of his best-known works during his periods of exile. His important political essays "On Fundamentals" and "On Factions," for example, were written in 1044, during his first banishment; and it was also at Yi-ling that he began work on his *Hsin Wu-tai shih* (New history of the Five Dynasties). His *ku-wen* theory of substance, validity, and objective reality was developed during his second exile; and it was at Ch'u-chou that he wrote the "Record of the Old Tippler's Pavilion."

Much of Ou-yang Hsiu's bibliographical and historical work was completed before he was 50: his participation in the compiling of the *Ch'ung-wen tsung-mu* (General catalogue of the Imperial Library; 1034–41) was behind him, as was his account of the Five Dynasties. By the middle of the eleventh century, he had already begun work on the imperially commissioned *Hsin T'ang shu* (completed 1060) and on the *Chi ku lu* (Collection of ancient inscriptions; completed 1063), the first compilation of bronze and stone inscriptions to appear in China.

As the official in charge of the *chin-shih* examination in 1057, Ou-yang Hsiu created a furor by requiring the candidates to write in the *ku-wen* style. By 1069, when Wang An-shih began his monumental reforms and Su Shih his long opposition to them, Ou-yang Hsiu was already in declining health; he had no opportunity to intercede in the bitter political controversy between his brilliant protégés Wang An-shih and Ssu-ma Kuang. He is remembered by posterity as the model of an accomplished, temperate, and this-worldly scholar-official in the Confucian tradition.

Many of the literary doctrines in Ou-yang Hsiu's theory of *ku-*

*wen*, such as "objective validity" or "credibility" (*hsin*), "simplicity" (*chien*), and "universality" (*ch'ang*), can be seen as criticisms of, and reactions to, the T'ang *ku-wen* heritage. They give his writing a significantly different theoretical and stylistic orientation from that of Han Yü. The pivotal idea of *hsin* in Ou-yang Hsiu's theory, for instance, has two aspects: its role in literature and as a criterion of value.[11] The basis of *hsin* in literature, according to Ou-yang Hsiu, is twofold: the truthfulness of the content of a work and the normality of the feelings expressed by the work. *Hsin* is closely associated in stylistic terms with *chien* and the related concept *yi*, both of which mean "simplicity" (with *yi* sometimes meaning "ease," "facility"). Some theoretical justification for this emphasis on simplicity can be found in Ou-yang Hsiu's idea of *tzu-jan* ("the natural," "nature").

*Tzu-jan* does not play a direct role in Ou-yang Hsiu's literary theory; rather, as in the case of Liu Tsung-yüan, it underlies the world view that is manifest in some of his most popular imaginative writings. *Tzu-jan* is also the one concept in Ou-yang Hsiu's critical thinking that he did not draw directly from the Six Classics but owed to the intellectual ferment of his time.

In early Sung times and for Ou-yang Hsiu, *tzu-jan* was neither natural landscape nor animal nature pure and simple. First and foremost, this term implied the metaphysical principle of *li*, the rational principle of order in the universe. Early Sung thinkers conceived of this rational principle of *li* in several different ways: to some it meant the principle behind change; to others the principle behind the unchanging. To Su Shih, for example, *li* was at once the principle behind change and behind the unchanging. His famous "Rhymeprose on the Red Cliff" is conceived exactly in terms of his bipartite view of nature as simultaneously changing and unchanging. Ou-yang Hsiu, however, like Han Yü, was not primarily a philosopher. He did not have a demonstrated taste (again like Han Yü) for either metaphysics or cosmology; his preference was to approach the principle of things in their natural and human— that is, their social and political—manifestations. Therefore, in literary theory and practice, instead of probing the ultimate reality of existence in terms of *ch'i*, *shu*, and *li* and in terms of their bearing on the phenomenal world as Chou Tun-yi, Shao Yung, and Chang Tsai did, he stressed the immediate and the tangible (*shih*), discussing only what is perceptible and rationally accessible to all men. The principle of good writing, he therefore affirmed, is not abstract or remote but lies in the goodness of the substance: "Like the glitter of gold and jade, it does not come from grinding, chiseling, dyeing, or rinsing, but is a *natural* emanation of their hard, solid substance."[12]

The question of *shih*, and Ou-yang Hsiu's insistence on its objective validity, as a criterion of value in literary writing arose largely from his reflections on the historical and moral significance of the Six Classics. It is intimately related to his personal perception of the principle of "universality" (*ch'ang*) as manifested in the *tao* of the Six Classics. *Ch'ang* literally signifies the permanent and the universal, but can sometimes also be used in the sense of "ordinary" and "common." For Ou-yang Hsiu, *ch'ang* is the normative principle of existence inherent in life. That the Six Classics comprehend this principle is proved by the fact that they have stood the dual test of time and of common and universal application in life. In a letter to a friend, Ou-yang Hsiu wrote:

> What a superior man pursues in his study is realization of the *tao*. In order to pursue and realize the *tao*, he must first understand antiquity. Only when he has learned to know antiquity and has comprehended the *tao* can he begin to realize it in his own conduct, put it into practice in daily affairs, disseminate it in his writings, and so establish his objective validity [*hsin*] for posterity. The *tao* is what the Duke of Chou, Confucius, Mencius, and their followers universally realized in their personal conduct; it is manifested in the writings of the Six Classics, and it still commands belief in the present time. The *tao* manifested by the Six Classics is easy to comprehend and can serve as a guideline for individuals. The teaching of the Six Classics is also easy to understand and can be put into practice in daily affairs....
>
> After Confucius, Mencius knew the *tao* best. However, his idea of *tao* as embodied in his teachings is no more than to instruct people to plant mulberry trees and hemp and to raise chickens and pigs. He regards care for the living and proper burial for the dead as the very foundation of the kingly way.... What Mencius called the way, is it not the *tao*? In practical terms, it is all so simple and near to every man. This is because he brings the *tao* to bear on the practical and the real.[13]

The tradition of the Six Classics, according to Ou-yang Hsiu, is the only tradition since antiquity to comprehend the principle of universality. This universality is demonstrated by the continuous transmission in time of these works and is further upheld by the fact that the Classics, being the works of sages, are solidly based on reality and firmly grounded in normal human feelings. They are therefore acceptable and accessible to all men. From this view of the Six Classics, Ou-yang Hsiu derived three conditions for a principled man's pursuit of the *tao*: to realize it in personal conduct, to apply it to daily affairs, and to transmit it in writings. Later, in a different context, these three conditions become the three prerequisites to Ou-yang Hsiu's idea of man's "immortality" (*pu-hsiu*) —an idea that expresses the closest possible approximation of the universal *tao* in human pursuit. In a "valediction" for his disciple Hsü Wu-tang (1054), he said:

> Things like plants, trees, birds, beasts, and man manifest themselves differently in life; yet when dead they are all alike—they fall into decay and eventually become extinct. However, there are sages and worthies among men who, although they lived and died like the rest, are different from plants, trees, birds, beasts, and other men in one respect: after they die, they remain immortal (*pu-hsiu*) and survive time. They are sages and worthies because they cultivate [the principle of immortality] in themselves, apply it to practical affairs, and manifest it in their writings. It is by virtue of this triple practice that they are able to become immortal and to survive time. . . .
>
> Once I read the "Treatise on Bibliography" by Pan Ku and the "Catalogue of the Four Categories [of Writings]" of the T'ang Dynasty and saw all that was listed there; so numerous are the writers since the Three Dynasties, Ch'in and Han—the more prolific ones with over one hundred titles, the least prolific of them with thirty or forty titles—that it is impossible to count them all. But most of their writings are scattered, are lost, have worn away, and have become extinct; fewer than one or two out of a hundred of the total survive. It grieves me to see what happened to these people. Their writings were indeed brilliant, and their expressions skillful. Yet, what such brilliance and skill amount to is no different from the blossoms of plants and trees that are blown by the wind, or the lovely sounds of the birds and beasts that drift by our ears. When we compare the pains these writers took in thinking and working, are they any different from the hustle and bustle of the common people so quickly overtaken by death? Sooner or later, even their works, too, will fall

into oblivion and become extinct, just like the other three things mentioned [the blossoms, the lovely sounds, and the common people]. Writings are as unreliable as that. Present-day students all aspire to become immortal like the ancient sages and worthies. They slave all their lives and waste their minds on writing. It's too bad.[14]

In terms of all three conditions for pursuit of the *tao*, the Six Classics are again perfect. Hence the conclusion seems inevitable that any literary principle that acts against the three necessary conditions of the *tao* acts also against the principle of *ch'ang* and so will have at best a secondary value, or at worst a negative value.[15] The two ideals of "loftiness" (*kao*) and "extraordinariness" (*ch'i*) to which the heroic school of Han Yü aspired are the exact opposite of what Ou-yang Hsiu considered the normative principles of the Six Classics—"simplicity" (*chien*) and "ease" or "facility" (*yi*). It should therefore come as no surprise that Ou-yang Hsiu severely criticized *kao* and *ch'i* as misguided attempts to exceed the universal (*ch'ang*).

His criticism of the cult of the pretentious, the lofty, and the extraordinary in art is forcefully expressed in a letter of 1035 to his friend Shih Chieh (1005–45), an impressive presence in the Imperial Academy:

> You make a diagonal line when it should be level and draw a circle when it should be a square, and you call your actions "truly practicing the way of Yao, Shun, the Duke of Chou, and Confucius." You could do nothing worse . . . Although calligraphy is a lesser art, yet one should still follow its regular rules and should not attempt to achieve the bizarre. . . . You have not read my last letter correctly. What I said there had nothing to do with what constitutes good calligraphy; I only expressed my anxiety over the fact that you, by keeping such close company with the bizarre and by regarding yourself as unusual, will inevitably mislead the young.[16]

The idea of "craft" or "artistry" (*kung*) and that of "fineness" or "perfection" (*ching*) present a problem of a different nature in Ou-yang Hsiu's literary theory. Unlike *kao* and *ch'i*, which are definitely to be avoided in writing, he saw *kung* and *ching* as desirable and, up to a point, even necessary to good literature. However, it is possible to imagine the theoretical difficulty Ou-yang Hsiu was likely to encounter, at a time when the excessive artistry of *shih-wen* was provoking criticism from all quarters, as he tried to accommodate such ideas in his own theory. To admit *kung* without qualification as a positive criterion of value would be fatal to his theory of objective validity and universality. *Kung*, being the privileged possession of poets and artists, encourages an author to make absolute claims for *individual* emotions, for individual caprice, and for poetic imagination. Because it is essentially not oriented toward truth, *kung* frequently conflicts with objective validity and with universality. Ou-yang Hsiu stressed many times that a writer cannot transcend the contingencies of time and circumstances by *kung* alone. In his famous preface to the collected poems of his close friend Mei Yao-ch'en (1002–62), he lamented the adversities that so often accompany the more admirable achievements of skillful writers and often prevent them from attaining an even higher order of achievement like that of the poets and historians of the *Shih ching* and the *Shu ching*.

> Of the poems that survive, many are the works of ancient men in adversity. When a man of letters fails to realize himself in the world, he frequently goes into voluntary exile among the mountain tops and by the riverbanks. There he sees the insects, fish, plants, trees, wind, clouds, birds, and beasts and often seeks out the strangest among them. All the grievances and indignation that are pent up inside him rise up in the form of rancor and ridicule, and he adopts the poetic device of a banished minister's complaint or a widow's lament. In this way, he finds expression for human feelings ordinarily difficult to articulate; the greater the adversity he is in, the more skillful is his expression. This is not to say that poetry requires adversity; rather, it means that a poet in adversity is more likely to develop his skill.
>
> My friend Mei Sheng-yü [Mei Yao-ch'en], ... had he been fortunate enough to find employment at court to sing the achievements and virtues of the Great Sung during sacrifices at the dynastic temple, might have rivaled the authors of the Shang Hymns, the Chou Hymns, and the Lu Hymns [in the *Shih ching*]. Would he not then have been truly eminent? What a pity that he was allowed to grow old without realizing his ambition, writing the verse of a man in adversity, expressing himself through images of insects, fish, and such things, and through the melancholy reflections of a grieving wanderer. The world enjoys his artistry [*kung*], but it has no idea that he had long suffered adversities and was growing old.[17]

Artistry alone, then, does not achieve the highest order of creation for a writer. Only when he bases his feelings on what is normal and correct (*cheng*),[18] and thereby partakes of the principle of *ch'ang*, as did the poets of the *Shih ching*, and only when he can realize in his life the three necessary conditions of immortality will he be able to achieve lasting fame and be remembered by posterity.

The correlation between the formal beauty (*k'o-ai*) of a natural object and the formal beauty of literary skill is also recognized by Ou-yang Hsiu in his concept of *ching*. But in *ching*, his focus has shifted from the concepts of transiency and immortality to the idea of "mutual exclusiveness" (*pu-chien*). *Ching*, a differentiated kind of skillfulness, is unique in its realization. Yet it is the law of nature and of human art that no two forms of *ching* ever exist in a single object. The peony, for instance, is the most beautiful of flowers, and the lichee tree bears the most perfect of fruits, but it is the nature of things that neither the peony nor the lichee tree has the other's fruit or flower.[19] Similarly, there is a natural limitation to the achievement of literary excellence in a work. If a writer excels in fineness of discourse, he cannot be simple and direct at the same time. If a poet excels in giving perfect articulation to his profound personal feelings, he cannot aspire to be universal as well. This idea of mutual exclusiveness in formal expression arrives rather late in Ou-yang Hsiu's literary theory. It reflects a maturity of thought as well as a rueful acceptance that technical perfection and universality of substance do not ordinarily coexist in practice; the paths to technical perfection and universal substance seldom cross. Writers are often compelled by their own nature and by circumstance to choose the one and to abandon the other. But in theoretical terms, universality in writing, to Ou-yang Hsiu, is indisputably of a higher order of value than artistic perfection because perfection in art, when realized, contains the good of only one thing at one time, whereas universality, when realized, comprehends the good of all things for all time.

## Nature and Man in the "Record of the Old Tippler's Pavilion"

Let us now consider Ou-yang Hsiu's own writings to observe how he put his literary theory into practice. The "Record of the

Old Tippler's Pavilion," written in 1046 during his exile in Ch'u-chou, is a well-known prose piece representative not only of Ou-yang Hsiu's personal *ku-wen* style but also of the humanistic spirit characteristic of Sung *ku-wen* writing in general—a spirit that defines and resolves problems in human terms within the limits of man's own sociopolitical order.

Even before the end of the Sung dynasty, "The Old Tippler's Pavilion" was noted for its original conception, its simplicity of style, and its unusual use—21 times—of the sentence particle *yeh*.[20] The meaning and function of the 21 *yeh* have intrigued readers and critics for centuries. Interpretation of the work, however, is generally based on a literal reading of one of the concluding lines in the first part: "The Old Tippler's delight is not so much in wine as in the mountains and waters." "The Old Tippler's Pavilion" is customarily read as the expression of a scholar-official's simple enjoyment of wine and nature. But simplicity can be a deceptive artistic device; behind it often lies a sober and oppressive reality. In considering the superficial simplicity of "The Old Tippler's Pavilion," it would be wise to reexamine its structural elements and explore more deeply their underlying thematic relationships.

All around Ch'u-chou are mountains. Those toward the southwest are especially lovely with their woods and ravines. The one that looks so luxuriant and lush is Mount Lang-yeh. After a walk of six or seven *li* into the mountains, one begins to hear the burbling sound of water as it gushes out from between two peaks; that is Jang Spring. Where the mountain turns and the footpath winds around, there stands a pavilion with its roof soaring wing-like over the spring; that is the Old Tippler's Pavilion. Who built the pavilion? A monk, inhabitant of these mountains, called Chih-hsien. And who gave it its name? The magistrate, in reference to himself. The magistrate and his guests gather here for drinking parties. He quickly becomes tipsy after only a few drinks, and as he is also the oldest among the company, he has bestowed on himself the sobriquet "Old Tippler." The Old Tippler's delight is not so much in wine as in the mountains and waters. He holds the joy of mountains and waters in his heart, and he finds expression for this joy in wine.

When the sun rises, the mists in the woods disperse; when the clouds return, the caves in the cliffs become dark: the alternation of darkness and light marks the mornings and evenings in the mountains. The wildflowers bloom and emit a subtle fragrance; the handsome trees put forth leaves and cast a dense shade; the wind blows high, and the frost is pure; the stream becomes clear, and the rocks are exposed: such are the four seasons in the mountains. Going thither in the morning, returning home at dusk, one finds the scenery different in the four seasons, and one's enjoyment is endless.

Men carrying loads sing along the road, and passersby rest under the trees; those ahead call out, and those behind respond; [elders] with stooped backs and [children] led by the hand pass to and fro unceasingly—these are the people of Ch'u-chou on an outing.

Some fish by the stream and find the brook deep and the fish fat; some draw water from the spring[21] and brew the wine and find the spring-water sweet and the wine clear; mountain delicacies and wild vegetables are spread out at random before [the gathering]—such is the magistrate's feast. The gaiety of the drinking and feasting needs neither strings nor woodwinds; pitch-pot players hit the target;[22] chess players win their games; wine cups pass back and forth as the drinking game goes on. Now getting up, now sitting down, shouting noisily—such is the merrymaking of the company. The one with a dark complexion and white hair, slumping languid among them, is the magistrate, tipsy with wine.

Presently, with the setting sun on the mountain, men and their shadows scatter pell-mell; the magistrate leaves and the guests follow. The woods are cloaked in darkness, and birdcalls are heard everywhere; the strollers are gone, and the birds rejoice. But although the birds may know the joy of woods and mountains, they do not understand the joy of men. Men may know the joy of the magistrate's company, but they do not understand the magistrate's joy in the joy of his guests. When tipsy with wine, he can share in their joy; when sober, he can recall it in writing. Such a person is the magistrate. But who is this magistrate? He is Ou-yang Hsiu of Lu-ling.[23]

"The Old Tippler's Pavilion" appears to be a simple prose piece. For centuries, readers and critics have appreciated it as a direct expression of a scholar-official's unaffected enjoyment of wine and nature.[24] The close relationship between wine and poetic inspiration has been a recurrent theme in Chinese writing, as well as in Western literature. From the works of the Seven Sages of the Bamboo Grove in Chin times through the works of Li Po in the T'ang and those of Su Shih in the Sung, wine has acted as a liberating force for the poetic spirit; it has the power to break down conventional bonds and set the poet free to roam in a realm where imagination is reality.

Yet considering Ou-yang Hsiu's view of life, art, man, and reality, such a flight of romantic imagination is almost inconceivable in him. Such "untold heights of poesy and imagination" would have given him acrophobia.[25] A manner he scorned when sober, he certainly would not abandon himself to when drunk, or at least he would not leave a record exalting it once he had regained sobriety. He always, when in control of his senses, preferred the tangible and the rationally accessible; early in his literary career, he expressed his distaste for people who shun their normal responsibilities and attempt to "escape the fetters of mortality" through wine and the cult of eremitism.[26] During Ou-yang Hsiu's exile to Yi-ling (1036), he abstained from drinking and maintained an impeccable code of conduct.[27]

During his exile at Ch'u-chou (1045–48), however, the earlier stoic stance disappeared. Wine not only appeared in his writings as a constant companion, it came to have so prominent a part in his life that he was forced to invent a persona—the Old Tippler—to apprehend its life dimension and assess its moral significance. In the poems and letters that refer to the Ch'u-chou period, wine is represented not so much as an open passage to spontaneous enjoyment of nature but rather as the only means by which the Old Tippler can lighten the oppressive burden of things: the burden of world-weariness and the overwhelming sense of the transience of life, of decay and death, and of the confusion of good and evil in human affairs, confusion that the apathetic cosmos also seems to manifest. In the following poem, for instance, the Old Tippler speaks of his own alienation from the human world and the pacifying effect wine has on him.

*Song of the Old Tippler*

When the Old Man first came to the mountain,
The beasts hid themselves,
And the birds flew off at the sight of him.
He goes to the mountain sober,
And returns home drunk.
Sober in the morning and drunk in the evening,

The four seasons do not exist [for him].
Birds call happily in the forest,
Animals come out and saunter on the paths;
They twitter and jabber in front of the Old Man, but he is
   too drunk to notice.
When a man has a heart, how can he have no feelings?
For every union there is a parting.
Waters burble, but the Old Man abruptly leaves and heeds
   not the sound;
The mountain stands lofty as the Old Man returns without
   noticing the seasons.
Waving in the wind, the mountain trees drop their leaves;
Every year in spring, the mountain grass is luxuriant.
Alas! I have no beneficent influence on the people,
My feelings are only for the wild fowl and deer of the
   mountains.
Ah, worthy Master Shen,
You have truly captured my emotions [in your lute music],
   and it soothes my thoughts.[28]

This poem, like the one following, was written in 1056 or 1057,
several years after Ou-yang Hsiu had left Ch'u-chou. He was
moved to write it one evening when a friend named Shen played a
song he had composed about the Old Tippler's Pavilion in Ch'u-
chou. The emotional and psychological tone of the poem clearly
recalls Ou-yang Hsiu's feelings of the Ch'u-chou period, especially
if we compare the confused rhythm of the Old Man's movement
and the regular rhythm of the plant and animal lives around him in
the poem above and the similar rhythms of the magistrate and his
environment in the "Record." The rapid movement of the seasons
here is also reminiscent of that of the seasons in the "Record"; both
reflect the anxiety and the skipping consciousness of their observer.
   Two aspects of nature, in particular, are accented in the poem,
one manifesting the continuity of life (birds and beasts), the other
manifesting the evanescence of life (leaves that fall and the luxuriant grass that passes with the spring). The Old Man is moved to
feel ("When a man has a heart, how can he have no feelings?"), but
he feels more strongly the evanescent aspect of nature and is not as
responsive to the joyous, vital aspect ("The four seasons do not
exist [for him]" and "birds call happily in the forest, . . . but he is
too drunk to notice"). This inability to harmonize with vital nature

is related to the Old Tippler's moral alienation from his fellow men ("Alas! I have no beneficent influence on the people"). The Old Man, for reasons not stated in the poem, is out of joint with the human world.[29] The realization that he can no longer relate to other people changes his outlook on life. The result is that he can no longer respond freely to the signs of joy in normal life. The world is apathetic to him, like the mountains that ignore his coming and going, and he is like the leaves and grass that wither with time. This conversion of normal human life into an oppressive intimation of time and death is too much for him to bear. It is at this point that wine appears, the anodyne to the Old Man's suffering: "Sober in the morning and drunk in the evening, the four seasons do not exist [for him]." When consciousness is put to sleep, pain no longer stings.

In another poem, the Old Man straightforwardly acknowledges his troubles. Ou-yang Hsiu depicts him as toying with the idea of abandoning himself to the traditional role of an educated drunkard:

*Song Presented to the Academician Shen*

The vicissitudes of life are too much for my feeble strength;
With blighted mien and hair turned grey at the temples,
I have truly become an old man.
My heart is besotted by worries, how can it know joy?
Master Shen said to me, "Old Sir, why do you say such
    woeful things?
In the hundred years of a man's life,
How much time does he have for drinking?"[30]

But nothing comes of this invitation to abandon himself to drinking. At the end of the poem, the Old Sir, "Gathering up his robes and pushing aside the lute, got up to look into the night. / Up in the sky, he watched the Milky Way moving southwestward." The pose here is one of tacit rejection and further questing. Thus, the same torment of alienation and the same longing for lost joy are acted out in different settings. In the following poem, written at Ch'u-chou in 1046, the Old Tippler is back again in nature, caught by the same urge to recapture joy and the same struggle to free himself from the dark elegiac mode of a tormented self. Here, yet another answer is contemplated and rejected.

*Written on the Old Tippler's Pavilion at Ch'u-chou*

Forty years of age is not yet old.
As I, the Old Tippler, incidentally write these lines.
In my drunkenness, all creation drops out of my
    consciousness;
How then can I remember my years?
I love the water at the foot of the pavilion,
That flows from between the unruly peaks,
Whose sound seems to fall from the sky.
       . . .
So pure, it is not like the music of strings and woodwinds,
Not that I don't find beauty in strings and woodwinds,
But their sound is too intricate.
So I frequently take some wine,
And walk a long distance to burbling water.
Wild birds spy on me as I get drunk,
And clouds in the brook invite me to sleep there.
Mountain flowers merely know how to smile;
They are unable to converse with me.
Only the wind from the cliff comes by
Sobering me up with its breeze.[31]

Here, wine and freedom are tentatively accepted for their
worth, and the old man's spirit probes beyond them to explore
the moral potential of an aesthetic harmony between man and nature. If nature is beautiful and man is sensitive to its beauty, if "all
creation" can "drop out" of his consciousness by means of wine,
and if the complexity of human affairs—"music of strings and
woodwinds"—can be replaced by the purer activities of nature,
then it should be possible for man—the Old Man—to recover his
inner joy through a harmonious relationship with nature.

This possibility, however, is dubious at best: "Mountain flowers
merely know how to smile; / They are unable to converse with
me." Harmony with nature may satisfy the spirit so long as man
remains in a natural state of existence, free of all traffic with the
human world. But that state cannot last: "The wind from the cliff
comes by / Sobering me up with its breeze." After the Old Man has
been sobered up by the wind, once his reason regains its consciousness after the effect of wine wears off, what then?

The theme that connects these three poems is by no means a simple one. Clearly, the relationship between the Old Man, nature, and wine is intricate and profound, bearing on the question of man's place in a world of flux. The Old Man in these poems is deeply disturbed by this question; he is caught in a net of pain and suffering, the result of a sudden awareness that the world is constantly changing and that the moral center of his life has no definite or permanent lodging but can easily be moved and shifted about by changes in the outside world. When this awareness becomes acute, the feelings it stirs up are too difficult to bear. Then the Old Man turns to wine, not for an answer or a resolution, but to find some relief from the unbearable feelings of his heart. Wine is therefore symbolic of a mode of feeling in the Old Man, a feeling informed by the conflict between the Old Man's urge to rediscover a meaningful relationship with the external world and his overwhelming sense of alienation and moral confusion in that world.

Between these poems and the "Record of the Old Tippler's Pavilion," however, there is a noticeable difference. In the "Record," the relationship between the Old Tippler, nature, and wine has a different focus: the perspective is one not of flux and pain but of joy. The solitary delights and sorrows of the alienated Old Man in the poems are resolved in the "Record" into a universal joy in life embracing the different kinds of living beings. The cause of this transformation of one man's sorrow into a multitude of common people's joy is suggested by the order and structure of the "Record."

The text of the essay is skillfully constructed in three parts. The lines beginning with "all around Ch'u-chou are mountains" and ending with "he holds the joy of mountains and waters in his heart, and he finds expression for this joy in wine" constitute the opening section, an exordium of sorts. The second section begins with the line "when the sun rises" and ends with the line "the one with a dark complexion and white hair, slumping languid among them, is the magistrate, tipsy with wine." The closing section begins with the line "presently, with the setting sun on the mountain" and ends with a revelation: "But who is this magistrate? He is Ou-yang Hsiu of Lu-ling."

The customary interpretation of the work is derived primarily from a partial reading of the first part and based on the deceptively picturesque quality of the Old Tippler's personality and his seemingly aphoristic line "the Old Tippler's delight is not so much in wine as in the mountains and water"; such a reading focuses on the first section of the essay as containing the only message of the entire work. The text of the essay, however, shows us quite unambiguously that the first part is only an introductory section in which the origin and significance of the pavilion and the Old Tippler in the title are defined and explained in the established tradition of "records of excursion" (*yu-chi*, to which Liu Tsung-yüan's "Eight Records of Yung-chou" belong). What Ou-yang Hsiu has done is to fulfill this traditional requirement of a *yu-chi*, but with a very personal note. In the second part, by its central position and length the main body of the work, the theme of joy unfolds in its multiple splendor. In contrast to the solitary delight of the Old Tippler in the first section, here a symphony of voices expresses a universal joy—the joy of being alive and of living at a time when, no matter how precarious the situation may appear to an Olympian eye, the earth is nevertheless bounteous and communal life is free from natural and human calamities.[32] In this symphony of universal joy, whatever tension may have characterized the Old Tippler's ambiguous feelings is dissolved in his tipsy participation in the normal business of his community. Wine, then, becomes not a symbol of alienation but an agent of communion in the second section. The man whom suffering has alienated from his fellowmen is now reunited with them in joy.

The symphony of man's joy in natural landscapes and in human society in the second part of the essay also has its own internal structure. The enjoyment of nature ("When the sun rises, the mists in the woods disperse.... One finds the scenery different in the four seasons, and one's enjoyment is endless") is juxtaposed with the joy of man ("Men carrying loads sing along the road.... The one with a dark complexion and white hair, slumping languid among them, is the magistrate, tipsy with wine"). Within man's joy, there are many degrees: that of the strolling people of Ch'u-chou, the merriment of the magistrate's guests, and the happiness of the tipsy magistrate himself. The significance of these differentiated joys, which are mutually contingent, is not revealed until the concluding section of the essay. Throughout the second part, we witness only a resonant celebration of natural beauty, of human gaiety, captured and immortalized as in a frieze. The transience of natural life is dissolved in the eternal alternation of morning and evening, and time becomes a constant cycle of the four seasons. Within this continuous revolution of time, human life is harmonized with the beauty of nature and is presented as eternally happy.

Then, beginning with "presently," rhapsodic description turns into sober reflection in the third section of the essay. In the conclusion, the differentiated joys of the second section are briefly recalled, their significance and internal relationships reflected on, and their relative values made explicit in terms of the varying degrees of intelligence of the creatures expressing this emotion: "Although the birds may *know* the joy of woods and mountains, they do not *understand* the joy of men. Men may *know* the joy of the magistrate's company, but they do not *understand* the magistrate's joy in the joy of his guests."

The magistrate finds joy in his people's innocent enjoyment of the simple things in their life of peace and plenty; and his joy is enhanced by an acute awareness of the larger situation—awareness that their joy is possible only because they live in a time of peace, protected by the life-bestowing virtue of their emperor. And Ou-yang Hsiu, who emerges in the last sentence and identifies himself with the magistrate and with the magistrate's persona, has understood the perceptual conditions of each of the joys described, has penetrated their inherent bias of time, place, and person, and has gone beyond the limitations of each of their individual joys and perils. Having thus understood the experiences of these many personalities, he has gained the insight that the universal in life is never confined to a single example but must be understood from the ever-continuing, ever-recreating principle behind its myriad manifestations. In this sense, "The Old Tippler's Pavilion," despite its extremely beguiling simple prose style, is not a simple work about joy alone; it is a serious effort on the author's part to come to terms with the constant (*ch'ang*) in life and with the permanent and universal in the world, the physical manifestations of which are necessarily and always in flux.

This attention to the constant and the permanent is formally underscored in "The Old Tippler's Pavilion" by the distinctive use, 21 times, of the sentence particle *yeh*, which is a grammatical marker of sentences in the declarative mode. The constant repetition in such a relatively short prose work of this sentence marker was certainly intended by the word-conscious Ou-yang Hsiu to serve an artistic and thematic purpose.[33] First, this repeated construction dictates a positive mode of understanding.[34] When used to the exclusion of other modes such as the interrogative and the subjunctive, this use of declarative mode accentuates the author's affirmative conception of the subject (man's life), the thematic counterpart to which in "The Old Tippler's Pavilion" is universal joy.

In the second part, especially where the theme of ever-present joy is developed, *yeh* comes invariably at the end of a passage descriptive of nature or of human activities and renders the preceding verbal phrases into nouns. For example, in the section "Men carrying loads sing along the road, and passersby rest under the trees; those ahead call out, and those behind respond; [elders] with stooped backs and [children] led by the hand pass to and fro unceasingly—these are the people of Ch'u-chou on an outing," the noun marker *che* and the declarative sentence marker *yeh* transform the whole sequence of busy activities—singing, resting, calling, responding, leading by the hand, passing to and fro—into an "A is A" nominal sentence structure.

This grammatical transformation parallels the author's perspective on nature and life—the actions of fluctuation and change, expressed by verbs, are but appearances in time, and the essential principle of nature and life is static and noun-like. Eternally present and unchanging, this principle generates change, comprehends change, and is itself expressed through change. That is to say, *yeh*, by transforming verbal constructions into nouns, expresses in grammatical form Ou-yang Hsiu's ultimate view of the universal in life as at once change (verb) within the changeless (noun), sorrow within joy, and mutability within the constant (*ch'ang*). The universal in life is immanent in the changing. Even perfection, as long as it belongs to the world of realized form, cannot escape change. Only by recognizing and accepting the contingencies in existential conditions and by penetrating beyond them to base one's vision of reality on the principle of universal life, which is infinitely self-recreating, is man able to transcend change and lift himself above the contingent in existence into the realm of immortality.

It was at this juncture, probably, that Ou-yang Hsiu began to develop the concepts of mutual exclusiveness of perfectly realized form (*pu-chien*) and immortality (*pu-hsiu*) and relate them to his theory of literature and his philosophy of life. In his writings after the Ch'u-chou period, he is constantly meditating on the regrettable tendency of the perfect realization of beauty and of desirable forms of life to exclude one another. He who delights in nature cannot at the same time enjoy the pleasures of wealth and fame;[35] the lichee tree, which bears the most perfect of fruits, cannot also have the peony's flower.[36] But in "The Old Tippler's Pavilion," Ou-yang Hsiu's dual vision of the forms of perfection, which are mutually exclusive, and the patterns of life and change, which are universal, has found artistically integrated expression in a *ku-wen* style that is at once simple in expression and easy to understand. This simplicity and accessibility reinforce the apparent theme of joy in life and express what he believed to be fundamental in all enduring works: objective validity of substance, normality of feelings, and universality of application and moral balance.

The unique and the perfect, the outstanding and the unusual that the T'ang *ku-wen* writers esteemed, still command an important place in Sung *ku-wen* theory. But the personal joy and sorrow of the Old Tippler, in spite of their beauty and genuineness, play only a partial role in the three-part essay "Record of the Old Tippler's Pavilion." The vista described by Ou-yang Hsiu is now much broader, the time span much longer. The descent from the heroic to the common has begun. "I want to ride on the wind and return [to the celestial abode]," Su Shih still yearns, but "I am afraid that in the jade towers and buildings there on high, the coldness will be too severe for me to endure." [37] The rational awareness that loftiness (*kao*) is incompatible with continuity of life (at least in an everyday context) renders pursuit of such heights daunting and prohibitive. Which of the two is to be preferred, the mountain peak or the plain, the unique or the universal, is a question that T'ang and Sung *ku-wen* writers bequeathed to later ages. And their varied resolutions of this question yielded a corpus of work that has since become a permanent part of the Chinese literary heritage.[38]

# 4

## SU SHIH

A Theory of Perception in Art

SU SHIH (1036–1101) was 30 years younger than his patron Ou-yang Hsiu, and so their careers and thoughts were not as closely intertwined as those of Han Yü and Liu Tsung-yüan. Politically, Su Shih, like Ou-yang Hsiu in his later years, was part of the conservative opposition to the New Law Reform. In literary theory, they are frequently mentioned together in the context of the *ku-wen* revival of the early Sung. Although intellectually and artistically they were of different generations and differed in almost every essential aspect, again like Han Yü and Liu Tsung-yüan, they have been perceived by critics and literary historians as the principal advocates of *ku-wen* in the Sung and as leading stylists who so perfected *ku-wen* and its theoretical basis that they determined its development for centuries to come.

### The Impact of Political Exile

Like his father, Su Hsün (1009–66), and his younger brother, Su Ch'e (1039–1112), Su Shih commanded a formidable prose style, which won him a great reputation in the famous *chin-shih* examination of 1057, administered by Ou-yang Hsiu, and in a special examination of 1060, for which Ou-yang Hsiu sponsored him. He was promoted from the provinces to the capital in 1065, but his career there was interrupted at the outset by the compulsory mourning for his father, and he returned only in 1069, just as Wang An-shih was coming to power. Because of his outspoken opposition to Wang's administrative reforms, Su Shih was demoted in 1071 and served in a series of provincial posts until he was dismissed from office in 1079 and banished to Huang-chou (in modern Hopei).[1] He returned to the capital in 1085, after the fall of the reform party, and briefly held high posts in the central government at various times in the following eight years. When the reformists regained power in 1094, they banished him to the extreme south, where he remained until shortly before his death.

Su Shih was thus only superficially involved in the great struggle between the conservative party of Han Ch'i and Ssu-ma Kuang and the radical reformist party of Wang An-shih; despite his early promise and ambition, he never quite attained sufficient eminence to become a central participant. Even when his party was in power, it denied him preferment during most of his career, distrusting his independence of mind. Su Shih, then, was unsuccessful in public life, and his preeminence in the eyes of posterity largely results from his prodigious literary talent.

As the twentieth-century scholar Kuo Shao-yü has noted, Su Shih was not primarily interested in literature for the sake of reviving the Confucian *tao*, or any *tao* for that matter. He was interested in the *art* of literature.

> The literary theories of Su [Hsün], Su [Shih], and Su [Ch'e] were basically different from those of Ou[-yang Hsiu] and Tseng [Kung, 1019–83]. The reason they were different was their different underlying attitude toward literature.... The Confucians Liu [K'ai], Mu [Hsiu], and Tseng [Kung] studied the literary works of the ancients with a view to seeking the *tao* embodied in those works. Although they did not necessarily find the *tao*, they never dared to announce boldly to the world, as Su Hsün did, that they were studying literature for literature's sake.... The Sus theorized only about the style of literature, not its content.... This is what was seminal about the literary theories of the three Sus.[2]

It is important to note here that the relationship between *tao* and *wen* in Su Shih's thinking marked a decisive turn away from Han Yü's and Ou-yang Hsiu's idea of "literature as a vehicle for the *tao*." Su Shih's "way of literature" approximated the ancient concept of art or consummate skill in the *Chuang-tzu*. Therefore, in discussing his theory and practice of *ku-wen*, we must pay special attention to his distinctive tendency to equate *ku-wen* with *wen* in general and the *tao* of *ku-wen* with the *tao* of the arts in general. Reflecting his reorientation of *ku-wen* theory toward a general theory of art and letters, Su Shih explicitly included technique (*fa*) among the criteria for evaluating literature. This addition of *fa* to the theory of literature was unprecedented, and it marks the second significant departure in the Sung development of *ku-wen*, the first being Ou-yang Hsiu's introduction of the ideas of simplicity and universality.

Philosophically, Su Shih stood with the generation of Neo-Confucian thinkers that included Chou Tun-yi, Shao Yung, and Chang Tsai, rather than with his patron Ou-yang Hsiu; he shared his older Neo-Confucian contemporaries' fascination with the "ultimate" and with the metaphysics derived from the *Yi ching*. He was interested in Chou Tun-yi's attempt "to explain how the countless differentiated phenomena of existence derive from an original source which is itself... undifferentiated."[3] Shao Yung's theory of a numerical universe, of number as an essential concept for interpreting existence, influenced Su's thinking on the nature of change and its meaning for man's life.[4] From Chang Tsai he borrowed the idea that the primal material force (*ch'i*) "is a constant process of change, integrating to form human beings and the other creatures of the world, disintegrating again to return to the state of the Great Vacuity. Man's task in the world is to comprehend this process of change and to harmonize his action with it."[5]

In discussing Su Shih's intellectual and literary development, it is expedient to focus on the years 1071 to 1085, from his demotion to the provinces through his first banishment. It was during this time, especially during his exile at Huang-chou, that his ideas crystallized and matured and found expression in several of his greatest works. It is clear from his writings that in exile Su Shih relied heavily on Buddhism to forget his frustrations in the political sphere. Buddhism helped him to maintain his intellectual and emotional equilibrium—he did not indulge in the bitter rage and self-pity of Liu Tsung-yüan or the immoderate drinking of Ou-yang Hsiu— and in his works of this period, he arrived at a transcendent view of life in the general scheme of things that could be called positively optimistic.[6]

## Nature and the World of Art: *Yi, Fa,* and *Kung*

The reorientation of the literary ideal in the eleventh century from the extraordinary (*ch'i*) to the universal (*ch'ang*), as we now know, was related to a revised view of nature among Sung writers. Writers like Ou-yang Hsiu came to identify the universal in nature with a life-affirming and life-sustaining constant. Su Shih, by contrast, saw the universal as a process of dynamic fluctuation that is essentially inconclusive: dissolution succeeds growth, completion is followed by destruction. All things in nature dissolve in time, and in time they assume new forms and appearances. Thus, change, when viewed not as a finite phenomenon in human life but as an infinite succession of dissolution and growth flowing through time, becomes continuity. This new vision of an infinite process forming the content of the universal gave rise to an immensely productive idea in Su Shih's writings—the notion that dissolution and growth, change and continuity, death and life, are but two phases of a single and harmonious whole. The phenomenon of change and the impermanence of life merged in Su Shih's thought into a central concept, which I shall call the "two-oneness" of change and continuity in time. The concept is important because it offers a rare point of focus for discussing visible turning points in the Sung development of *ku-wen*.

Su Shih formulated his idea of continuity-in-change after his arrival at Huang-chou in 1080. Thereafter, he elaborated various aspects of the concept in his correspondence and in miscellaneous writings and applied these different aspects in his creative works. In the following, I first consider Su Shih's views after 1080 on the vicissitudes of nature as represented in the art of painting and refer to earlier remarks he made on literary style that contained germs of his mature conception of art in general. Then I examine his famous "Rhymeprose on the Red Cliff" (1082) as an illustration of how he used these ideas in his creative writings and of how they elucidate some difficult passages in that work.

The impressive transformation in Su Shih's writings after his arrival at Huang-chou was noted by his younger brother, Su Ch'e:

Once he said to [me] Ch'e, "In my opinion, you are the only one among today's scholars who can compete with me." When he was demoted and banished to Huang-chou, he closed his door to the world and gave full rein to his brush and ink. His writings suddenly changed, becoming like [the rush of] a river in flood;[7] and [I] Ch'e was left staring, never able to equal him again.[8]

The simile of a river in flood suggests a considerable growth of vitality and resources, an expansion of vistas, and a proportionate loosening of set, conscious bounds. To appreciate what Su Ch'e meant by the simile in terms of Su Suih's literary style, it would be useful to examine some of the principles that had guided Su Shih's writings before the Huang-chou period.

The Preface to the *First Volume of the Journey South* (1059) contains a revealing passage:

> For the writers of former times, [literary] craft did not mean merely that one was able to write in this or that manner; craft meant that one could not but write in this or that manner. Like the clouds above mountains and rivers, like the flowers and fruits of plants and trees, it was the outward manifestation of [innate] fullness and luxuriance; even if they had wished not to have such a manifestation, would that have been possible?
>
> Ever since my youth, I have heard my father discourse on literature, remarking that the sages of ancient times composed because they could not but do so. [I] Shih and my younger brother, Ch'e, wrote a great deal, but never with the conscious intent [*yi*] to compose anything. In the year *chi-hai* [1059], we accompanied our father on a trip to Ch'u. There was nothing to do on the boat, because gambling, chess playing, and drinking are not what a family should enjoy together. The beauty of the scenery, the simplicity of the local customs, the historical associations of former worthies [with the region], and all that with which our senses came into contact stimulated our hearts and issued forth in lyrical verses.... These verses were done while we were talking and laughing together; they were not labored writings.[9]

Su Shih was 24 years old when the preface was written. His distinction here between writings that are noted for their literary craft or artistry (*kung*) and writings that are distinguished for their level of conscious intent or conception (*yi*) is significant, as is his distinction between literary craft that stems from effort and literary craft that is spontaneous and free from human control. Of these two kinds of craft, Su Shih valued the latter more, and he seemed pleased that it informed most of his own writings at that time. Of writings distinguished for their level of conscious intent, he gives us no criterion of value judgment here except to hold up the compositions of the ancient sages as the ideal.

As Su Shih's critical thinking developed, the emphasis on *yi* over *kung* in evaluating a work became more pronounced. For example, although Su Shih did not dispute that novelty (*hsin*), extraordinariness (*ch'i*), loftiness (*kao*), and ornateness (*hua*) are characteristics of *kung*, he looked on them with distaste when the intent (*yi*) behind these skillful displays was nothing more than to gain conventional approval.[10] By 1072, Su Shih had begun to emphasize change and to criticize the exaltation of the constant or universal (*ch'ang*), the cornerstone of Ou-yang Hsiu's critical theories, when it reflected man's conceptual manipulation of the natural course of events. In his Preface to the *Collected Poems of Shao Mao-ch'eng*, he wrote: "It is indeed difficult for human desires to coincide with the natural course.... How can [the coincidental] be universal? When such a coincidence occurs by chance, people then insist that it should be universal. This is why men are mostly discontented and lacking in understanding."[11]

In Su Shih's mature reflections on art, after 1080, we find a consistent tendency to emphasize nature (*t'ien*) over man (*jen*) and a shift of focus from craft or artistry (*kung*) to intent or conception (*yi*); in Ch'ien Chung-shu's words, there was a propensity in Su Shih's thinking on art to "turn from the work of art to the mind of the artist."[12] In contrast to Su's definition of literary craft quoted above, the basis of evaluating *kung* shifted from the criterion of spontaneity, which pertains to the stylistic quality of a literary *work*, to the writer's mode of *thought*, which reflects his philosophical thinking as well as his ethical outlook. For example, in contrasting nature and man, Su Shih ceased to identify *yi* with the writings of sages alone and began to link it with nature (*t'ien*). At this point, *yi* became an increasingly important critical concept in his literary theory.[13] A given subject, when seen from the detached perspective of the natural course of events, assumes a form of expression and dictates a set of technical rules very different from those of the same subject seen from the perspective of individual human bias.

Much of Su Shih's critical discussion of *yi* dealt with the art of painting, and not by coincidence. Painting communicates and represents nature directly, and to Su Shih, an accomplished painter himself, it was the art of nature par excellence: the painter's art, insofar as it seeks to approximate that which naturally exists in the absence of human agency, mirrors the working of nature (*t'ien kung*) and its *yi* (*t'ien yi*). An examination of Su Shih's discussion of painting is illuminating not only because he obviously considered the arts of painting and poetry in unison but also because ideas concerning the two forms of art can generally be conveyed more vividly and more convincingly in terms of the visual art. Cyril Drummond Le Gros Clark deemed "the close comparison between the painter and the poet" to be "important to an elucidation of Su Shih's philosophy of art."[14] However, what is crucial in Su Shih's association of the poet with the painter is not so much a comparison as a convergence of the painter's and the poet's minds on the conceptual level with regard to an understanding of the working of nature and an appraisal of the role of artistic expression in the total process of creating a work of art, whether verbal or pictorial.

Water, especially water in motion, is a favorite symbol in Su Shih's criticism of literature and art. It symbolizes spontaneity, freedom, change, continuity, and all aspects of nature in which man aspires to participate. In his "Postscript to the Paintings of P'u Yung-sheng" (ca. 1081), Su Shih commented:

Most painters of water, ancient and modern, have painted it as extending far over a level surface with fine ripples. Those skilled at this technique can at best make it rise and fall in waves, so that people touch it with their hands, thinking it really three-dimensional; this they take to be the highest achievement. But in merit, these paintings hardly differ by a hair's breadth from the craftsmanship of representing water on block-print sheets.

During the Kuang-ming era [880–81] of the T'ang dynasty, the private scholar Sun Wei first formulated an original conception [*hsin-yi*] [in painting water]. He painted [it in] dashing torrents and huge waves, turning and twisting with the mountains and rocks, taking its form from whatever things [*wu*] it encountered.[15] He showed water in all its various aspects, and his work was pronounced "creative and preeminent" [*shen-yi*].[16] Later, two natives of Shu, Huang Ch'üan and Sun Chih-wei, mastered the technique [*fa*] of his brush strokes.... In recent years, P'u Yung-sheng of Ch'eng-tu ... began to paint water in motion. He showed a grasp of the original conception [*yi*] of the two Suns.[17]

In the postscript, Su Shih states that three things are to be considered in the painting of water: *yi*, *fa*, and *kung*—that is, the painter's conception of the subject, his technique, and his execution. Of the three, *yi* prescribes the technique and determines the merit of the execution. The character of water, when conceived in its essentially changeable nature, is expressed as "taking its form from whatever things it encountered" in the painting. But when conceived in its local appearances, it is generally represented as "extending far over a level surface with fine ripples." The difference between the two conceptions (*yi*) of water is reflected in the technique (*fa*), resulting in two methods of painting water. Sun Wei was able to realize the first conception of water, and so Su Shih describes his painting as "creative and preeminent." Sun Chih-wei mastered Sun Wei's technique and was able to execute the same effect, but because the original conception did not come from him, his painting is praised only for its forcefulness.[18] P'u Yung-sheng recreated the *fa* and the *yi* of the two Suns in making water come alive in his painting, but it is hard to imagine that Su Shih regarded his accomplishment as anything more than skillful execution since neither the *yi* nor the *fa* of painting water in motion originated with him.

Su Shih, indirectly through a postscript that discussed three painters and their representations of water in motion, underlined the close and well-ordered relationship among *yi*, *fa*, and *kung* in a finished work of art. In his "Discourse on Literature," he described his own style:

> My writing is like ten thousand barrels of spring water, gushing from the ground, choosing no specific outlet. On level ground, it floods and covers thousands of miles in a day without the least effort. Turning and twisting with the mountains and rocks, it takes its forms from whatever things it encounters, unpredictably. All that can be foretold is that it always goes where it should go, and it always stops where it cannot but stop. That is all. As for the rest, I myself am unable to tell.[19]

And in his "Letter in Answer to Hsieh Min-shih" he said,

> I have perused the letters and verses and miscellaneous essays you sent me. On the whole, they are like moving clouds and flowing water, without any fixed quality, just going always where they

should go and stopping always where they cannot but stop. Your style is natural, and it expresses itself exuberantly.[20]

Critics are wont to quote these two passages as indicative of Su Shih's ideal of literary style. However, once the inherent relationship among *yi*, *fa*, and *kung* is clear, we can see that there is a qualitative difference between the two styles. Like the two painters of "living water" in the "Postscript," the lack of an expressed source of being in Hsieh Min-shih's writing precludes the presence of a vital, productive *yi*. Su Shih's own writing, on the other hand, has a definite origin (gushing from a spring underground) and a well-formulated method of expression (taking its forms from whatever things it encounters). The spring is an admirable image of a great, abundant, and natural reservoir of vitality, accumulated over time (fed by constant practice, continued reflection, and vast learning) and the fountainhead of his literary output. Once above ground, its spontaneity in action is to be understood in the same sense as the lack of self-consciousness of the master carver in the *Chuang-tzu*, whose skill is already one with the *tao* and no longer needs the mediation or guidance of conscious method.[21] Such spontaneous skill, as a natural expression of the artist's spiritual communion with the *tao*, is certainly not to be compared to the moving clouds in Hsieh Min-shih's case, which, to all appearance, have no real connection with the topography of the sky.

To attain such unconscious skill, which implies a direct communication between the *tao* and execution, it is imperative that the conceiving spirit (*shen*) be free of all emotional affect. In his "Postscript to the Calligraphy of the Six T'ang Masters" (1081), Su Shih pointed to the undesirable effect of emotional and moral bias in a work of art : "In the case of petty men, even if their calligraphic art is craftsmanlike (*kung*), it invariably carries an expression that is smug and ingratiating. The fact is that a man's feelings always show through with his thoughts. Is this not what Master Han said about the axe thief?"[22]

When affected by emotion, the conceiving mind, the agent of direct communication between man and nature and between nature and art, becomes individualized and consequently carries the taint of a localized and unnatural form.[23] How is a writer to attain a style of writing comparable to the category of creative and preeminent (*shen-yi*) in painting and be freed, so to speak, from the appearance of an axe thief?

In another passage of the letter to Hsieh Min-shih, Su Shih elaborated on the concept of *tz'u-ta* ("language must communicate") as the ultimate achievement in literary skill, the stylistic equivalent of *shen-yi* in painting.

> Confucius said, "Language not in good style will not travel far." He also said, "It is sufficient if language communicates the meaning." However, language that merely communicates [the author's] intent [*yi*] is often suspected of being less than good style; this is greatly in error. To seek out the innermost mystery of things is like trying to tether the wind or capture a shadow. Not one man in thousands can have a perfect understanding [of the mystery] in his mind, much less be able to make it perfectly intelligible in speech or in writing. To be able to do this is what is meant by "language communicating the meaning." When language communicates, it is in more than sufficiently good style.[24]

What language communicates, after all, is *yi*. And to make language communicate, a writer, according to Su Shih, must first have "the mystery of things" clearly conceived in his mind—that is, he must conceive his subject as a painter conceives nature, with his mind detached from personal emotions; his mind must also be free of moral bias, so that things will communicate by themselves in speech or in writing. One way to accomplish this is to see the subject in the way a painter sees water, through a series of external changes,[25] because change is the visible way in which things express themselves in nature: dashing torrents, huge waves, and gushing springs, all changing form at every encounter with things, express the nature of water.

## The "Two-Oneness" of Change and Continuation in the "Rhymeprose on the Red Cliff"

Once this conception and expression of change in nature are transferred to the conception of change in the human world, man's life and history, with all their ups and downs and their monumental events, become one with the twists and turns of the torrents and waves. The "Rhymeprose on the Red Cliff" (1082) may be viewed as a literary recreation of this transference of perspective, the natural rhythm of change applied to the vicissitudes of human life and history; as the transient in man merges with the continual process of dissolution and growth in nature, the boundaries between finite mind and infinite nature dissolve.[26]

### Rhymeprose on the Red Cliff, Part I

In the autumn of the year *jen-hsü*, on the night after the full moon in the seventh month, Master Su and his guests went on a boat ride at the foot of the Red Cliff. A cool breeze blew softly, and no ripples rose on the water. Raising his cup, he toasted the guests, and they chanted the poem on the bright moon and sang the verse about the lovely maiden. Presently the moon rose over the eastern hill and lingered between the Dipper and the Herdboy.[27] Clear dew spread over the river; the glistening water blended with the sky.

Letting the reed-like boat go where it would, and drifting over the vast expanse, immense and boundless, was like leaning on the void and riding on the wind, bound they knew not where; soaring weightless, it was as if they had left the world and stood alone, transformed with feathered wings to ascend to the realm of immortals.

And so [Master Su and his guests] drank the wine, and their spirits grew extremely high; and tapping on the edge of the boat, they sang a song that went:

[Our] cinnamon oars Oh, rudder of orchid plant.
Hit the transparent brightness Oh, going upstream on
   floating light.
Far away, far away Oh, are my feelings,
Longing for the lovely one Oh, under the other sky.

A guest played the flute and accompanied the song.[28] Its *wu-wu* sound, now plaintive, now longing, now sobbing, now pleading, lingered on in a long drawn-out coda like an endless thread; [a melody] such as might stir the dragon hidden in the secluded gorge to dance, or a widow in her lonely boat to weep.

With a melancholy look, Master Su straightened his lapel, sat upright, and asked the guest, "Why do you play this way?" The guest said,

"'The moon is bright, stars are sparse;
Crows and magpies are flying to the south.'

"Are these not Ts'ao Meng-te's [Ts'ao Ts'ao, A.D. 155–220] lines?[29] Facing Hsia-k'ou to the west and Wu-ch'ang to the east, mountains intertwining with the river and forming a dense layer of dark green—is this not the place where Meng-te was cornered by young Chou [Yü, A.D. 175–210]? At the time when [Meng-te] had just taken Ching-chou and was moving downstream to the east, his ships aligned stem to stern for a thousand *li*, his flags and banners screening the sky, [Meng-te], pouring a libation on the river, held his lance level and composed these lines. He was indeed the hero of his time—but where is he now? Not to speak of you and me, who fish and gather firewood on the river islets, companion of fish and prawn and friends of deer and elk; we ride in this boat as small as a leaf, raise the gourd and toast each other, as transient as mayflies between heaven and earth, tiny grains in the boundless sea. It grieves me that our life is so short, and I envy the endlessness of the Long River. Would that I could cling to some flying immortal and wander off [into the void], there to embrace the bright moon and live forever. But I know that such a thing cannot be readily achieved, and I commit my lingering notes to the sad air."

Master Su said, "Does my guest understand how it is with the water and the moon? The one is constantly flowing but is never gone; the other is constantly waxing and waning but in the end never diminishes or grows.[30] That is to say, if we consider that which changes in things, then heaven and earth can last no longer than the wink of an eye. But if we consider that which is unchanging in things, then we and all creation alike are without end. So what do we have to envy?

"Moreover, everything between heaven and earth has its own master. If something does not belong to us, we cannot get even a hair of it. Only the bright moon in the hills, which are music to anyone who has ears for them and beauty to anyone who has eyes for them—these we can take without their ever coming to an end and use them without their ever being exhausted. They are the inexhaustible treasures of the Creator, the very things that you and I are now enjoying together."

The guest was delighted, and he laughed. They washed their cups for another round of drinks. After the meats and fruits were finished, and the cups and dishes were all in disarray, Master Su and his guests lay down to sleep in the boat, each one pillowed on another, not knowing that light was already in the eastern sky.[31]

*Rhymeprose on the Red Cliff, Part II*

In the same year [1082], at the time of the full moon in the tenth month, I was walking back to Lin-kao from the Snowy Hall. Two guests were with me, and we traversed the Huang-ni Slope. Frost and dew had already fallen, and the trees were completely bare of leaves. Our shadows were on the ground, and looking up, we saw the bright moon. Looking around us, we were delighted, and we sang to one another as we walked.

Presently, I sighed and said, "I have guests but no wine; and if I had wine, there would be no meat [to serve with it]. The moon is clear and the wind is cool; what shall we do on such a fine night?" One of my guests said, "Today toward sunset I cast my net and caught some fish. Large-mouthed and fine-scaled, they resemble Sung River perch. But where are we to get wine?"

When we arrived home, I consulted my wife about it. My wife said, "I have a jug of wine that I stored away long ago to meet your unexpected need." And so we took the wine and the fish, and once again we went on an outing to the foot of the Red Cliff.

The river flowed roaring by, the bank rose sharply for a thousand feet. The mountain was high and the moon was small; the water had fallen and the rock lay exposed. Not many days and months had passed since my last visit, yet I could scarcely recognize the hills and the river.

I then tucked up my robes and climbed upward. Walking along steep cliffs, pushing my way through thick undergrowth, stepping over tiger- and leopard-shaped rocks, and mounting tree roots gnarled like dragons, I clambered all the way up to to where the falcon's nest was precariously perched[32] and looked down into the dark palace of Feng Yi [the river god]. My two guests were unable to follow me there.

I let out a long, piercing whistle. Grass and trees trembled and shook; mountains rang and valleys resounded; the wind rose and the waters rolled in torrents. I felt a stilling sadness, an awful apprehension; so chilly [was the place] that it was impossible for me to stay.

I turned back and boarded the boat; we set it loose in midstream and let it go wherever it would. At the time it was nearly midnight. Looking around, all was lonely and desolate. Just then a solitary crane came across the river from the east. Its wings were like chariot wheels, and it was clad in a black garment below and a plain white silk jacket above. With a long, hoarse cry, it swooped over our boat and flew toward the west.

Presently my guests left, and I too returned home to bed. I dreamed that two Taoist priests,[33] with feather robes fluttering, were passing by Lin-kao; they bowed to me and said, "Was your outing at the Red Cliff enjoyable?" I asked their names, but they lowered their heads and did not answer. "Ah ha! I now know. The one who cried and flew over me last night, was it not you?" The Taoist priests looked back and laughed, and I woke up with a start. I opened the door and looked for them but could not see where they were.[34]

One question often raised about the "Rhymeprose on the Red Cliff" is whether the work is to be read as two pieces or one. In fact, the first part is much more often read than the second, which is not infrequently omitted from anthologies. This practice is based on a failure to appreciate the underlying unity of the two parts. Another question concerns the discrepancy between the single crane and the two feather-robed Taoist priests in the second part; this problem is closely related to the issue of whether the "Rhymeprose on the Red Cliff" is one work or two. The problem of the crane has elicited the interest of many scholars and created much discomfort among critics. A common solution has been textual emendation: "*two* Taoist priests" is changed to "*one* Taoist priest," and the discrepancy conveniently disappears, although some editions of Su Shih's collected works persist in printing "*two* Taoist priests."[35] But this textual problem of two or one can probably best be solved by an examination of the themes of the rhymeprose and of the idea of two-oneness.

Part I of the prose poem opens with Su Shih and his guests riding in a boat under the Red Cliff by the light of the full moon in the seventh month of the year. They are in a convivial mood, drinking and chanting poetry. Presently one of the guests begins to play his flute. The plaintiveness of the music rouses Su Shih to ask why he plays so sadly. The guest replies that the scene has reminded him of a poem written below the Red Cliff by the great hero Ts'ao Ts'ao in his prime, nearly 900 years before. That reminder has caused him to reflect on his own mortality. He envies the river, which flows endlessly, and wishes that he could roam the heavens forever as a companion to the moon. But knowing that his wish is impossible, he can only express his sadness in music. Su Shih counters the guest's lament by pointing out that the river and the moon remain ever the same despite the appearance of continual change. There is no occasion for envy or sadness, Su Shih says, since from the standpoint of change, nothing ever endures, and nature cannot be possessed by the force of human desires and aspirations. All that man can do is to enjoy what is offered him in his encounters with nature. Thereupon, the guest takes heart, and all present continue their carousal till daybreak, when they are all drunk and pillowed on one another.

The first piece, then, is a statement on human mortality and freedom cast in the form of a dialogue between Su Shih and his guest. The guest mourns the transience of man's life and fame and aspires to immortality. According to Su Shih, however, there is no such thing as mortality or immortality; these are merely human concepts prompted by human desires and aspirations. If one can contemplate the manifestations of mortality and transience in life and in history in the same way in which he contemplates the water and the moon in nature—detached from personal sentiments and desires—then he will see that there is no cause to mourn.

Part II of the rhymeprose recounts another visit to the Red Cliff three months later. The season and the mood are both quite different. It is again a clear, moonlit night, but in place of the soft breeze on the water, there is a heavy frost on the ground. The conviviality of the occasion is not so pronounced since food and drink are not ready at hand. Su Shih's conversation with his guests, which bears on the latter problem, is in sharp contrast to the earlier exalted discourse on the exploits of past heroes and the impermanence of life. There is again a boat ride, but the center of action shifts to the land.

Su Shih is seen walking with two guests through a winter landscape from his country retreat to his home. Presently, having obtained fish and wine, they are on their way to the Red Cliff. Su Shih then leaves his guests and climbs to the top of the cliff. The scene has changed beyond recognition since his last visit, and Su Shih is oppressed by its bleakness. High above the river, he sits alone and whistles to the wind; but it is too cold to stay there long, and he descends and returns to the boat. It is almost midnight. A solitary crane flies by. Shortly after, the guests leave and Su Shih goes home to sleep. In a dream, he encounters two Taoist priests, in feather robes, who inquire about his excursion that night. Suddenly realizing that the priests are the very crane that flew by his boat earlier, he awakes with a start. He looks out of his door, but there is no sign of the priests.

In comparison with the first part, the second is quite low-keyed. It is tempting to interpret its subdued tone in the same light as that

in which some critics interpret the change in scenery and mood—
that is, as a deliberate attempt to bring out by contrast the theme of
change and transience in life. Such an interpretation, however, en-
tails serious contradictions not only in the development of the two
parts of the piece itself but also with regard to what we have already understood of Su Shih's appreciation of the phenomenon of
change in nature. Within the rhymeprose itself, Master Su has already argued in the first part that there is no basis for melancholy
over the passing of good moments in history and in life; he has
offered the moon and the running water as two arresting images of
how things can be seen from the dualistic perspective of change-
continuity. The moon and the water are still present in the second
part. Which of the two, then, are we to accept as representing the
basic theme of the whole piece—the changing mood of Su Shih
under two different circumstances or the consistently unchanging
moon and water? This issue, a highly speculative one, is visibly
projected in the one-crane two-priests enigma.

Before we examine the conception of change implied in the shift
of number from one to two, let us consider the use of the dream
in literature as a device for expressing speculative thought. One
example that comes readily to mind is the dream in the second
chapter of the *Chuang-tzu*, where, after a long discussion of dreams
and their interpretation, it is said that Chuang Chou dreamt that he
was a butterfly.

> Once Chuang Chou dreamt he was a butterfly, a butterfly flitting
> and fluttering around, happy with himself and doing as he pleased.
> He didn't know he was Chuang Chou. Suddenly he woke up and
> there he was, solid and unmistakable Chuang Chou. But he didn't
> know if he was Chuang Chou who had dreamt he was a butterfly,
> or butterfly dreaming he was Chuang Chou. Between Chuang
> Chou and a butterfly there must be *some* distinction! This is called
> the Transformation of Things.[36]

The dream in the *Chuang-tzu*, as in the second part of Su Shih's
rhymeprose, suggests a move away from reality toward medita-
tion on what constitutes reality. The issue in question in the *Chuang-
tzu* is not whether it is Chuang Chou dreaming or the butterfly
dreaming. The dream is the framework in which the idea of the
"transformation of things" is expressed. Poised between two pos-

sible modes of reality—Chuang Chou dreaming and the butterfly dreaming—but committed to neither, one is forced by the lack of resolution on a realistic level to take notice of the idea of "transformation," which presents a resolution on the speculative level; namely, the merging of the two differentiated states of being in time—Chuang Chou and the butterfly. This merging in time constitutes the formal structure of the idea of "transformation."

Similarly, the lack of a resolution between the apparently contradictory positions of Su Shih in Parts I and II forces one to seek a unifying standpoint on the speculative level—that is, through the idea of two-oneness as projected in the dream: the transformation of one crane into two Taoist priests. What the dream in the second part seeks to communicate is essentially the same speculation about change as that expressed in the dialogue between Master Su and his guest in the first part. But now there is an implicit exchange of positions: Su Shih assumes the position of the guest, and the dream speaks for his own previous position. In the dream, not only is emotional bias verbally excluded from the depiction of the coexistence of change and continuity, but differentiated time, the usual context of change, is eliminated as well. In terms of differentiated existence over time, one that approximates the numerically rational correspondences of nature seen in distinct, arrested moments, one crane should indeed "change" into one Taoist priest (or vice versa provided that that kind of change is considered more possible than changing into two). But if existence is seen in terms of undifferentiated continuity, the crane, on the speculative level, is at once itself and the Taoist priest, which makes two. The dream, therefore, is a poetic marker of this shift in modes of thought; it is the author's way of calling attention to the fact that what is under consideration is only a speculative idea—a theme, so to speak—which is not something that can be proved in realistic terms or be called true or false.[37]

In an early controversy over the two-one problem, a Sung scholar remarked that the passage about the crane and two Taoist priests may contain an allusion to a story about the T'ang emperor Ming-huang. According to the story, the emperor Ming-huang went hunting on the Double Ninth and shot a solitary crane flying in the mountains. The crane flew away to the southwest with the arrow. Nearby was a temple that an itinerant Taoist priest was accustomed to visit three or four times every year. One day, the priest arrived with an arrow in his hand. He told the residents of the temple that the owner of the arrow would be there two years later and that they should return the arrow to him. Two years later, the emperor visited the temple. When he saw the arrow and the date inscribed on it, he realized that the crane he had shot on that ninth day of the ninth month was the very same itinerant Taoist priest.[38]

The inference here is, of course, that Su Shih may have been alluding to the crane in the story of the emperor Ming-huang and translating the possibility of their being one and the same crane into the presence of two Taoist priests in the dream (for what more apt image could one use to express the idea of possibility?). Or, if one wants to be witty, the crane of the rhymeprose could merely have joined the crane of the story of the emperor Ming-huang, and both cranes continued their existence as priests. At any rate, "playing" with the allusion also collapses the chronology, making the Ming-huang crane a contemporary, in some way, of the rhymeprose crane. This collapse of time is achieved by the image of two priests walking together. One priest would constitute a simple allusion to the previous test. However, even if we grant this playfulness to the author, this is still a local solution, which explains the dream but does not elucidate the total unity of the two prose poems.

The "Rhymeprose on the Red Cliff" was, in my opinion, certainly conceived as one piece twice enacted in different moments of life. The theme is that of time and life as conceived from the two complementary viewpoints of change and continuity. From the first part to the second, there is a steady progression from the concrete to the abstract, from the human to the natural, and from change-in-time (historical moments such as Ts'ao Ts'ao's battle at the Red Cliff) to timeless becoming (the dream). The order of progression in the two parts strongly suggests that the abstract and timeless (one crane) encompasses the concrete and differentiated (two priests). This idea of "two-oneness" is at once the beginning and the origin of all successive changes in time.

L. E. J. Brouwer, the Dutch philosopher and mathematician, said the following about man's intuition of two-oneness as the origin of numbers:

This neo-intuitionism considers the falling apart of moments of life into qualitatively different parts, to be reunited only while remaining separated by time, as the fundamental phenomenon of the intellect, passing by abstracting from its emotional content into the fundamental phenomenon of mathematical thinking, the intuition of two-oneness, the basal intuition of mathematics, creates not only the numbers one and two, but also all finite ordinal numbers, in as much as one of the elements of the two-oneness may be thought of as a new two-oneness, which process may be repeated indefinitely.[39]

This pregnant passage can be seen as bringing Su Shih's fundamental insight on change and continuity to the highest level of abstraction, removing all specificity from every concrete phenomenon of change and grasping the absolute essentials of identity and difference. The abstraction of all emotional content contrasts well with Su Shih's similar demand for the less austere purpose of avoiding bias. But, of course, Su Shih's crane image is much more evocative than a simple mathematical concept. The crane suggests not only two-oneness but a whole process of change and continuity, a variation on a theme that takes on its own life and escapes abstraction.

Change, or transformation, need not be a tragic phenomenon; it may simply be the process of coming into being or passing from one state of being to another. Change may be the law governing not decline and death but the incessant process of generation, as in the Yi ching; it may be the law governing incipiency, birth, and the phenomenal world. In other words, death is tragic and the phenomenon of existence impermanent only if one insists on seeing them from the perspective of a single life-death succession (sheng-ssu). Su Shih, in his "Rhymeprose on the Red Cliff," has eliminated the sense of the tragic view of life (which is not the same as eliminating the sense of the tragic in life) by broadening the span of life beyond the confines of one life-death succession to the life-[death]-life succession (sheng-sheng) of the Yi ching tradition. He has thereby escaped the law governing change as decline and death and has attained freedom from the necessity of the tragic, as Han Yü, Liu Tsung-yüan, and Ou-yang Hsiu did before him.

Han Yü attained freedom through identification with the orthodox Confucian tradition, thereby transcending time. Liu Tsung-yüan attained it through an affirmation of the necessity of moral good in man, thus transcending the necessity of physical law (*tzu-jan*) of nature and history. Ou-yang Hsiu liberated himself through a firm grasp of the irreducible facts in life, which comprehend different phases and levels of man's achievement and which make reality credible. Su Shih achieved the same end by dissolving the boundary between the real and the unreal, between the desirable and the undesirable, and finally between life and death. Because all four men ultimately derived the inspiration for their affirmation of life from the schools of thought of ancient times (*ku*) and because each produced a body of prose works expressing that affirmation, they are usually considered together as writers of the ancient-prose style (*ku-wen*). The fact that Su Shih articulated his most penetrating statement on *tao* and *wen* in rhymeprose—which is not purely a prose form—need not prevent us from considering him within the framework of the *ku-wen* movement. The keynote of dissolution of the boundary between manifested (literary) forms in Su Shih's concept of literature and art is eminently present in this work of literary art. This dissolution of boundary in Su Shih's thinking about *wen* and *tao* (whether in terms of the *Yi ching* or Buddhism or Taoism) marks a second turn away from the norm established by Han Yü in his program for *ku-wen* writers, which insists on a pure integration of the ancient (Confucian) *tao* with established, classical literary forms.

As many of Su Shih's critics charged in his lifetime, he was an eclectic and unorthodox thinker. A central characteristic of his eclecticism is that he seems never to have followed any one line of thought to a definitive position; his conclusions were intuitive rather than formal. This eclecticism is probably the reason why he has never been accorded a conspicuous place in Chinese intellectual history, and why so few literary historians and critics have tried to place his works in their contemporary intellectual context. On the whole, when we look at the concepts of *ch'i* and *li* and the principle of generation (*sheng-sheng*) of the *Yi ching*, which informed his method (*fa*) of literary creation and art criticism, it is apparent that he was more a disciple of contemporary Neo-Confucian thinkers like Shao Yung (1011–77), Chang Tsai (1020–77), Ch'eng Yi (1033–1108), and Ch'eng Hao (1032–85) than of the T'ang *ku-wen* masters. Therefore, his *ku-wen* theory and practice must be understood not primarily in terms of what he had in common with his mentor Ou-yang Hsiu or his much-admired predecessors Han Yü and Liu Tsung-yüan but in terms of what was current, volatile, and revolutionary in the intellectual trends of his own time. Only then can we begin to appreciate the complexity of the process in the *ku-wen* movement that transformed T'ang classicism into Sung Neo-Confucianism.

# CONCLUSION

## The Harsh Logic of History and the Gentle Voice of Poetry

IN HIS FAMOUS "Letter in Reply to Jen Shao-ch'ing" (93 B.C.), Ssu-ma Ch'ien wrote that he had permitted himself to survive the cruel and unjust punishment inflicted on him only so that he might be able to complete the *Shih chi*. Through that work, he aimed to "inquire into the boundary between heaven and man and to comprehend change between the past and the present and to form an independent school of thought."[1]

The *Shih chi*, Ssu-ma Ch'ien hoped, would preserve for posterity the deeds, persons, and values neglected by his contemporaries. That aspiration became a tradition for Chinese historians. Some eight centuries later, we find in Liu Chih-chi's preface to his *Shih t'ung* (completed 710) the following statement:

> Alas! Although I held the job [of an official historian], my way was not put into practice. I was known to my contemporaries, but my fine plans were not implemented. I had no means of expressing my frustration, discontent, isolation, and indignation. Had I remained silent and said nothing, remained speechless and transmitted nothing, I feared that after my death no one would know about me. And so I retired from office and took it upon myself to write the *Shih t'ung* in order to make manifest my ideas.[2]

Liu Chih-chi here is almost writing in Ssu-ma Ch'ien's voice to explain his own need to write.

In the preceding chapters, we have seen that Han Yü, Liu Tsung-yüan, Ou-yang Hsiu, and Su Shih had each to a greater or lesser degree suffered wrongs and been disgraced. Like the historians, they wished to transmit to posterity certain ideas and values that were not manifested in the events of their times. Han Yü in the T'ang and Ou-yang Hsiu in the Sung were commissioned as court historians to set down "the boundary between heaven and man . . . change between the past and present." However, the ideal of the historian is to be comprehensive, precise, objective, factual, and just in the treatment of historical materials. Unfortunately, the *tao* of history as it unfolded in their times seldom coincided with the *tao* as it ideally should have developed. Within the limitations imposed, and with often inadequate materials, Han Yü and Ou-yang Hsiu were hard-pressed to illustrate and substantiate the ideals of just and virtuous rule. The basic problem confronting the *ku-wen* masters, whether or not they were writing in the capacity of official historians, was the need to compensate for these factual deficiencies somewhere in their writings to show their awareness of these ideals and their belief in them.

Han Yü, Liu Tsung-yüan, and Ou-yang Hsiu all served as high government officials. They all participated at one time or another in the implementation of governmental policies and in policy-making at the highest level, and in both roles they created the materials of history. Not only were they exposed at first hand to the workings of historical forces, but they were also in a position to guide and shape events in accordance with their individually envisioned ideal *tao*. Their privileged position allowed them to write about the actual *tao* of history as well as the ideal *tao*.

Han Yü identified with the *tao* of history and man as it ideally should have been. In his most representative and most controversial works, he invariably spoke up for the ideal *tao*. There is little distance between his voice as a writer and his voice as spokesman for the ideal *tao*. Whether he was writing dogmatically as in "On the True Way" and "On the True Nature of Man," historically as in the "Huai-hsi Inscription," formally as in the "Address to the Crocodiles," or informally as in the "Valediction to Li Yüan," his commitment to Confucian orthodoxy as the ideal *tao* is always present. That history, essentially a collective record, refuses to conform to any individual set of values is demonstrated in Han

Yü's case by mixed reception of his historical and his *ku-wen* writings. In spite of Han Yü's effort to merge the truth of history with the ideal *tao*, his *Veritable Record of the Emperor Shun-tsung* (815) was accepted as history, after some revision, whereas his "Huai-hsi Inscription" was rejected out of hand. In the "Inscription," Han Yü injected his personal thoughts and feelings into his account of events, forcing these events to conform to his own sense of commitment to values that he labeled as the orthodox *tao*. This effort to force the *tao*, in the form of an ideal political order, onto the events of history disqualified the inscription as historical record, but it also created an important distinguishing feature of *ku-wen*: the injection of historical materials and subjects into informal prose writings and the treatment of these materials with the poetic vision and sensibility of the individual writer.

Liu Tsung-yüan, for his part, never endorsed the position that literature should serve only as the vehicle of the ideal *tao* or that the writer should always be its spokesman. He made a clear distinction between the two functions of formal writings: the function of history was to praise and blame; that of poetry was to instruct and satirize. The *tao* could not be transmitted in the writings of any one person. Liu's biographical sketches of Camel Kuo and of the snake-catcher illustrate through the words and deeds of ordinary people how man can achieve the *tao* on the common, everyday level. For those in power, other ways exist; such possibilities are recognized in his "Three Admonitions" and in the other animal fables. The distance that Liu Tsung-yüan carefully preserved in his writings between his personal views and the *tao*, whether of those in power or of the common man, gave him greater freedom than Han Yü had had. Whatever the *tao* may be, so far as Liu Tsung-yüan was concerned, it could not be realized by verbal assertion alone. Between the *tao* as ideal and the *tao* as implementation lies the entire world of the collective life, which is history, *and* the world of individual lives, which poetry and other forms of literary writings represent. Liu Tsung-yüan considered himself a critic as well as a poet in both realms.

This view of the multiple voices of a writer and the different functions of literary forms brought a controlled richness to his *ku-wen* style, with its flexibility in the use of literary forms and critical control over their substance. Liu Tsung-yüan also used historical subjects in his informal prose writings, infusing them with a poet's vision and sensibility. He contributed as much as Han Yü did to formulating a distinct T'ang *ku-wen* style, yet he still maintained a conscious distance between his role as a private writer and his role as purveyor of the *tao*.

This movement in prose writing toward greater freedom for writers to express their personal views on public and historical subjects and to introduce a poetic voice to such lesser prose forms as correspondence, fables, and biographical sketches continued into the early Sung. In the *ku-wen* writings of Ou-yang Hsiu and Su Shih, the concept of the *tao* dissolved into that of the conceptualizing mind (*yi*) of the writer.[3] The *tao* could then be identified as a writer's private idiom, his mode of understanding history and man. The classicism of Han Yü as an objective norm in literature was no longer an issue for Sung *ku-wen* writers. Their major concern was what is universal in life on the everyday level. This tendency to emphasize the everyday *tao* for everyman over the ideal Confucian *tao* envisioned by men of principle can be illustrated by a comparison of four works from the T'ang and Sung that employed natural landscape to address the common theme of "the boundary between heaven and man": the "Valediction to Li Yüan" by Han Yü, the landscape essays of Liu Tsung-yüan, "The Old Tippler's Pavilion" by Ou-yang Hsiu, and the "Rhymeprose on the Red Cliff" by Su Shih.

In the "Valediction to Li Yüan," landscape is nature idealized in images drawn from two ancient poetic traditions—the *Shih ching* and the *Ch'u tz'u*. Li Yüan's return to this idealized nature constitutes a public pledge to the ancient *tao* embodied in those traditions: the world of nature is the symbolic home for the spontaneity, purity, and harmony lost in the world of man. In the landscape essays of Liu Tsung-yüan, the unappreciated beauty of the natural scenery of Yung-chou serves as a counterpart to heaven's indifference to the ideals of man. The world of nature, like the world of man, is not a home for human ideals since it is equally unsympathetic to man's aspirations. Man searches in vain for a union with his ideals in external worlds.

In "The Old Tippler's Pavilion," man has found a way of coming to terms with life independent of an idealized concept of nature. In fact, union with nature is recognized as inadequate for the full realization of human ideals, as at best providing a temporary refuge from the troubled world of man. In the "Red Cliff," man's fulfillment is no longer an issue; success and failure are but different phases of a comprehensive whole. There is no boundary "between heaven and man" any more than there is division by dynasties in historical time. From the perspective of the all-embracing One, all changes in nature or in history are but a phase. In other words, for Su Shih, nature need not be perfect or history just; man finds his peace in self-contemplation.

This ultimate return of man to himself as self-sufficient has profound implications for intellectual thought and literary history after the early Sung. Scholars will eventually have to investigate the relationship between this return of man to a self-contained world in the Sung and the rise of verisimilitude as a creative principle in Chinese fiction and drama in the Yüan and Ming. But for our study of the development of ku-wen in T'ang-Sung times, this gradual emancipation of ku-wen writing from the tyranny of natural law and concrete history and the accompanying process of the introjection of a lyric voice into a context of writing that was at its origin predominantly political and rational is evidence of literary development in a different direction; namely, of the evolution of ku-wen from a prose form to a literary genre that is both a style and a principle of artistic creation.

This study has shown that, since Han Yü's time, the theoretical orientation of ku-wen has moved from the predominantly ideological to the predominantly aesthetic: from ku-wen to wen in general and from an emphasis on the ancient (ku) and the way (tao) to an emphasis on the individual artist's perceptive mind (yi) and his artistic technique (fa). Tao, which in the ancient tradition addresses primarily the tao of government and presumes a harmony between the political and the natural to be its ideal manifestation, has lost its monopoly on the claim to the ideal through the rethinking of T'ang and Sung ku-wen writers. It is evident from the writings of Liu Tsung-yüan, Ou-yang Hsiu, and Su Shih that the political and the natural no longer dominate over the human and moral and that harmony between the political order and the natural order no longer categorically occupies a position of moral supremacy over man's will to self-assertion.

This new development in the intellectual thought of T'ang-

Sung *ku-wen* writers may at first glance seem to delineate only a reorientation of their attitudes toward the *tao*. But in retrospect, we can see that this fall of nature out of the realm of the ideal has a momentous impact on the principle of mimetic art in both verbal and pictorial media. If nature is no longer ideal, then life and death, in the form of the life-and-death span of one plant, one animal, and one man, need not be the archetypal metaphors for truth and beauty, good and evil. All states of human affairs, death and political disorder included, are no more than manifestations of a same universal movement of energy (*ch'i*) in the realm of perpetual being (*yu*).[4] The structure of reality no longer pivots on the concept of change but begins to describe the continuous coming-into-being (*sheng*).

This fundamentally transformed world view gave rise to new possibilities of verbal mimesis and intellectual investigation. And this view constitutes the one encompassing similarity among T'ang-Sung *ku-wen* literature that sets it distinctly apart from the free prose of pre-Ch'in times and the even more subjective prose of the Ming and enables us thereby to approach a discussion of T'ang-Sung *ku-wen* as a literary genre.

In *Beyond Genre*, Paul Hernadi distinguishes four main types of similarity as possible bases for theories of genre: similarity between the mental attitudes of the authors, which some critics see as responsible for the similarity between literary works; the similar effect some works are likely to have on a reader's mind; similarity between literary works considered as verbal constructs; and similarity between the imaginative worlds that different verbal constructs evoke.[5] This study of T'ang-Sung *ku-wen* has concentrated predominantly on an investigation and clarification of the first and fourth types of similarity and their interrelationship. In a way, it complements the work of *ku-wen* anthologists, modern critics, and literary historians toward the construction of a genre theory of *ku-wen*.

Ming and Ch'ing anthologists largely used similarity between literary works considered as verbal constructs as the basis for their selections. As a criterion of inclusion, they employed for the most part the similarity between the verbal medium of the works; in the case of *ku-wen*, the use of the nonparallel free prose modeled on pre-Ch'in works in minor prose forms developed out of court documents and historical writings.[6] The similarity that justifies inclusion of rhymeprose (*fu*) and songs in the Ch'u style (*tz'u*) is not that of verbal medium but that of the authors' mental attitudes and the imaginative world evoked.[7] Modern critics and literary historians like Kuo Shao-yü and Lo Ken-tse concentrate more on the similarity between the mental attitudes of the authors, focusing specifically on the similarity of attitudes toward the two key concepts of *tao* and *wen*.

As James R. Hightower says in his study of the *Wen hsüan* and genre theory, the concept of genre underlies all anthology making and literary criticism, although no particular concept of genre is self-evident. Every genre, as Hernadi quotes from Paul Van Tieghem, is a "mold first designed by invention, then adopted and perfected by experience . . . once a genre becomes part of a literary tradition, one associates with it certain subject matters as well as patterns of thought and sentiment."[8] Tieghem's formulation emphasizes the similar effect some works are likely to have on a reader's mind, and this formulation approaches the concept of genre diachronically, whereas the other formulations are essentially synchronic. The analysis in the preceding chapters has consisted of a combination of the two approaches: I have followed Tieghem in finding the invention of a *ku-wen* "mold" in my study of Han Yü and traced the process of adaptation and perfection in the writings of Liu Tsung-yüan, Ou-yang Hsiu, and Su Shih. The reorientation of attitudes on *tao*, *wen*, and *tzu-jan* in Sung times toward an emphasis on the freedom of the writer's mind brought these underlying principles of the *ku-wen* world view to an apogee of artistic self-consciousness. These principles become the bases of a program of "art for art's sake," rather than one of art in the service of the state. A critical investigation of the main types of similarity among *ku-wen* writings becomes feasible because of this evolution of a body of consciously created *ku-wen* literature.

Since the time of Su Shih, the sense of the word *ku-wen* seems to have developed in yet another direction and came to denote increasingly a style rather than a genre; that is, it became a designation for a certain way of writing that could be used in composing in many different genres rather than a style of writing that distinguishes one genre. In Ming times, for example, the so-called T'ang-Sung school of *ku-wen* represented by such writers as T'ang Shun-chih (1507–60), Kuei Yu-kuang (1506–1571), and Mao K'un (1512–1601) developed a theory of prose around the pivotal idea of *fa* (technique). In what sense this further development in the Ming contributed or ceased to contribute to the formulation of *ku-wen* as a literary genre will not be known until many more studies are done of Ming prose and of its intellectual and artistic content.[9]

From an initial commitment to imitation of the freedom and originality expressed in the free prose of the ancients, the development of T'ang and Sung *ku-wen* led to the realization of freedom and originality in its own way of thought and its own structure of literary expression. The literature that this movement produced over four centuries of adaptation and perfection is supported by a sufficiently coherent theory of its own form and style and illustrated by a sufficiently rich body of works that modern readers may even explore the possibility of defining it as a genre. The *ku-wen* literature of the T'ang–Sung period marks its writers' transcendence, in their intellectual and aesthetic pursuits, of the limits of the laws of physical nature and of history. It is a transcendence achieved by the introduction of the lyric voice into an essentially ideological and political prose medium, an introduction that freed the medium from the confines of rationality.

REFERENCE MATTER

# GLOSSARY

ch'ang 常 common, universality, constants in human affairs
chen 眞 genuineness
ch'en tz'u 陳詞 clichés
cheng 正 normal and correct
cheng-t'ung 正統 the legitimate line of succession
chi 寄 to take refuge
chi chih pen 己之本 nature in the self
ch'i 奇 extraordinary
ch'i 氣 material energy, vital force
chien 簡 simple
chih 志 personal aspirations
chih 智 wisdom
ching 經 constants in human affairs
ching 精 fineness, perfection
ch'ing 情 emotions
ch'iung 窮 at the end of one's resources
ch'u T'ang ssu chieh 初唐四傑 the four outstanding authors of the
early T'ang
ch'uan-ch'i 傳奇 tales of marvels
ch'üan 權 the expedient and the efficient
ch'un 純 purity

chung tao　中道　steering a proper and balanced course
fa　法　art of representation, technique
fu　賦　rhymeprose
hsia　下　low
hsiao-shuo　小說　small talk, fiction
hsin　心　heart, spirit, universal mind
hsin　信　the credible
hsin　新　novelty
hsin-yi　新意　originality
hsü　序　preface
hsüeh　學　learn, study
hua　華　ornateness
jen　仁　human-heartedness
kao　高　lofty
k'o-ai　可愛　formal beauty
ku-wen　古文　ancient prose
ku-wen yün-tung　古文運動　the *ku-wen* movement
kung　工　craft, artistry
li　理　the principle underlying physical nature
mao　貌　appearance
ming　銘　bronze inscription
ming　明　analytical power
ni　泥　muddled
pei　碑　stele inscription
pien-wen　變文　transformation texts
p'ien-wen　駢文　parallel prose
pu-chien　不兼　mutual exclusiveness
pu-hsiu　不朽　immortality
pu-t'ung　不通　lack of understanding
shen　神　conceiving spirit
shen-yi　神逸　creative and preeminent
sheng　生　coming-into-being
sheng-sheng　生生　life-life
sheng-ssu　生死　life-death
shih　時　contemporaneity
shih　師　to model after, to hold as a teacher

shih 勢 sociopolitical reality

shih 實 the real

shih-wen 時文 current style (of parallel prose, early Sung)

shu 數 mathematical principle

shu 書 letters

sung-hsü 送序 valediction

T'ang-Sung pa ta chia 唐宋八大家 the eight prose masters of the T'ang and Sung

tao 道 way

tao yang feng yü 導揚諷諭 to serve a didactic or satiric function

te 德 virtue

t'ien 天 Heaven, nature

t'ien-chüeh 天爵 natural endowment

t'ien-kung 天工 the working of nature

ting ch'i shih fei 定其是非 to determine right and wrong

tsa 雜 impure

ts'ai 才 talent

tzu-jan 自然 natural and spontaneous

tz'u ling pao pien 辭令褒貶 to praise or blame

tz'u-shih hsiang ch'eng 辭事相稱 expression appropriate to the topic

tz'u-ta 辭達 language must communicate

wei 偽 artificiality

wei 位 roles

wen 文 literature

wen-chih pin pin 文質彬彬 balance between plainness and adornment in literature

wen tao 文道 the way of literature

wen yi ming tao 文以明道 literature is meant to clarify the *tao*

wen yi tsai tao 文以載道 literature is meant to be a vehicle for the (Confucian) *tao*

wen yu erh tao 文有二道 literature serves two basic functions

wu 無 nothingness, emptiness

wu-ssu 無私 freedom from personal bias

yen 言 language

yi 易 simple

yi 意 mind, intent

yi 義 righteousness

yi li hsi chih 以理析之 to analyze in accordance with the inherent principle of things

yu 有 being

yu-chi 遊記 records of excursions

yü 愚 foolishness

# NOTES

COMPLETE AUTHORS' NAMES, titles, and publication data, as well as Chinese characters, are given in the Selected Bibliography, pp. 219–30. A list of abbreviations used in the notes and bibliographic references is on pp. 219–20.

## INTRODUCTION

1. Lo Ken-tse, *Sui T'ang*, p. 103. See also Goodrich.

2. Hightower, "Parallel Prose"; idem, *Topics*, pp. 38–40. "Parallel Prose (*p'ien-wen*) is characterized by a tendency to use four-and-six word parallel phrases, a somewhat florid and artificial style, an emphasis on verbal parallelism, attention to tonal euphony, occasional rhyme, and frequency of allusion. It is a form of prose that makes use of most of the devices peculiar to Chinese poetry. Parallel Prose flourished during the Six Dynasties, especially during the Ch'i and Liang Dynasties (479–556), going under the name of 'Modern Style.' The *Anthology* (*Wen hsüan*) of Hsiao T'ung (501–531) is the great repository of specimens" (p. 38).

3. "Biography of Li E," *Sui shu*, 66:2a–b.

4. Wei Cheng, Preface to the "Biographies of the Literati," *Sui shu*, 76:1a. Li Yen-shou adopted the same view in his Preface to the "Biographies of the Garden of Letters," *Pei shih*, 81:2a–8b.

5. The same criticism appeared in the "Appraisal of the 'Biographies of Wang Pao and Yü Hsin,'" *Chou shu*, 41:18a–21b; Li Yen-shou's Preface, *Pei shih*; and later in Liu Chih-chi, "Miscellaneous Notes, II," *Shih-t'ung*, ts'e 4, chap. 8, p. 35.

6. Liu Chih-chi, "Treatise on Language," *Shih-t'ung*, chap. 20, pp. 1-2.

7. Pulleyblank, "Neo-Confucianism," esp. pp. 89-114.

8. Ibid., p. 89. Awareness of the issue can also be discerned in Han Yü's "Reading Hsün-tzu" and "Reading *Ho-kuan-tzu*," *HCLWC*, pp. 20-21; and in Liu Tsung-yüan, "Explicating the *Annals of Yen-tzu*"and "Explicating the *Analects*: Two Essays," *LHTCC*, *chüan* 4, pp. 48-50.

9. Ch'en Tzu-ang, Preface to "Poem on the Tall Bamboos," written for Tung-fang Tso-ch'iu, 1:9b; Li Po, *Li T'ai-po ch'üan-chi*, "Extravagance in detail ruins what is natural in art" (2:23b) and "The ancient sage kings valued the unsullied and the genuine" (2:34a).

10. Yang Chiung, Preface to the *Collected Works of Wang Po*, *CTW*, *chüan* 522; Wang Po, "Address to Vice-President P'ei of the Ministry of Personnel, *CTW*, *chüan* 180.

11. Li Hua, Preface to the *Collected Works of Ts'ui Mien*, *CTW*, *chüan* 315

12. Significantly, Hsiao Ying-shih, under whom Han Yü's eldest brother, Han Hui, studied *ku-wen*, was like Han Yü also concerned with the idea of a "legitimate line of succession" (*cheng-t'ung*). According to Pulleyblank ("Neo-Confucianism," pp. 86, 97), Hsiao wrote a continuation of the *Ch'un-ch'iu* from the Han dynasty to the Sui dynasty, bypassing the Ch'en dynasty because it had usurped the rule of the Liang (Hsiao's ancestral house) and therefore should be excluded from the "legitimate line of succession," and at a slightly later date, Lü Wen also mentioned the "line of succession" in connection with Confucian teaching, many years before Han Yü took up the issue.

13. Tu-ku Chi, Preface to the *Collected Works of Li Hua*, *CTW*, *chüan* 388.

14. See "Biography of Han Yü," *CTS*, *chüan* 160.

15. Liang Su, Preface to the *Collected Works of Commissioner Li*, *CTW*, *chüan* 518.

16. Ts'ao P'i, "Discourse on Literature," *Weh-hsüan*, *chüan* 52.

17. Cf. Seng Chao (d. 414) and his discussion of the origin of the world; Feng Yu-lan, chap. 8, sect. 4 (Eng. tr.: pp. 258 ff).

18. The same cosmogonic *ch'i* was discussed by Tsung Mi (fl. 804). Interest in the topic seems to have persisted since the times of Seng Chao. See Feng Yu-lan, chap. 9, sect. 6.

19. Before the rise of the T'ien-t'ai sect in Chinese Buddhism around 760, "universal mind" (*hsin*), "the nature of man" (*hsing*), and "emotions" (*ch'ing*) were the chief concerns of the Hua-yen sect. They were widely discussed by intellectuals, lay and Buddhist alike, throughout Han Yü's time. Li Ao, a disciple and son-in-law of Han Yü's, even wrote a defense

of the idea of *hsing* in his famous "The Recovery of the Nature." For a discussion of these ideas, see ibid., chaps. 8–10 (Eng. tr.: pp. 413–22).

20. Liu Mien, "Collected Essays" (*CTW*, *chüan* 527), especially his three essays on literature and literary theory: "A Letter in Answer to Minister P'ei of Chin-nan About Literature" (*CTW*, 527:8b–9b); "A Letter Discussing Literature with Lu *ta-fu* of Hua-chou" (*CTW*, 527: 7b–8a); and "A Letter Thanking T'u *hsiang-kung* for His Discussion of the Works of Fang *hsiang-kung* and Tu *hsiang-kung*" (*CTW*, 527:4a–6a).

21. *HCLWC*, pp. 98–100.

22. Han Yü's *tao* and *te* differ significantly from those of Lao-tzu. The present interpretation is based on Han Yü's "On the True Way" (*HCLWC*, pp. 7–11), where his source for the concepts of *tao* and *te* seems to be the *Analects* and not the *Tao-te ching*. See *Analects*, 4:19: "A scholar, whose mind is set on *truth* [tao] and who is ashamed of bad clothes and bad food, is not fit to be discoursed with" (Legge, p. 168). See also *Analects*, 7:16: "Let the will be set on the path of duty. Let every attainment in what is good be firmly grasped. Let relaxation and enjoyment be found in the polite arts" (Legge, p. 196).

23. *Analects*, 19:19–23: "Tzu Kung said, 'The wall of my master is several fathoms high. If one does not find the door and enter by it, he cannot see in the ancestral temple with its beauties, nor all the officers in their rich array" (Legge, p. 347).

24. *Li yen*, cf. *Tso chuan* (The Tso commentary):

When Muh-shuh [P'aou] went to Tsin, Fan Süen-tsze met him, and asked the meaning of the sayings of the ancients, "They died but suffered no decay." ... Muh-shuh said, "I ... have heard that the highest meaning of it is when there is established [an example of] virtue; the second, when there is established [an example of] successful service; and the third, when there is established [an example of wise] speech. When these examples are not forgotten with length of time, this is what is meant by the saying—"They do not decay." As to the preservation of the surname and the giving of clan branches, by which the ancestral temples are preserved, and the sacrifice continued without interruption from age to age, where is the state in which we have not that? The preservation of the greatest dignity cannot be called that freedom from decay." (Legge, pp. 505–7)

The source of Han Yü's "li yen" in the "Letter to Li Yi" is this passage from the *Tso chuan*. He was also talking about achievement through the verbal medium (*yen*); the vocabulary is the same.

25. Han Yü's use of the "fruit" metaphor here probably had a literary

antecedent in Liang Su's reference to Tu-ku Chi's well-known phrase *"hua erh pu-shih"* ("It has blossoms but bears no fruit"). See Liang Su, "An Elegy [on the Death] of Tu-ku [Chi] of Ch'ang-chou," *CTW, chüan* 522.

26. For the idea that what is true must also be perfect, see *Mencius,* 7A:24: "The superior man who sets his mind on truth (*tao*) will not consider himself accomplished unless he can express himself in perfectly ordered writings" (my trans.).

27. For "cultivation, nurture" (*yang*), cf. *Mencius,* 6A:8: "Therefore, if it received its nourishment, there is nothing which will not grow. If it lose its proper nourishment, there is nothing which will not decay away" (Legge, p. 409). The concept of proper "cultivation" is an important one throughout the *Mencius.* The most famous passage is the one that discusses *chih-yen* and *yang-wu hao-jan chih-ch'i* in *Mencius,* 2A:2.8–17 (Legge, pp. 188–90). Liu Tsung-yüan later incorporated this idea in the notion of "growth" in his "Biography of Camel Kuo."

28. It is customarily believed that Han Yü borrowed his concepts of *ch'i* and *yen* from the famous discussion of them in *Mencius* 2A:2.8–17 (see preceding note). Han Yü certainly had Mencius in mind when he wrote the letter since much of its vocabulary and ideas of cultivation seem to be derived from *Mencius.* However, it is my belief that his mention of *ch'i* in this context is more a gesture of courtesy to his master Liang Su, who first introduced the concept of *ch'i* into *ku-wen* theory, than a serious attempt at reviving *Mencius.* Liang Su was a lay disciple of the T'ien-t'ai sect. The water analogy had been prevalent in Hua-yen and T'ien-t'ai discussions of reality and the appearance of the universe. Therefore, Han Yü's use of the terms had a contemporary as well as a classical reference.

29. For *chün-tzu* ("man of principle") and *ch'i* ("utensil"), see *Analects,* 2:12: "The master said, the accomplished scholar is not a utensil" (Legge, p. 150). Also, *Analects,* 13:25: "The superior man is easy to serve and difficult to please. If you try to please him in any way which is not according with right, he will not be pleased. But in his employment of men, he uses them according to their capacity" (Legge, p. 273). Here, Han Yü has fused the language of these two passages.

30. For *fang* as "art"(or, as I translated it in this particular instance, "direction"), cf. the *Analects,* 6:26, 3: "To be able to judge of others by what is nigh in ourselves;—this may be called the art [*fang*] of virtue" (Legge, p. 194).

31. After Han Yü got his *chin-shih* degree in 792, he tried unsuccessfully to obtain a post in the capital. In 794, he left Ch'ang-an. In 796, he served on the staff of the military governor of Pien-chou. When Tung Chin, the military governor, died, he left Pien-chou to serve on the staff

of the military governor of Hsü-chou, Chang Chien-feng. See his biography in *CTS, chüan* 160.

32. For the first reference to this custom, see Chao Yen-wei, p. 111. See also note 22 to Chapter 1.

33. A second letter probably was written in the same year; see *HCLWC*, p. 100. Judging from the way Han Yü answered Li Yi and from his very brief reference to Li Yi's talent and character in his recommendation of the following year ("Letter to Lu Yüan-wai of the Ministry of Sacrifices," *HCLWC*, pp. 116–18), Han Yü did not think very highly of him and was rather impatient with his eagerness to succeed.

34. "On the True Way" is Han Yü's most famous polemical attack on the false claims of Buddhism and Taoism to the term *tao*. For a translation, see Chan, pp. 454–56.

CHAPTER 1

1. Su Shih, "Inscription on a Stele at the Shrine of Han Wen-kung at Ch'ao-chou," *STPC*, vol. 2, *ts'e* 9, 15:20–22.

2. Kuo Shao-yü, vol. 1, pp. 132–41, 242–50.

3. The first official articulation of this view is in the "Appraisal" in the "Biography of Han Yü," *HTS*, 176:6b–7a.

4. Ch'ien Mu, "Tsa-lun."

5. Pulleyblank, "Neo-Confucianism."

6. Some earlier works on Han Yü's achievements are Ch'ien Chi-po; Li Ch'ang-chih; Kuo Shao-yü, vol. 1, pp. 242–50; Lo Ken-tse, *Sui T'ang*, pp. 127–34; Ch'en Teng-yüan; Ch'en Yin-k'o, "Lun Han Yü"; Ch'ien Mu, "Tsa-lun"; Li Chia-yen; and Lo Lien-t'ien, *Han Yü*.

7. By "literary transformation," I refer to the transformation of ideology into literature by means of certain technical devices. For an example of this, see the discussion of Han Yü's "Stele Inscription on the Lo-ch'ih Shrine in Liu-chou" later in the text.

8. *HCLWC*, pp. 120–21, 142–44, 274–80, 284–86.

9. "Appraisal" in "Biography of Han Yü," *CTS*, 160:1a.

10. *HCLWC*, p. 121; see also "Postscript to Obituary of Ou-yang Chan," p. 176.

11. Cf. *Chuang-tzu*, 26, "Wai-wu," pp. 398–99. For a translation, see Watson, *Chuang-tzu*.

12. For example, see Ku Yi-sheng, "Han Yü."

13. Li Chia-yen.

14. Wang P'u, *chüan* 50.

15. See note 9 to Introduction.

16. See Wang T'ang; Li Chao; Su E; Niu Seng-ju; Li Fu-yen; and Tuan Ch'eng-shih.

17. For the three types of parallelism—phonic, grammatical, and metrical—see Hightower, "Parallel Prose."

18. See "Letter Written While Attending the Civil Service Examination," *HCLWC*, p. 120.

19. Chou Yi-liang.

20. P'ei Tu, "Letter to Li Ao," *T'ang wen ts'ui*, 84:1a:

> I have known Han Yü of Ch'ang-li for a long time. I like him very much, and unexpectedly, I find myself admiring him. To be sure, he is a man of excellent talent. But I have recently heard remarks from his friends and peers that he frequently relied on his special talent and let it gallop unbridled. Is it justifiable that he should use his talent thus, not for the purpose of establishing models but to amuse himself? Writers today who do not possess the same talent as he does should be warned against such practices.

21. Ch'ien Mu, "Tsa lun," pp. 132−34.

22. The date and the nature of the "Examination Letter" and that of four other of Han Yü's short prose works collectively entitled "Tsa shuo" ("Miscellaneous tales" *HCLWC*, pp. 18−20) show that it is very possible that these works are the *wen-chüan* ("literary samples") that Chao Yen-wei (8:111) mentioned:

> In the T'ang dynasty, the degree candidate first made his name known to the principal examiner through the channel of illustrious persons of the time. This was followed by presentations of his sample works. The presentations were repeated after a few days and were called *wen-chüan*. The *Yu-kuai-lu* and tales of marvels were all examples of such presentations. These works comprehended all styles and showed the writer's ability to write history, poetry, and to hold a discourse. The *chih-shih* candidates, however, frequently presented poetry [instead]. Their poetry constituted the many hundred collections we see in circulation today.

(Chao's work discusses events that occurred from 1170 on.) For a detailed study of the practice, see Mair, "Scroll Presentation."

23. Chang Shih-chai, "Rectifying Mistaken Views", *Wen-shih t'ung-yi, ts'e* 2, *chüan* 4, *nei-p'ien* 4, p. 23.

24. K'ung An-kuo, Preface to the *Shu ching*, *Ch'üan Han wen*, 6b−7b; P'u Shang, Preface to *Shih ching*, *Mao Shih* 1:1a−3b; Ssu-ma Ch'ien.

25. Shih Ch'ung, Preface to the *Chin-ku Poems*, *Ch'üan Chin wen*, 33:13a−b. Wang Hsi-chih, Preface to the *Lan-t'ing Poems*, *Ch'üan Chin wen*, 26:9b−10a.

26. See Ch'ien Mu's discussion of the origin of *sung-hsü* in his "Tsa-lun."

27. Both these criteria were proposed by Ch'ü Wan-li.

28. For samples, see *T'ang wen ts'ui, chüan* 97, 98.

29. For another translation, see Yang and Yang, "Li Yuan."

30. See note 34 below. Han Yü's second portrait of the *ta-chang-fu* ("great man") is also a negative one. The peril of the useful and the preservation of life are two constant themes in the *Chuang-tzu*. It is interesting to note Han Yü's adaptation of these themes here and of the specific image of the knives and saws to denote punishment. Cf. *Chuang-tzu*, 4, p. 81. For a translation, see Legge, *The Texts of Taoism*, vol. 1, p. 220 (Watson's translation [p. 64] does not have the image of the axe): "The trees in consequence do not complete their natural terms of life, and come to a premature end in the middle of their growth under the axe and bill;—this is the evil that befalls them from their supplying good timber." See also Legge's translation of *Chuang-tzu*, 18, pp. 272–73:

> When Chwang-tze went to Chu, he saw an empty skull, bleached indeed, but still retaining its shape. Tapping it with his horse-switch, he asked it, saying, "Did you, Sire, in your greed of life, fall in the lessons of reason and come to this? Or did you do so, in the service of a perishing state, by the punishment of the axe? Or was it through your evil conduct, reflecting disgrace on your parents and on your wife and children? Or was it through your hard endurance of cold and hunger? Or was it that you had completed your terms of life?"

31. *HCLWC*, p. 42.

32. Two contemporaries of Han Yü seemed to be named Li Yüan. Ch'ing scholars believed that the Li Yüan of the "Valediction" was not the same one as the brother of Li Su (the general who led the Huai-hsi expedition). See Ch'en Ching-yün, 3:7b; and Yao Fan, *chüan* 44, 42:19a.

33. The image was first created in Han times. See Tung Chung-shu, "The Unemployed Gentleman," *Ch'üan Han wen*, 23:1a–b, *Ku-wen yüan*, 3:3a–b, and *Yi-wen lei-chü*, 30:20b–21a; for a translation, see Hightower, pp. 200–203. Ssu-ma Ch'ien, "Lament for the Unemployed Gentleman," *Ch'üan Han wen*, 26:4b–5a, *Yi-wen lei-chü*, 30:21a–b; for a translation, see Hightower, "Lament."

34. *Mencius*, 7B:34 (Legge, p. 496):

> Mencius said, "Those who give counsel to the great should despise them, and not look at their pomp and display. A hall several times eight cubits high, with beams projecting several cubits;—these if

my wishes were to be realized, I would not have. Food spread before me over ten cubits square, and attendants and concubines to the amount of hundreds;—these though my wishes were realized, I would not have. Pleasure and wine, and the dash of hunting, with thousands of chariots following after me—these, though my wishes were realized, I would not have. What they esteem are what I would have nothing to do with; what I esteem are the rules of the ancients—why should I stand in awe of them."

For Mencius's idea of the "great man," see the *Mencius*, 3B:2 (Legge, p. 265):

To dwell in the wide house of the world, to stand in the correct seat of the world, and to walk in the great path of the world, when he obtains his desire for office, to practice his principles for the good of the people; and when the desire is disappointed, to practice them alone, to be above the power of riches and honours, to make dissipated, of poverty and mean condition to make swerve from principle, and of power and force to make beck:—these characteristics constitute the great man.

35. Cited by Kao Pu-ying, p. 239 notes. The citation originally comes from the *Tung-p'o t'i-pa*, a work said to be largely apocryphal; it does not appear in any of the standard editions of Su Shih's works.

36. *Tz'u-shih hsiang-ch'eng* ("expression worthy of the subject matter") is a phrase that occurred in Han Yü's "Memorial to the Throne on the presentation of the Memorial Inscription on the Huai-hsi Rebellion" (818), *HCLWC*, p. 350.

37. *Ch'iung tse yi kung* ("writing becomes the more skillful when one is in extremity") is a phrase from Ou-yang Hsiu's Preface to the *Collected Poems of Mei Sheng-yü*, *OHCC*, 42:7a–b. It admirably summarizes Han Yü's concept at this particular period of *ch'iung* and its relationship to *kung*.

38. *CTS*, 160:1a.

39. *HCLWC*, pp. 7–13.

40. Ibid., pp. 136–37. For a translation, see Yang and Yang, "Meng Chiao."

41. Pulleyblank, "Neo-Confucianism" (p. 334, note 158), states:

Han Yü's biographies in the histories attribute his dismissal to a memorial criticizing the abuses in purchasing for the palace in the markets of the capital, but there is no such memorial in his works. Li Ao's *hsing-chuang* [An outline of life and deeds] (*CTW*, ch. 639, pp. 220 ff) says that he was hated by a favorite of the Emperor. A memorial inscription by Huang-fu Shih mentions the memorial about famine conditions and says that he was in consequence hated by those in charge of the government (*CTW*, ch. 687, pp. 14a ff). Han Yü's epitaph for Chang Shu, one of the men who was banished with him, also says that they were slandered by a "favorite."...It is a natural inference that the person offended was Li Shih....

On the other hand, in a long poem written at the end of 815, Han Yü refers to the memorial but says that it was appreciated both by the Emperor and Tu Yu and wonders if his words have been repeated to his friends the two Lius.

One of the two Lius Han Yü suspected was Liu Tsung-yüan. The other was Liu Yü-hsi (772–842).

42. See "Farewell to *Ch'iung*," *HCLWC*, p. 328, "Preface to Poems Written During a Gathering at Ching-tan," ibid., pp. 153–54; "Explications of the Method of Learning," ibid., pp. 25–28; "Letter in Answer to Li *Hsiu-ts'ai*, ibid., pp. 102–3; and "Link Verse on the Theme of Taking Shelter from the Summer Heat," *HCLSHN*, pp. 189–92.

43. *HCLWC*, pp. 328–29. For a translation of the complete essay, see Hightower, "Han Yü," pp. 20–22.

44. See *HCLWC*, p. 99; and translation in the Introduction.

45. *HCLWC*, pp. 36–37.

46. See Ssu-ma Kuang, *chüan* 225, 229.

47. "Biography of Han Yü," *CTS*, *chüan* 160.

48. The poem, allegedly "found" by Su Shih during the Shao-sheng era (1094–98) when he was exiled to the extreme south, is not included in standard collections of Su Shih's poetry. It is cited in Chao Te-lin, vol. 20, and in Hu Tzu, *Ts'ung-hua*, *chüan* 39. Chao mentioned the demolition of Su's "Shang-ch'ing Ch'u-hsiang Palace Inscription" during the Shao-sheng era (1094–98) and the rewriting of the text by Ts'ai Ching without explicitly suggesting a parallel between Han Yü's case and Su Shih's case. But Hu made the parallel with Han's case explicit.

49. *Li-pu shih-lang* ("vice-minister of the Ministry of Civic Offices") was the highest post Han Yü attained in his life. A person was frequently referred to in later ages by the highest official title he held in life, or by his posthumous title, as a sign of respect.

50. For other examples, see Yao Fan, 42:20b–21a; and Ch'ien Ta-hsin, p. 176. See also notes 63, 65, 67–70, and 73 below.

51. *HCLWC*, pp. 350–51.

52. Ts'ai Yung, "Discourse on Bronze Inscriptions," *Ch'üan Hou-Han wen*, 74:4a 5a.

53. For example, Ch'ien Ta-hsin (pp. 176–177) pointed out: "[When Han Yü] said, 'On the day *keng-shen*, I will come personally to see you off

at the gate,' he gives only the date but not the month and the year. This is where he imitated the *Shang shu* and erred [by deviating from the T'ang usage]." See note 70 below.

54. "Evil" here refers to the rebellion of An Lu-shan and Shih Ssu-ming (755−63).

55. The "weeds" refer to the subordinate generals of An Lu-shan and Shih Ssu-ming who surrendered to the T'ang government and were made governors of various provinces.

56. See "The Basic Annals of Emperor Hsien-tsung," *CTS*, 14.7b.

57. See "The Basic Annals of Emperor Hsien-tsung," *HTS*, 1.10b; and the "Biography of Liu P'i," *CTS, chüan* 140, *HTS, chüan* 158.

58. See "The Basic Annals of Emperor Hsien-tsung, *HTS*, 7.12ab; and "Biography of Chang Mu-chao," *CTS, chüan* 141, *HTS, chüan* 148.

59. See "The Basic Annals of Emperor Hsien-tsung," *HTS*, "Biography of T'ien Hung-cheng," *CTS, chüan* 141, *HTS, chüan* 148.

60. See "The Basic Annals of Emperor Hsien-tsung," *HTS*, "Biography of Wu Shao-yang," *CTS*, chüan 145, *HTS, chüan* 215; and "Biography of Wu Yüan-chi, *CTS, chüan* 145, *HTS, chüan* 214.

61. "Four generals with three different surnames": in the seventh month of the first year of the Pao-ying era (762), Li Chung-ch'en was made governor of Huai-hsi. In the third month of the fourteenth year of the Ta-li era (779), Li Hsi-lieh, a subordinate of Li Chung-ch'en's expelled Li Chung-ch'en and took over the governorship. In the fourth month of the second year of the Chen-yüan era (786), Ch'en Hsien-ch'i poisoned Li Hsi-lieh and became the governor of Huai-hsi. Three months later, Wu Shao-ch'eng killed Ch'en Hsien-ch'i and became governor. When Wu Shao-ch'eng died in 809, Wu Shao-yang killed Wu Shao-ch'eng's son Wu Yüan-ch'ing and pronounced himself the *liu-hou* ("acting governor") of Huai-hsi. The "four generals" are Li Hsi-lieh, Ch'en Hsien-ch'i, Wu Shao-ch'eng, and Wu Shao-yang, and the "three surnames" are Li, Ch'en, and Wu. See Kao Pu-ying, p. 278, note.

62. For the quotation, see "The Basic Annals of Emperor Hsien-tsung," *CTS*, 15:6a−b.

63. The appointments of Li Kuang-yen and Wu Ch'ung-yin were made in the ninth year of the Yüan-ho era (814); see ibid., 15:6a−b.

64. The appointments of Han Hung and Li Wen-t'ung were made in the tenth year of the Yüan-ho era (815); see ibid., "The Annals of Emperor Hsien-tsung," 15:7a−b. However, the difference in time here between these appointments and the appointments of Li Kuang-yen and Wu Ch'ung-yin is eliminated by Han Yü for the sake of stylistic polish. This discrepancy was noted by Ch'ien Ta-hsin, pp. 176−77, on Han Yü's "Inscription on the Pacification of the Huai-hsi Rebellion."

65. The appointments of Li Tao-ku and Li Su were made in the eleventh year of the Yüan-ho era (816). Here again, Han Yü ignored the time difference to achieve stylistic streamlining and polish.

66. For the appointment, see "The Basic Annals of Emperor Hsientsung," *CTS*, 15:10b.

67. The appointment of P'ei Tu was made in the tenth year of the Yüan-ho era (815); see ibid., 15:8a.

68. Han Hung was appointed commander-in-chief; see ibid., 15.8b.

69. Liang Shou-ch'ien was sent out in the eleventh year of the Yüanho era (816); see ibid., 15:10b.

70. On the third day of the eighth month in the twelfth year of the Yüan-ho era (817), P'ei Tu left for Huai-hsi: "On the day *keng-shen* [the third day] in the eighth month [of the twelfth year of the Yüan-ho era], P'ei Tu set out for the mobile camps. [Emperor Hsien-tsung] assigned three hundred soldiers from the Shen-ch'e Army to be his bodyguards. His Majesty drove to the T'ung-hua Gate [of Ch'ang-an] to see him off" (ibid., 15:12a).

T'ung-hua Gate is one of the three eastern gates in the capital city of Ch'ang-an. According to Ch'ien Ta-hsin (pp. 176–77): "[When Han Yü] said, 'On the day *keng-shen*, I will come personally to see you off at the gate,' he gives only the date but not the month and the year. This is where he imitated the *Shang shu* and erred [by deviating from the T'ang usage]." Cf. note 53.

71. See "Biography of Li Su," *HTS*, *chüan* 154.

72. *Ch'eng-hsiang* ("chief minister") is again a misuse of terms. In T'ang times, the leading minister was called *tsai-hsiang* and not *ch'eng-hsiang*. See Ch'ien Ta-hsin, pp. 176–77.

73. See "The Basic Annals of Emperor Hsien-tsung," *CTS*, 15:13a–14b.

74. The correct title is *chien-chiao shang-shu tso-pu-yi*, which is a titular post. Han Yü here is again criticized by Ch'ien Ta-hsin (pp. 176–77) for not giving the exact title. If *chien-chiao* is omitted, there is no way to distinguish a titular post from a real one. Of the posts mentioned in the rest of the paragraph, all are titular posts except those awarded to P'ei Tu.

75. "The generals north of the river" refers to rebel generals such as T'ien Ch'eng-ssu, who rebelled in 775, and Chu T'ao, Wang Wu-chün, and T'ien Yüeh, who rebelled in 782, "Those south of the river" are Li Na, Li Hsi-lieh, and Wu Shao-ch'eng, who all rebelled around 782.

76. "The four sage ancestors" are Emperor Su-tsung (756–62), Tai-tsung (763–79), Te-tsung (780–805), and Shun-tsung (805).

77. "The general of Wei" is T'ien Hsing; see "The Basic Annals of Emperor Hsien-tsung," *HTS*, 7:12b.

78. The "old practice" was to select their own general and then petition for the emperor's recognition. See note 61.

79. "The miscreant neighbors" were Li Shih-tao of Yün-chou and Wang Ch'eng-tsung of Heng-chou. See "Biography of Wang Ch'eng-tsung," *CTS*, 142:10b, which notes that when the imperial army went on an expedition against Wu Yüan-chi, Wang Ch'eng-tsung and Li Shih-tao presented a memorial to the throne beseeching pardon for Yüan-chi. They plotted many times to frustrate the dispatch of imperial troops.

80. Wu Yüan-heng, the chief minister, was assassinated on the third day of the sixth month in the tenth year of the Yüan-ho era (815). The assassin, sent by Wang Ch'eng-tsung and Li Shih-tao, also made an attempt on the life of P'ei Tu, but did not succeed. See "The Basic Annals of Emperor Hsien-tsung," *CTS*, 15:8a; "Biography of Wu Yüan-heng," *CTS, chüan* 158, *HTS, chüan* 152; and "Biography of P'ei Tu," *CTS, chüan* 170, *HTS, chüan* 173.

81. Cf. "The Great Plan," *Shu ching*: "If you have doubts about any great matter, consult with your own heart; consult with your nobles and officers; consult with the masses of the people; consult with the tortoise and milfoil.... If you, the tortoise, and the milfoil all agree, while the nobles and common people oppose, the result will be fortunate" (Legge, p. 3). Han Yü seemed to have "The Great Plan" in mind when he wrote here: "The emperor heeded not such counsel, and he consulted the spirits." Near the end, he again echoed it: "When the Ts'ai expedition was first suggested, the dignitaries and the officials would not endorse it. During the four years of the expedition, all men, high and low, questioned its wisdom."

82. For the battle at the Ling-yün Gate, see "The Basic Annals of Emperor Hsien-tsung," *CTS*, 15:9b-11a.

83. The battle was led by Li Kuang-yen.

84. *Hsüan* ("to proclaim"): it is suggested that Han Yü here echoes the "Chiang Han" poem in the *Shih ching*. See Kao Pu-ying, pp. 293-94 notes. The "Chiang Han" stanza wherein *hsüan* occurs is as follows (Legge, p. 554):

> The king gave charge to Hoo of Shaou.
> You have everywhere diffused [and carried out my order].
> When Wan and Woo received their appointments,
> The duke of Shaou was their strong support.
> You do not [only] have a regard to me the little child,
> But you try to resemble that duke of Shaou.
> You have commenced and earnestly displayed your merit;
> And I will make you happy.

The possibility that Han Yü deliberately used the somewhat archaic *lai-hsüan* ("and carried out my order") to invoke a literary association with the *Shih ching* ode is enhanced by the similarity of the occasions behind the two works. The "Huai-hsi Inscription" celebrates the pacification of the Huai-hsi Rebellion; the "Chiang Han," interestingly enough, celebrates "an expedition against the more southern tribes of the Hwae" (Legge, p. 554). If Han Yü intended to ingratiate himself with P'ei Tu, as some critics believe, then he could not have conceived a higher compliment than to compare P'ei Tu to the duke of Shao.

85. A threat of similar vividness occurs in the "P'an-keng" section of the *Shu ching*. After he had moved his people to the new city, P'an-keng threatened to cut off the noses of those who dared to create trouble in the new city.

> Ah! I have now announced to you my unchangeable purpose:—do you people really respect my great anxiety; let us not get alienated and removed from one another; share in my plans and thoughts, and be prepared to obey me; let every one of you set up the true rule of conduct in his heart. If there be bad and unprincipled men, precipitously or carelessly disrespectful to my orders, and taking advantage of this brief season to play the part of villains or traitors, I will cut off their noses, or utterly exterminate them. I will leave none of their children. I will not let them perpetuate their seed in this new city. (Legge, p. 241)

Parallels between the occasions of the two passages and their threats of extermination of the clan and of violent physical punishment suggest that Han Yü wrote his lines with the "P'an-keng" in mind and was actually executing his intention of emulating the purport and style of the *Shih ching* and the *Shu ching*.

86. "All Men, high and low, questioned its wisdom" (Legge, *She King*, p. 616):

> Pleasant is the semicircular water,
> And we gather the cress about it,
> The marquis of Lu is coming to it,
> And we see his dragon-figured banner.
> His banner waves in the wind,
> And the bells of his horses tinkle harmoniously.
> Small and great, all follow the prince in his progress to it.

This ode also has to do with the conquering of the "tribes of the Hwae." The ode is "in praise of some marquis of Loo, celebrating his interest in the state college, which perhaps he had built or repaired, testifying to his virtues, and auspicing for him a complete victory over the tribes of the Hwae, which would be celebrated in the college" (ibid.).

87. The *Ming-t'ang* ("Hall of Distinction") was a symbol of imperial rule. *The Book of Rites* has a chapter on it; but its actual existence is half-legendary. See Legge, *Li Ki*, p. 29, "Introduction to the "Ming-t'ang wei":

> The Treatise commences with but does not fairly describe, the great scene in the life of the duke of Kan, when as regent of the kingdom, he received all the feudal lords and the chiefs of the barbarous tribes at the capital, on occasion of a grand audience or durbar....
> The Hall of Distinction was a royal structure. Part of it was used as a temple, at the sacrifice in which peculiar honor was done to King Wan (The Shih IV i, 7). It was also used for purposes of audience as on the occasion referred to in this Book; and governmental regulations were promulgated from it (Mencius I ii, 5).
> The principal Hall was in the capital; but there were small ones with the same name at the four points where the kings halted in their tours of inspection to receive the feudal lords of the different quarters of the kingdom.

For a discussion, see Schafer, pp. 16−18.

88. Cf. "Sheng-min" in the "Great Odes," which celebrates the founding of the Chou; "Ch'ing-miao" and "Ch'en-kung" in the "Chou Sung," which celebrate the origin and first ancestors of the Chou; and "Hsüan-niao" and "Ch'ang-fa" in the "Shang Sung," which celebrate the origin and first ancestors of the Shang. Legge, *She King*, pp. 465, 569, 582, 636, 638.

89. The importance of *tuan* ("to decide, to determine") was already emphasized by Han Yü in his "On the Proper Course of Action Concerning Huai-hsi" (814), *HCLWC*, p. 372: "To have the broken, wearied, and greatly harassed [people] of three little *chou* to withstand the full force of the entire world, one can just stand there and watch them be defeated. What is yet unknown is whether Your Majesty will take the decisive act or not."

90. "P'an-keng," Legge, *Shoo-king*, pp. 233−47.

91. "Reading the Inscription [on the Pacification of the Huai-hsi Rebellion] of Han Yü," Li Shang-yin, 1 : 1a. For a complete translation, see James J. Y. Liu, "Li Shang-yin's Poem."

92. *HCLWC*, pp. 25−28.

93. Ch'en Yin-k'o, "Han Yü and the T'ang Novels." Ch'en's article set off a series of controversies. Wu Keng-shun, for example, opposed Ch'en's

thesis that *ku-wen* arose in T'ang times from attempts to write *ch'uan-ch'i* in the *ku-wen* style; see Y. W. Ma for an elaboration of Ch'en's thesis.

94. Kuo Hsi-liang.

95. Jao Tsung-yi, pp. 98–102.

96. Ts'en Chung-mien recently argued that the "Lo-ch'ih Inscription" was written in 823, and not, as it is sometimes believed, in 824. One of Ts'en's strongest pieces of evidence is the phrase "in the third year" in Han Yü's text. Ts'en stated that "the third year" has to be "the third year" after Liu Tsung-yüan's death because it was only in the seventh month of that year (822) that *hsin-mao* and *ping-ch'en* both occurred. The "Lo-ch'ih Inscription" was therefore written in the following year. (See Ts'en Chung-mien, p. 47.)

97. Liu Tsung-yüan was made prefect of Liu-chou in the tenth year of the Yüan-ho era (815); see "The Basic Annals of Emperor Hsien-tsung," CTS, 15.7b.

98. *Pu* ("ford," or "crossing"): a place along riverbanks where people can pull a boat by ropes. See Liu Tsung-yüan, "A Local History of the T'ieh-lu-pu at Yung-chou," *LHTCC, ts'e* 4, *chüan* 28, p. 71.

99. Cf. Han Yü, "Epitaph for Liu Tzu-hou," *LHTCC*, pp. 294–97.

100. Cf. Liu Tsung-yüan, "Inscription for the Newly Renovated Temple of King Wen-hsüan at Liu-chou," *LHTCC, ts'e* 2, *chüan* 5, pp. 4–5.

101. This episode's literary antecedents in Chin dynasty supernatural tales are discussed below.

102. Liu Tsung-yüan died in 819, the fourteenth year of the Yüan-ho era. "The third year" here means the third year after his death, which was 822, and not the third year of the Ch'ang-ch'ing era, which was 823, See note 96 above.

103. *Ching-ch'en* should have been *ping-ch'en*. Han Yü here used *ching* for *ping* to observe the taboo on the name of Li Ping, one of the earlier T'ang emperors.

104. After the fall of Wang Shu-wen and Wei Chih-yi in 805, Liu Tsung-yüan, as one of their associates, was banished to be the *ssu-ma* of Yung-chou in the south; he was never reinstated to service in the capital. See Han Yü, "Epitaph for Liu Tsung-yüan"; and "Biography of Liu Tsung-yüan," *HTS* 168: 5a, *CTS*, 160: 11a–b. For a detailed description of Liu Tsung-yüan's fate after 805, see Chapter 2 of this book.

105. In the T'ang, one of the local ceremonies at Liu-chou when its people received their god was to sail a boat in the stream and then guide it from the shore to the shrine. The boat had two flags, and the god presumably rode in it. The boat carried carved wooden figures of human beings and horses. For a description of the rite, see note by Chu T'ing-yü, 31 : 11b.

106. The "hills of E" and the "waters of Liu" were local landmarks in Kwangsi province.

107. "Biography of Han Yü," *CTS*, 160:4b.

108. "Biography of Han Yü," *HTS*, 176:9a—10b. The *HTS* mentions the "Lo-ch'ih Inscription" only in the "Biography of Liu Tsung-yüan."

109. Wu Kuang-sheng, pp. 62—63.

110. Earlier "records" of the same kind are Ch'iu Ch'ung "Record of the Renovation of the Lo-ch'ih Temple" (1111), and Fu Kao's "Record of the Repair of the Lo-ch'ih Inscription of Marquis Liu" (Wu Kuang-shen, pp. 38—39). The entire trend began in 1090 when the Sung emperor Che-tsung officially recognized the establishment of the Lo-ch'ih Shrine and bestowed on it the new designation "Ling-wen Shrine." In 1105, the emperor Hui-tsung further honored the memory of Liu Tsung-yüan by bestowing on him the posthumous title *Wen-hui hou* (Marquis Wen-hui). See Ch'en Ching-yün, 82a—b.

111. This is what Liu Hsü meant by "substantiate."

112. Lin Shu, pp. 25b—26a.

113. *Chiang* ("to descend") first appeared in the nonpoetic writings in the *Tao chuan*:

> [Duke Chwang, thirty-second year]: In autumn, in the 7th month, there was the descent of a Spirit in Sin [Sin belongs to Kwoh]. King Kwuy asked Ko, the historiographer of the Interior, the reason of it, and he replied, "When a State is about to flourish, intelligent Spirits descend in it, to survey its virtue. When it is going to perish, Spirits also descend in it, to behold its wickedness. Thus, there have been instances of States flourishing from Spirits appearing, and also of States perishing. (Legge, p. 120)

There are also numerous instances in the *Shih ching* where *chiang* is used. However, *chiang* in the *Shih ching* is used mostly in connection with the ancestral spirits of the royal houses. It does not offer as close a comparison to the present case as the *Tso chuan* does.

114. "Biography of Han Yü," *HTS*, 176:9a—10b.

115. Li Fang, *chüan* 370, p. 1707.

116. T'ao Ch'ien, pp. 23—25.

117. Kan Pao, p. 44.

118. Ibid. There is a textual variation on the word *ch'ing*. In some editions, *ku ch'ing* ("the bones were black") is read as *ku ch'ing* ("the bones were uncontaminated"). Ch'en Yin-k'o ("Lun *Tsai-sheng-yüan*," p. 75) thought the first reading more accurate.

119. Kan Pao, pp. 44—45.

120. "Biography of Han Yü," *CTS*, 160:4b.

121. *HCLWC*, p. 312. The phrase is from Han Yü's "Epitaph for Fan Shao-shu of Nan-yang."

122. *HCLWC*, pp. 325–31. The model for the "Address to the Crocodiles" seems to be works like the "Charge to the Demons," *Hung ming chi*, 14 : 4a–9a.

123. Lo Lien-t'ien, *Han Yü*, esp. pp. 24–25, 45–55. Lo's chapter is the most exhaustive treatment of the subject that has come to my attention. In retrospect, what Lo makes of the first meeting between Han Yü and Liu Tsung-yüan sounds convincing (p. 46). The question remains, however, why Lo places the date of their first meeting so late (in 798) and attributes the meeting to circumstances that are so convoluted. Han and Liu were both in Ch'ang-an from 788 to 795. In 789, they both unsuccessfully took the *chin-shih* examination. In the years immediately following, both of them again were preparing for and took the *po-hsüeh hung-tz'u* examination. There were plenty of opportunities, to follow Lo's line of reasoning, for them to meet before 798 when, according to Lo, Han Yü was introduced to Liu by one of their common family friends. The friends would have had more opportunities to introduce the two previously, between 788 and 795.

124. Hou Wai-lu, *Chung-kuo ssu-hsiang*, vol. 4, part I, pp. 320–21; Ch'ien Mu, "Han-Liu chiao-yi."

125. See note 41 above.

126. See Hou Wai-lu, *Chung-kuo ssu-hsiang*, vol. 4, part I, pp. 320–21.

127. Liu Tsung-yüan, "A Letter to Han Yü Discussing the Role of an Official Historian," *LHTCC*, *chüan* 31, pp. 331–33.

128. The two other works are "An Elegy [on the Death] of Liu Tzu-hou," *HCLWC*, pp. 187–88 (for a trans. into French, see Margouliès, p. 216); and "Epitaph for Liu Tzu-hou," *HCLWC*, pp. 294–97 (for a trans. into English, see Yang and Yang, "Liu Tzu-hou.") All three works mention the disgrace and banishment of Liu Tsung-yuan.

129. Liu Yü-hsi, "An Elegy [on the Death of] Liu Yüan-wai," *LHTCC*, pp. 564–65; see also idem, "A Second Elegy [on the Death of] Liu Yüan-wai," p. 565.

130. See *HCLWC*, pp. 187–88.

131. I am referring here primarily to his ancestors who served under the T'ang. Han Yü's distant ancestors of the sixth and seventh generations had been distinguished military generals under the T'o-pa Wei, but they were too distant to be of influence in the 780's and 790's.

132. *Po-hsüeh hung-tz'u* ("erudites"): in T'ang times, a *chin-shih* degree holder who wished to serve in the central government in the capital had to pass one of the civil service examinations administered by the Ministry of Civil Offices or one of the examinations administered by the emperor himself. The latter were not offered every year, whereas the former were

conducted annually. The *po-hsüeh hung-tz'u* was the most prestigious of the annual examinations. Those who passed this examination were usually appointed to the post of secretary or of collator in the Imperial Secretariat (a ninth-grade rank). Those who failed usually found employment with local military governors.

133. *Ssu-men Po-shih* ("scholars of the Ssu-men Academy"): in T'ang times, the Imperial Academy was divided into six divisions, enrolling students from families of civil and military officials of different ranks. The National Scholars Academy was the highest ranking of the six divisions. It enrolled students from families of civil and military officials of the third-grade rank and above and appointed two scholars with the fifth-grade rank. Its total enrollment was 300. The Ssu-men Academy was the third-highest-ranking division. It enrolled 500 students from families of civil and military officials of the seventh-grade rank and above and 800 students from nontitled households and appointed three scholars with the seventh-grade rank (Lo Lien-tien, *Han Yü*, p. 9).

134. "*Hsin T'ang shu* Biography," in *HCLWC*, pp. 435–46.

135. Wu Wen-chih, *Liu Tsung-yüan p'ing-chuan*, pp. 17–22.

136. Lo Lien-tien, *Han Yü*, pp. 18–19; Wu Wen-chih, *Liu Tsung-yüan p'ing-chuan*, pp. 26–27.

137. *HCLWC*, p. 42; *LHTCC*, pp. 75–77.

138. According to the biography of Han Yü in the *HTS*, it was his criticism of palace purchasing practices that caused his exile. According to Hung Hsing-tsu's *Han-tzu nien-p'u*, both memorials, the one on purchasing practices and the one on famine and drought, were the causes of Han Yü's exile. But according to Fang Sung-ch'ing's notes to Hung's *nien-pu*, Wang Shu-wen and his clique were responsible.

139. Wu Wen-chih, *Liu Tsung-yüan p'ing-chuan*, pp. 40–43; Shih Tzu-yü, p. 50.

140. According to Shih Tzu-yü (pp. 61, 65), Ts'ui Min, who became a good friend of Liu Tsung-yüan's, was sent to Yung-chou in 807 to be the prefect there. Wu Wu-ling was demoted to Yung-chou in 808; in that year he showed Liu the collected works of his father. In 809, Liu Tsung-yüan's father-in-law, Yang P'ing, was demoted to Ling-ho. He and his son Yang Hui-chih passed by Yung-chou on their way to Ling-ho. They brought Liu Han Yü's "Biography of the Brush." In Liu Tsung-yüan's two letters to Yang Hui-chih, especially in his second letter of 811, he mentioned that a letter from Yang had been brought to him by a friend named Chang. These are only a few examples of how friends and acquaintances of Liu's served as couriers to keep communication with the outside world open.

141. Liu Tsung-yüan, "Notes on My Reading of the 'Biography of

the Brush' by Han Yü," *LHTCC*, pp. 246–47: for a translation, see Nienhauser, "Allegorical Reading."

142. Liu Tsung-yüan, "An Appraisal of Yi Yin's Presenting Himself to Chieh Five Times"; "Poem on Historical Events"; "Poem on the Three Ancient Worthies"; and "Poem on Chin K'o"; *HLTCC*, pp. 228, 495–97.

143. Hsü Meng-jung was a friend of Liu Tsung-yüan's father. In 809, Liu Tsung-yüan wrote a long letter to Hsü in which he expressed through references to historical precedents a strong hope that someday he would be cleared of the charges against him and reinstated to service (*LHTCC*, *chüan* 30, pp. 331–33). In the same year, Liu also wrote a letter to Hsiao Mien in which he expressed the same wish for reinstatement (ibid., pp. 327–29). Hsiao Mien served as an imperial secretary around 814. Han Yü was appointed a compiler in the Imperial History Bureau in 813; he was appointed a *lang-chung* (chamberlain) of the Examination and Review Board in 814.

144. In 820, Han Yü recommended Han T'ai to take his place as prefect of Ch'ao-chou (see "Recommending Han T'ai to Take My Place," *HCLWC*, p. 363). Han T'ai was one of the eight prefects (of which Liu Tsung-yüan was also one) banished after the 805 reform. Liu Yü-hsi and Han Yü were the two friends to whom Liu Tsung-yüan entrusted his bequests: Han Yü was given responsibility for his sons and Liu Yü-hsi for his collected works. On Han Yü's death, Liu Yü-hsi wrote the "Elegy [on the Death of] Han *li-pu*," *CTW*, *chüan* 610.

145. Both of them were acknowledged leaders of the *ku-wen* movement at the time.

146. Liu Tsung-yüan, "Notes on My Reading of the 'Biography of the Brush' by Han Yü," *LHTCC*, *chüan* 21, pp. 246–47.

CHAPTER 2

1. Yung-chou was a second-class prefecture. In the T'ien-pao period (742–55), it had 27,494 households and a population of 176,168. It was 3,274 *li* south of Ch'ang-an and 3,665 *li* from the Eastern Capital (Loyang). "Treatise on Geography," *CTS*, *chüan* 40, p. 182. For detailed information on the topography and products of Yung-chou, see Nienhauser, "Life and Works," notes, pp. 119–20.

2. During the T'ang dynasty, it was customary to conduct an annual review of demoted and banished officials. If the reviews were positive for six consecutive years (i.e., five reviews), the official would be recalled to the capital for reassignment. Liu Tsung-yüan's recall to the capital in 815 most likely falls under this category. On special occasions such as the ascension to the throne of a new emperor, the establishment of an heir ap-

parent (809), or a government victory in a large-scale military campaign (such as the pacification of the Huai-hsi rebellion in 817), there would be general amnesties. However, an emperor might choose to exclude special categories of people from the general amnesties. In the fifteenth year of the Chen-kuan period (642), for instance, those who were guilty of treason and whose sentences had already been reduced from capital punishment to demotion and exile were excluded from consideration for reappointment even though they had completed six years in exile (see "Demoted Officials and Exiles," *T'ang hui-yao, chüan* 41, p. 734). Liu Tsung-yüan and seven others banished in 805 were specifically excluded from all amnesties and due consideration accorded demoted officials and exiles by an imperial edict (see "The Basic Annals of the Emperor Hsien-tsung," *CTS, chüan* 14, p. 3107).

Liu-chou had jurisdiction over four *hsien* and 6,674 households, with a population of 7,637. During the T'ien-pao era, it had jurisdiction over five *hsien*, with 2,232 households and a population of 11,550. Liu-chou was 5,470 *li* from the capital and 5,670 *li* from Lo-yang (see "Treatise on Geography," *CTS, chüan* 41, p. 213).

3. Pulleyblank, "Neo-Confucianism," p. 84. See also Hartman, "Literary Background," p. 15; and Nienhauser, "Life and Works," p. 35, which expresses views similar to Hartman's.

4. See, e.g., Yeh Chia-ying; and Shimizu Shigeru. The Shimizu essay set the tone for many studies of Liu Tsung-yüan's records of excursions. See also Nienhauser et al. Most of the works of Liu Tsung-yüan discussed in this book are from the Yung-chou period.

5. *Ni* ("muddled") means "unable to circulate." Cf. the use of *ni* in "On the Judicial Application of the Penal Laws," *LHTCC*, p. 41: "Without the expedient, the constant will not circulate (*ni*); without the constant, the expedient will become perverted."

6. "Letter to Wu Wu-ling Responding to His View on My 'Rebuttal of the *Kuo-yu*,'" *LHTCC*, pp. 337–38.

7. These and other figures on the distribution of Liu Tsung-yüan's works by place of composition are based on Nienhauser, "Life and Works," p. 119, note 26, p. 123, note 64, and p. 125, note 84. Liu Tsung-yüan wrote 119 pieces during the Ch'ang-an period, 331 pieces during the Yung-chou period, and 103 pieces during the Liu-chou period.

8. See Ch'ien Mu, "Tsa lun," esp. p. 152, for Ch'ien's comments on the uniqueness of Liu Tsung-yüan's *yu-chi* and his contribution to the development of classical prose.

9. Ibid., *passim*.

10. "Biography of the Boy Ou Chi," *LHTCC, chüan* 17, pp. 208–9.

This biographical sketch, according to Shih Tzu-yü (p. 111), was written in 819, the last year of Liu Tsung-yüan's life.

11. Wu Wen-chih, *Liu Tsung-yüan p'ing-chuan*, for example, has made rather detailed comments on Liu Tsung-yüan's allegorical method and his iconoclastic thinking in his chapters on the Yung-chou period. But similar discussion is notably absent from his chapters on the Liu-chou period. Cf. chaps. 6–9 on the Yung-chou period with chaps. 13–14 on the Liu-chou period. Nienhauser ("Life and Works," p. 43) said the following of the Liu-chou corpus: "Among his other prose writings in Liu-chou are several landscape essays. They differ from the Yung-chou pieces in that they are merely objective descriptions of nature, rather than allegorical laments." I have noticed that Liu Tsung-yüan included no moralizing comments in the "Biography of T'ung Ou" as he did in the biographical sketches of Camel Kuo and the snake-catcher at Yung-chou.

12. Shao Po, a Sung scholar, once remarked of the prose writings of the four most renowned T'ang-Sung prose writers: "The writings of Han T'ui-chih derive their inspiration from the canonical works, the writings of Liu Tzu-hou derive their inspiration from the histories, the writings of His Honor Ou-yang [Hsiu] abound in temperance but have scant heroic air, the writings of His Honor Su [Shih] abound in heroic air but have scant temperance" (14.7a).

During the Yung-chou period, Liu Tsung-yüan was preoccupied with a theory of political *tao* firmly based on historical events. Hence his views on the questions of *tao, li, tzu-jan,* and *t'ien* were patently political. He had little interest in and even less patience for approaching the question of *li* and *tao* through the perspective of *hsing* (the nature of beings) and *ming* (fate, destiny—a religious or quasi-religious interpretation of the condition and purpose of man's life).

In "On the Theory of Seasonal Practices," Liu Tsung yüan said: "The way of the sages does not search out what is most unusual and call it divine. It does not call upon heaven's name to give it an aura of superiority. It merely takes care that the way is beneficial to the people and leaves no practical affair unattended" (*LHTCC,* p. 38).

In his "Outline of Biographical Events" of Liu Hun, he stated: "The principle that governs the destiny of man is a topic that the sages rarely spoke about. It is a topic that no educated gentleman will elaborate on. How can a shaman know everything about it? If I have to follow that to stay alive, giving up the teaching of the sages in order to follow the heretical art, it is much better to die a speedy death" (ibid., p. 78).

Liu Tsung-yüan denied that either *t'ien* or the sages had anything directly to do with the origination and continuation of political order or political institutions in history. It was all a matter of *wei* and *shih*. Man, admittedly, had an active role to play in history. But this role again was not determined by his natural endowment (*t'ien-chüeh*). Man relates to his historical role internally through his own perceptive and analytical powers (*ming*) and personal aspirations (*chih*) and externally through his understanding of his political environment (*wei* and *shih*). Hence, when discoursing on the basis of human virtues and human accomplishments, Liu Tsung-yüan made little allowance for what man receives from *t'ien*. In "On Nobility Coming from Heaven," he said: "When someone asks, 'What you have said about the natural endowment in man, do you mean that it is analogous to meting out what is each's due from the official treasury?' I would say, 'No, I just mean what one has in himself in terms of vital energy.' When Chuang Chou speaks about *t'ien*, he speaks about *tzu-jan*; I will accept that." (ibid., p. 36).

The essay that most clearly reveals Liu Tsung-yüan's political interpretation of *li* as the principle behind the peaceful order in the world is his "Disquisition on Feudalism" (ibid., pp. 31–34). The following quotation from the "Disquisition" sufficiently illustrates the point.

> Some may still argue, "Hsia, Shang, Chou, and Han continued for a long time because they adopted feudalism; and Ch'in lasted only a short while because it instituted the prefecture system." Those are really not [the kinds of opinion] one would consider to be informed about the principles behind political government. . . .
>
> With regard to the way of governing the world, it is only when the principle [of the relative position of the ruler and the ruled] is in harmony that the right persons are correctly placed in service. When persons of merit occupy high positions and persons of no merit occupy low positions, then the principle of government is able to function peacefully. Now in the case of feudalism, the principle of rule becomes a hereditary one. When the principle of rule and being ruled becomes a matter of heredity, who can say that the ones occupying high positions are indeed meritorious, and the ones occupying low positions are of no merit? Whether people will live in peace or disorder becomes unknowable. (ibid., p. 34)

In "Disquisition on the Six Violations," Liu stated *li* as the principle behind peaceful political order even more explicitly: "The way to choose the sovereign and set up the officials is the great fundamental [underlying principle] of order and disorder in the world" (ibid., p. 43).

13. See "Disquisition on Feudalism," ibid., *chüan* 3, p. 34. Cf. Liu Yü-hsi, "Disquisition on Heaven," Parts I–III, also in ibid. (pp. 195–99) following Liu Tsung-yüan's "Discourse on Heaven." The long transition in

Liu's viewpoint from seeing *t'ien* from the standpoint of *tzu-jan* to seeing *t'ien* from the standpoint of *hsing* is discussed in the section "Nature as Living and Growth."

14. In many ways, Liu Yü-hsi went beyond the concept of *t'ien* as spontaneously-being-so. In Part I of his "Disquisition on Heaven," he developed Liu Tsung-yüan's view that *t'ien* was indifferent to the ways of man:

My friend Liu Tzu-hou of Ho-tung, an intelligent man, wrote the "Discourse on Heaven" to refute the words of Han T'ui-chih. It is truly well written. However, he wrote under provocation and not expressly for the purpose of exhaustively studying the relations between heaven and man. Hence I am writing this disquisition to bring out all the arguments.

Whatever assumes physical form has what it is able to do and what it is not able to do. *T'ien* is the greatest among all that has form. Man is the most distinguished among all animals. What *t'ien* is able to do, man indeed is not necessarily able to do. But there are also things that man can do that *t'ien* cannot do. Therefore I say that *t'ien* and man surpass each other in their respective ways.... What *t'ien* can do is to engender life for all beings; and what man can do is to govern all beings.... If man wants to use his personal success and failure to challenge the existence or nonexistence of *t'ien*, he is misled. (*LHTCC*, p. 196)

Liu Yü-hsi thinks that *t'ien* and mankind interact, although their respective *tao* are very different. This differs significantly from Liu Tsung-yüan's view that *t'ien* stands aloof from man and is totally indifferent to man's ways.

In Part II of "Disquisition on Heaven," Liu Yü-hsi develops the important concept of *shu* (mathematical determinism, a concept that occupies no visible place in Liu Tsung-yüan's speculative thinking). Liu Yü-hsi held that *shu* can account for how and why things happen in certain ways and that *shih* is derived from *shu*. He gives the example of a man traveling in a boat to illustrate how the principle (*li*) behind what happens during the boat trip can be understood in terms of the man's role and in terms of how the water and the boat work together under the governing principle of *shu*. *T'ien* has nothing to do with what happens to man:

Do you understand the sailing of a boat? In cases of boats that sail on the Wei River, the Tzu River, the I River, and the Lo River, the speed depends on man; where they are to stop over for lodging depends on man. No strong wind can stir up enough waves [against them], and no countercurrent can be stiff enough to overcome them. Should the trip be swift and safe, it is all because of man. If the boat capsizes or gets stuck, it is also because of man. The people in the boats never speak of *t'ien*; why is this so? It is because the principle (*li*) [of why certain things happen in certain ways] is clear. . . . The one asking said, "I have seen boats sailing alongside each other, the wind and the current are the same, and yet there are some that sink and some that do not. If that is not *t'ien*, then what is the cause of the difference?" [Liu Yü-hsi] answered, "Water and boat are two things. When things come together, there is necessarily *shu* existing between them. Once *shu* is there, then *shih* is formed in between the things. One boat sinks; one boat crosses. That is how they respectively meet their *shu* and are propelled by their *shih*. . . ." The one asking said, "You said that once *shu* is there, then *shih* is generated; it does not concern *t'ien*. Is this to say that *t'ien* is more limited than *shu*?"

[Liu Yü-hsi] answered, "The form of *t'ien* is always round and its color is always blue. Its circumference is measurable. Its day and night are demonstrable. Doesn't this mean that *shu* resides therein? It is always high and is not low. It is always moving and does not stop. Does this not mean that it is propelled by its *shih*? Now this [*t'ien*] that is blue, once it has taken the form of being high and vast, it is not able spontaneously to return to being low and limited; once it is propelled by *shih* to function by moving, it is not able to stop for even an instant. How can it evade *shu* and rise above *shih*? Hence I firmly hold that the myriad beings go on and on without end because they interact and surpass one another in each of their own ways, and their respective functions serve one another's purposes. *T'ien* and man are only the most distinguished of all things." (ibid., pp. 197–98)

It is only one step from this to interpreting the animal fables of Liu Tsung-yüan as dramatic studies of the interaction of *shu* in life rather than arguing the issue in the terms Liu Yü-hsi uses in his "Disquisition on Heaven."

For scholarly and philosophical discussions of Liu Tsung-yüan's and of Liu Yü-hsi's theories of *t'ien*, *shu*, and *shih*, see Hou Wai-lu, "Liu Tsung-yüan"; Wu Wen-chih, "Liu Tsung-yüan"; and Chao Chi-ping.

15. As conceptualizations of forces governing events in human life, especially irrational or incomprehensible events, *ming* is used to evoke the supernatural in an attempt to understand, rationalize, and explain the incomprehensible, whereas the frame of reference of *shu* is confined to the physical and natural world only. In this sense, *ming*, instead of being a

deterministic concept, seems paradoxically to address those elements in an event that defy any rational and predetermined explanation. Liu Tsung-yüan, in a rare reference to *shu*, said the following about *ming* and *shu*:

> Nowadays, the emperor is promoting civilizing teachings [across the nation]. . . . That I and four or five others should [adversely] be entrapped in a ruinous state like this, is this not a matter of fate (*ming*)? Fate is something that resides with *t'ien*, not an institution formed by the ordinary run of men. What then is there to regret? . . . Your humble servant may indeed be guilty. But is that not in the number (*shu*) of things?

See "Letter to the Han-lin Scholar Hsiao Mien," *LHTCC*, p. 328. Cf. Lamont.

16. As a remedy to the hardships caused by the chronic droughts at Liu-chou, Liu Tsung-yüan mobilized the local people to dig wells. To commemorate the occasion, he wrote "Inscription for the Well, with a Preface" (816), *LHTCC*, pp. 240–41; and "To the God of the Well" (816), ibid., *chüan* 41, p. 439. For a record of his other deeds, see Han Yü, "Epitaph for Liu Tzu-hou," translated in Chapter 1; and Liu's "Stele Inscription for the Newly Renovated Temple of King Wen-hsüan at Liu-chou" (*LHTCC*, *chüan* 5, pp. 54–55); and "Stele Inscription for Yao E" (ibid., pp. 58–59).

17. See Han Yü, "Stele Inscription on the Lo-ch'ih Shrine at Liu-chou" (823), translated and discussed in Chapter 1.

18. Liu Tsung-yüan, "Disquisition on Feudalism," *LHTCC*, p. 32.

19. The T'ang-Sung *ku-wen* revival, like the May Fourth Movement in the twentieth century, was not purely a "literary" movement. Its advocates, like the May Fourth advocates, saw in literature an effective means of advancing their own political and ideological ends. Literary theories and literary writings played rather different roles in the cases of different writers. Just as not every May Fourth writer subscribed to the theory of "art for life" and hence did not practice some sort of realism in his writing, so not every *ku-wen* practitioner adopted the same ideological or literary stance and program. The literary theories of the *ku-wen* writers fluctuated considerably with their changing views of the world and of their own roles in the world. Hence, it is nearly impossible to find consistent positions on such questions as the nature and purpose of literature.

20. "Letter to the *Hsiu-ts'ai* Ts'ai An on Literary Writing," *LHTCC*, *chüan* 34, p. 364. Few scholars make the distinction between the didactic orientation of Han Yü's theory of *wen yi tsai tao* ("literature is meant to be a vehicle for the [Confucian] *tao*") and the implicit reflective and critical

approach in Liu Tsung-yüan's theory of *wen yi ming tao*. The two phrases are treated as almost interchangeable in most works on the *ku-wen* theories of Han and Liu.

21. "Disquisition on the Six Violations," *LHTCC*, *chüan* 4, p. 34:

When the ancients spoke about *li*, few were able to develop their ideas fully. As soon as an idea was advanced and a statement was made, one felt threatened and insecure. It was all right to say that the idea was correct; it was equally proper to say that it was incorrect. The issue was left in a state of ambiguity. When teaching it to posterity, no one knows which position to accept or reject. Men of clear thinking regret this situation. However, if any of them goes ahead to determine the rightness and wrongness [of the statement or of the idea involved], then those prudish academicians and ignorant students babble in chorus and confuse him, accusing him of being arrogant and bizarre.

22. Ibid., *chüan* 3, p. 34.
23. "Letter to Wei Chung-li on the Way of Being a Teacher," ibid., *chüan* 34, p. 359.
24. "Letter to Wu Wu-ling Responding to His View on My 'Rebuttal of the *Kuo-yü*,' " ibid., p. 338.
25. "Letter to the *hsiu-ts'ai* Yen Hou-yü Responding to the Question of the Way to Be a Teacher," ibid., *chüan* 34, p. 361.
26. "On Nobility Coming from Heaven," ibid., *chüan* 3, p. 36.
27. "Preface to [the 57] Poems Written on the Occasion of Seeing off My Cousin [Liu] Ch'eng to Chiang-huai after His Dismissal from Office [at the Capital]," ibid., *chüan* 24, p. 269.
28. "With regard to the way of governing the world, it is only when the principle behind the relative positions of the ruler and the ruled is in harmony that the right persons are correctly placed in service" (see note 12 above). A general and extensive discussion of the *sheng-jen chih tao* can be found in Liu's "Second Letter to Yang Hui-chih," ibid., pp. 348–53. "The way of the sages does not search out what is most unusual and call it divine. . . . It merely takes care that the way is beneficial to the people" (see note 12 above). In setting forth the achievements of Lu Chih, Liu Tsung-yüan said that Lu Chih was able to penetrate into the objectives of the sages and that the *tao* was thus reflected in his principal achievement. "He considered the livelihood of people as the fundamental, and the deeds of Yao and Shun as the goal" ("A Proposed Epitaph [*piao*] for the Late Master Lu Wen-t'ung of T'ang, Secretary of the Review Board, Tutor to the Heir Apparent," ibid., *chüan* 9, p. 90). On the *piao* genre, see Liu Hsieh, 5:9b: "*Piao* set forth a request"; and Hightower, "The *Wen Hsüan*," p. 525.

29. On *chün-tzu chih tao*, "Letter to Yang Hui-chih [son of Yang P'ing and Liu Tsung-yüan's brother-in-law]": "To be with what is central and not to be misled by the accidental is the way of the man of principle" (*LHTCC, chüan* 33, p. 347). On *ta-jen chih tao*, see "Stele Inscription for Chi-tzu": "The ways of the great man are three: his integrity brings him opposition; his measures are adopted by the sagacious; and his teachings extend to the people" (ibid., *chüan* 5, p. 51). The model of a "great man" is Chi-tzu of the Shang dynasty. On *chün-tzu*, Liu Tsung-yüan said, "To be flexible in manner and unbending at heart . . . then one earns the name of a superior man" ("Second Letter to Yang Hui-chih," ibid., *chüan* 33, p. 348).

30. "On the [Duke of Chou's] Argument in Favor of Enfeoffing the Younger Brother [of King Ch'eng] with a T'ung-tree Leaf"), ibid., *chüan* 4, p. 46. Liu Tsung-yüan's account here varies from the account given in "Hereditary House of Chin" in the *Shih chi* (39:1b), which names the Grand Historian Yin I, not the Duke of Chou, as the one who argued with the king that the latter should not joke about such a matter as enfeoffment. Also compare the account in Liu Hsiang, 1:4a-b.

"A Rebuttal of the Argument in Favor of Penalizing Those Involved in Vendettas," *LHTCC, chüan* 4, pp. 45-46. Han Yü also submitted a public statement on the subject in the same open debate; see "A Statement on the Legality of Vendettas," *HCLWC*, pp. 341-42. Behind the public debate on the proper handling of vendetta cases was an incident of the sixth year of the Yüan-ho period (811). A man named Liang Yüeh killed another man to avenge the death of his father and then gave himself up to the local government. For accounts of the incident, see "Biography of Chang Hsiu," *HTS*, 195.7a-b; "The Basic Annals of Hsien-tsung," *CTS*, 14.19a-b; "Treatise on the Penal Law," *CTS*, 50.13a-b.

"Explicating the *Annals of Yen-tzu*," *LHTCC, chüan* 4, pp. 49-50; "Explicating the *Analects*: Two Essays," ibid., pp. 48-49.

31. "Chung tao" is an important concept in Liu Tsung-yüan's approach to putting ideas into practice. It appears in practically all his statements on political and institutional matters. It is an essential characteristic of his concept of the *chün-tzu*, and it is a guiding principle in his advice to aspiring writers. It also marks his understanding of the way of the sages. See, e.g., "On the Judicial Application of the Penal Laws, Part II," ibid., p. 41; "On the Theory of Seasonal Practices, Parts I and II," ibid., pp. 38-40, esp. pp. 39-40; "On the Enfeoffment with the Leaf of a T'ung Tree," ibid., p. 46; "Letter to Han Yü Discussing the Role of an Official Historian," ibid., *chüan* 31, p. 332; and the two letters to Yang Hui-chih, ibid., pp. 347-53. For a discussion of the concept of "ta-chung" and its role in Liu's thinking and writing, see Chang Shih-chao, vol. 2, pp. 1290-99.

32. "Postscript to the Collected Works of Yang P'ing-shih [Ling]," *LHTCC, chüan* 21, p. 250.

33. Ibid., pp. 250−51. In the Sung, the concept of "difficult to excel in both" was given a different orientation by Ou-yang Hsiu in his discussion of immortality (see the conclusion of Chapter 3).

34. See Chang Shih-chao's discussion of Liu Tsung-yüan's "Odes on the Pacification of the Huai-hsi Rebellion" (vol. 1, pp. 7−9).

35. "Written on the Occasion of Building a Pavilion West of the Fa-hua Monastery" (809), *LHTCC, chüan* 43, p. 476.

36. Ssu-ma Ch'ien, "Biography of Ch'ü Yüan," 84:1a−6b. For a translation, see Watson, *Records of the Grand Historian,* vol. 1, pp. 499−508. For a detailed discussion of the issues involved in Ch'ü Yüan's life and his personal destiny, see Hightower, "Ch'ü Yüan Studies."

37. For the *p'eng* bird and the sparrow, see *Chuang-tzu chi-chieh,* "Free and Easy Wandering," pp. 1−2, and "Autumn Floods," p. 98. Insofar as Chuang-tzu's theory of nature concerns the naturally determined forms of being and the scale of action of those beings, it compares interestingly with Liu's theory of mathematical determinism (*shu*). See note 14 above.

38. For a comparison of the life and poetry of Hsieh Ling-yün with those of Liu Tsung-yüan, see Yeh Chia-ying. For the life and poetry of T'ao Ch'ien, see Hightower, *T'ao Ch'ien.* Interestingly enough, when Su Shih was in exile, he took with him only the works of T'ao Ch'ien and Liu Tsung-yüan. See "Six Letters in Answer to the *T'ui-kuan* Ch'eng Ch'üan-fu," *STPC, hsü-chi, ts'e* 12, *chüan* 7, p. 17: "Since I have come to this overseas place, it is as if I had run into a deep valley. There is nobody I can talk to, nor are there any books. I have only the collected works of T'ao Yüan-ming and several volumes of the poetry and prose of Liu Tzu-hou, which I always place by my side and look on as my two friends."

39. In his first five years at Yung-chou, Liu Tsung-yüan had an extremely difficult time adapting to the local climate and living conditions. His house burned down four times, and he was constantly ill with one disease or another. For descriptions of his life in the first years at Yung-chou, see his letters to Hsü Meng-jung, Yang P'ing, and Hsiao Mien, *LHTCC, chüan* 30, pp. 319−29.

40. Most of Liu Tsung-yüan's rhymeprose, especially his "Rhyme-prose on My Pitiful Life" and "Rhymeprose on Dream of Homecoming," lament his own exile to Yung-chou. See ibid., *chüan* 2, pp. 26−29. For Liu Tsung-yüan's self-reproaches, see the discussion of his "Foolish Brook" series in the following text. His most colorful attacks on his enemies can be found in "Curses on the Corpse Worms," "Chopping up the Crooked Side-Table," and "On the Abominable Monkeys," ibid., *chüan* 18, pp. 215−19. Tuan Hsing-min (pp. 103−36) treats all three of these works exhaustively as political invectives in an allegorical mode, directed by Liu against his enemies.

41. "Looking for the Foolish Brook After Rain on an Early Summer Day," *LHTCC, chüan* 43, pp. 481–82.

42. There are, in fact, nine "records"—the traditional eight and a ninth one, "Record of a Visit to Huang Brook," which, for some reason, is not included in the group. See ibid., *chüan* 29, pp. 313–18. For critical studies of the significance and literary quality of the *yu-chi*, see Shimizu Shigeru; Wu Wen-chih, *Liu Tsung-yüan p'ing-chuan*, pp. 125–266; and Nienhauser, "Landscape Essays."

43. *LHTCC, chüan* 29, p. 316.

44. Ibid., p. 318.

45. See note 42 above.

46. Nienhauser, "Landscape Essays," p. 75.

47. *Yü*, unlike *ni* ("muddled"), does not signify a lack of such positive qualities as *wen* ("good style"), *chih* ("wisdom"), or *ming* ("perception"). As can be inferred from the allusions to Ning-wu-tzu and Yen Hui in the translation of the Preface to the "Foolish Brook Poems," *yü* in Liu Tsung-yüan's usage means rather the nonassertive way in which a superior man (*chün-tzu*) conducts himself when the circumstances are such that it would be improper and unwise for him to act assertively.

48. "Valley of the Foolish Old Man": Morohashi (*Dai Kanwa jiten*, vol. 4, p. 1120) says this place is west of Lin-chih *hsien* in Shantung province, quotes the *Shui ching* as his authority, and notes that Liu Tsung-yüan mentioned it in his preface. He then quotes from the "Chen-li" chapter in the *Shuo yüan*: "Duke Huan of Ch'i was pursuing a deer and went into a mountain valley. He saw an old man (*lao kung*) and asked him, 'What valley is this?' [The old man] replied, 'This is the Valley of the Foolish Old Man (*yü kung chih ku*).'" Morohashi also quotes a long story from the "T'ang wen" chapter in the *Lieh-tzu* about a foolish old man who tried to move a mountain (see Graham, pp. 99–101), but this passage has nothing to do with a valley or with Shantung. See *Lieh-tzu, chüan* 5; and Liu Hsiang, *chüan* 7, 32:4a–4b.

49. *Analects,* 5:20: "The Master said, "When good order prevailed in his country, Ning Wu acted the part of a wise man. When his country was in disorder, he acted the part of a stupid man. Others may equal his wisdom, but they cannot equal his stupidity" (Legge, pp. 180–81).

50. *Analects,* 2:9: "I have talked with Hui for a whole day and he has not made any objection to anything I said; as if he were stupid. He has retired, and I have examined his conduct when away from me and found him able to illustrate my teachings. Hui! He is not stupid" (Legge, p. 149).

51. Compare the mimetic function of the Foolish Brook—a mirror to all creation (*chien wan-wu*)—with the reflective function (*ming yi chien chih*) of man's critical intelligence (*ming*), which, in Liu Tsung-yüan's "On No-

bility Coming from Heaven," appears as essential to a rational under-standing of the *tao*.

52. *LHTCC, chüan* 24, pp. 273-74.

53. Ibid., *chüan* 43, p. 481.

54. Ibid., *chüan* 43, p. 481.

55. The allusion here is to the "Pu Chü" in the *Ch'u Tz'u*. *Pu Chü*, as David Hawkes (p. 88) pointed out, really means "divining for the best course of action to follow"; and it is a satirical counterpart to the worldly wise "Fisherman" (*Yü fu*) in the sense that it "is strongly pro-Ch'ü Yüan and satirizes contemporary society; Yü Fu extols the simple wisdom of the rustic at Ch'ü Yüan's expense and satirizes the would-be-martyr who scorns the world."

56. The marquis of Shou-chang's name is Fan Chung, posthumously entitled *ching*. Fan Chung was the father of Fan Hung, who has a biography in *Hou-Han shu*. For Fan Chung's planting of the lacquer trees, see "Biography of Fan Hung," *Hou-Han shu*, 62:1a-b.

57. *LHTCC, chüan* 43, p. 481.

58. Ibid., *chüan* 14, pp. 149-50.

59. Ibid., pp. 147-49.

60. Ssu-ma Ch'ien, "The Hereditary House of Chin," 39:29a-b.

61. See ibid.

62. See Ssu-ma Kuang, 6b-10b. Ssu-ma Kuang's version is consider-ably more detailed.

63. *LHTCC, chüan* 17, p. 212.

64. Ibid., *chüan* 19, pp. 232-33. Su Shih, inspired by Liu Tsung-yüan's "Three Admonitions," wrote two admonitions, using the self-deceiving behavioral patterns of dolphin and squid as dramatic subjects. Su Shih's two works "About the Dolphin" and "About the Squid" can be found in the appendixes to ibid., p. 557.

65. Ibid., p. 232.

66. For recent expressions of this view, see Neighbors, pp. 84-85; and Tuan Hsing-min.

67. *LHTCC*, pp. 232-33.     68. Ibid., p. 232.

69. Neighbors, p. 87.        70. *LHTCC*, p. 232.

71. *Ku-wen* literature during the T'ang and Sung periods was part philosophy, part literature. It is not always easy, as in the cases of the animal fables and the biographical sketches by Liu Tsung-yüan, to deter-mine whether they can be better understood as philosophical writings or as literary writings. In any case, in interpreting Liu Tsung-yüan's fables, I try to go beyond the totally politicized approach adopted by Tuan Hsing-min, whose main thesis and examples are rendered by Hartman in "*Alieni-loquium*." Tuan performed an impressive task in ferreting out the possible historical identities of the people behind Liu Tsung-yüan's many animal

fables. However, I remain uncomfortable with his obvious conclusion that these works are no more than personal invectives against Liu's political enemies. In my opinion, Liu's fables go beyond the historical to the speculative, i.e., to philosophical thought.

In the West, it is a familiar idea that literature goes beyond history in capturing what is universal. "The distinction between historian and poet," according to Aristotle (*Poetics*, 1451), "consists really in this, that the one describes the thing that has been, and the other a kind of things that might be. Hence poetry is something more philosophical and of graver import than history, since its statements are of the nature rather of universal, whereas those of history are singulars." Nonetheless, the Western tradition, at least from Aristotle to Kant, tends to separate philosophy and literature more sharply than does the Chinese tradition. In the West, it is thought that philosophy must deal with the general *in abstracto*. For example, Kant (p. 31) wrote late in his life: "Among all peoples the Greeks first began to philosophize. For they first attempted to cultivate the cognition of reason *in abstracto* without the guiding thread of pictures, while other people sought instead to make concepts intelligible to themselves *in concreto* by pictures only. Even nowadays there are people like the Chinese and some Indians who indeed treat of things taken from mere reason, such as God, the immortality of the soul, and the like, but nevertheless do not seek to investigate the nature of these objects *in abstracto* according to concepts and rules. They make no separation between the use of reason *in concreto* and that *in abstracto*."

This view is somewhat one-sided even relative to the history of Western philosophy. It is a well-known fact that Plato often merges philosophy and literature. For the period after Kant, Kierkegaard, Nietzsche, Wittgenstein, Heidegger, and Sartre provide other examples. Admittedly, the style of these philosophers is more similar to that of Lao-tze and Chuang-tze than to that of Liu Tsung-yüan. But the difference is one of degree, and my attempt to look at these fables from a philosophical perspective follows a tradition in China that goes back to the *Chuang-tzu*.

72. *LHTCC, chüan* 17, pp. 206–7. According to the Ch'ing scholar Ku Yen-wu (*chüan* 19), there was no tradition in ancient times for writers who were not official historians to write biographies, and most "biographies" written by those who were not official historians were in essence fiction or hearsay. See entry "The ancients did not write biographies for others":

> The term "biography" began with the Grand Historian. It was a historical form. When not in the position of writing official histories, a person does not write biographies of others. Hence, there are stele inscriptions, records, and outlines of personal lives and deeds [of individuals], but no biographies [by private writers].

In Jen Fang's *On the Origins of Literary Forms*, written in Liang times, it was said that biography writing began with Tung-fang Shuo's "Mr. Never-Existed." That was an allegory in the form of a biography. There are three biographies in the *Collected Works* of Han Wen-kung—"Ho Fan, an Imperial Academy Student," "Wang Ch'eng-fu, the Plasterer," and "[Mr.] Brush." There are six biographies in the *Collected Works* of Liu Tzu-hou—"Sung Ch'ing," "Camel Kuo," "The Boy Ou Chi," "The Builder," "Li Ch'ih," and "Fu-pan." [Han Yü] selected only one anecdote from Ho Fan's life and called it a biography. Those people like Wang Ch'eng-fu were all lowly people, yet [the writers] called their stories biographies. "[Mr.] Brush," "Li Ch'ih," and "Fu-pan" are playful pieces, yet they were called biographies. Such is the kind of writings done by hearsay collectors. When it comes to [the life and deeds of] Commander Tuan, then it was not called a biography but an outline of his deeds. The reason the writer did not dare to write a biography of Commander Tuan was that he was not in the position of writing an official historical account.

From Sung times on, there were people who wrote biographies of others, encroaching on the duties of an official historian.

73. *HLTCC, chüan* 17, pp. 207–8.
74. "Harsh government is fiercer than tigers": the expression appears in the *Li Chi,* chap. 4, paragraph 56.
75. *HLTCC, chüan* 16, pp. 200–201.
76. Su Shih, "Written on the Back of Liu Tzu-hou's Memorial Inscription for the Zen Monk Ta-chien," *STPC, hou-chi, ts'e* 7, *chüan* 19, p. 67. See also Ch'ien Ch'ien-yi, 33:11b.
77. Ch'ien Ch'ien-yi, 23:14a–b; Wang Fu-chih, 25:1a–2b; Wang Ming-sheng, "Beneficial Deeds Recorded in the Annals of Shun-tsung," *chüan* 74b; and Chang Shih-chai, "Ethics of Writers," p. 56.
78. E.g., Hou Wai-lu, "Liu Tsung-yüan"; idem, *Chung-kuo ssu-hsiang,* vol. 4, part I, pp. 352–92; Wu Wen-chih, "Liu Tsung-yüan"; and Huang Yün-mei.

In the 1950's and early 1960's, most studies on Han Yü and Liu Tsung-yüan published in mainland China denigrated Han Yü and praised Liu Tsung-yüan. Hou Wai-lu's chapter on Liu Tsung-yüan in *Chung-kuo ssu-hsiang* (1959) and his 1964 article "Liu Tsung-yüan" created a place for Liu Tsung-yüan in the intellectual history of China. Wu Wen-chih's *Liu Tsung-yüan p'ing-chuan* has a long chapter (pp. 125–66) on the landscape essays of Liu Tsung-yüan, which in many ways echoes the themes and analyses of Shimizu Shigeru's article. Wu's criticism of Liu's works was on the whole sympathetic, and he was positive about Liu's political views and efforts toward reform.

Since the 1960's, the strongest champion of the idea of Liu Tsung-yüan as a political progressive and of the view that a powerful passion informed his prose writings has been Huang Yün-mei. His terse section on Liu (pp. 101–27) sparkles with the insight that often accompanies strong convictions. Huang's statement on the mandate of Heaven (p. 109) is penetrating and is supported in a different context by the modern scholar and historian Ku Chieh-kang, who argued that rulers in the Ch'in and Han dynasties succeeded, with the help of Confucian scholars and Taoists, in translating theories of the supernatural into political institutions that consolidated and strengthened the authority of the emperor.

Ch'en Yin-k'o's "Lun Han Yü" provided a definitive study of the historical significance of Han Yü's thought and literary endeavors in his own time and in later ages. His six-point exposition was attacked point by point by Huang Yün-mei in a rather lengthy rebuttal, "Tu Ch'en Yin-k'o 'Lun Han Yü'" (pp. 67–100). Huang's rather negative evaluation of Han Yü in another chapter of his book (pp. 5–66) specifically challenged the positive evaluations of Han Yü in the histories of Kuo Shao-yü and Lo Ken-tse (Sui-T'ang).

Whether the critical studies of Hou Wai-lu and Huang Yün-mei are the results of free and independent thinking, or are in part affected by the political necessities of the 1960's, is a question that need not concern us here. What is important here is that a different assessment of the historical significance and literary achievements of Han Yü and Liu Tsung-yüan had been made and was supported by documentation and new arguments.

Sun Ch'ang-wu's Liu Tsung-yüan chuan lun is essentially a compilation of information available from existing scholarship on Liu Tsung-yüan.

79. Cf. Dubs, pp. 263–65:

> In ancient times the travelling scholars were prejudiced—these were the erring schools of philosophy. Micius was prejudiced towards utility and did not know the elegancies of life. Suntze was prejudiced towards desire, and did not know satisfaction. Shentze was prejudiced towards law and did not know the worthy man. Shentze was prejudiced towards power and did not know wisdom. Hueitze was prejudiced towards words and did not know reality. Chuangtze was prejudiced towards Nature and did not know man. For if we consider life [tao] from the standpoint of utility, it will merely be seeking for profit. If we consider life [tao] from the standpoint of desire, it will merely be seeking for satisfaction. If we consider life [tao] from the standpoint of law, it will merely be an art.

If we consider life [*tao*] from the standpoint of words, it will merely
be dialectic. If we consider life [*tao*] from the standpoint of Nature,
it will merely be cause and effect. *These different presentations are all
one aspect of life* [*tao*] [italics added]. Now the right Way of Life [*tao*]
is constant and includes all changes; one aspect is insufficient to
express the whole. Those who have partial knowledge perceive one
aspect of the Way [*tao*], but they cannot know its totality. So they
think it sufficient, and gloss things over. On the one hand they confuse themselves, and on the other they mislead others.

For the Chinese text, see *Hsün-tzu chi-chieh*, pp. 261-62.

80. Other critiques of the inherent prejudices and biases in the ancient
schools of thought, including Confucian thought, can be found in
*Chuang-tzu*, "T'ien-hsia p'ien"; and Han Fei-tzu, "Fei shih-erh-tzu p'ien."

81. Lo Ken-tse, *Chung-kuo wen-hsüeh p'i-p'ing shih*, vol. 2, p. 147: "Han
Yü and Liu Tsung-yüan are to T'ang dynasty *ku-wen* what Mencius and
Hsün-tzu are to the pre-Ch'in Confucian school of thought."

82. See Hou Wai-lu, *Chung-kuo ssu-hsiang*, vol. 4, part I, pp. 320-60,
which deals with Han Yü's theory of *t'ien-ming*, the debates between Liu
Tsung-yüan and Liu Yü-hsi on *t'ien*, and the controversy over the role of
the historian.

For discussion of differences in Han Yü's and Liu Tsung-yüan's conception of *hsüeh*, see Kuo Shao-yü, vol. 1, pp. 246-53; and Lo Ken-tse,
*Chung-kuo wen-hsüeh p'i-p'ing shih*, vol. 2, pp. 150 ff.

Essential primary documents on Liu Tsung-yüan's views on learning
(*hsüeh*) and teachers (*shih*) are the letters to Wei Chung-li, Yen Hou-yü,
Yüan Chün-ch'en, and Tu Wen-fu (*LHTCC*, pp. 357-62, 365-66).

83. Kuo Shao-yü (p. 250) seemed to think that Han Yü might qualify
as a thinker whereas Liu Tsung-yüan could only be considered an excellent writer.

84. See note 12 and Kuo Shao-yü, p. 252. Liu Tsung-yüan was very
much in tune with the more progressive thinking of his senior contemporary historiographer-official Tu Yu. For example, arguments in Liu's
famous "Disquisition on Feudalism" show the unmistakable influences of
Tu Yu's idea of the natural evolution of institutions, and Liu's "Rebuttal
of the *Kuo-yü*" echoes Liu Chih-chi's Preface to the *Shih-t'ung*. In Liu
Chih-chi's "Author's Preface" (*Shih-t'ung*, *chüan* 10), Liu Chih-chi states
that he had "criticized on many occasions past sages and displayed a fond-
ness for stating what he considered to be right and wrong and hence it was
only right that he be incriminated by his contemporaries." Further on in the
same preface, Liu Chih-chi also said that in writing the *Shih-t'ung*, he had
more or less followed in the footsteps of Confucius; "however, if I forth-
with do what Confucius did without the name of Confucius, I am afraid

that I will startle the public and be found guilty by my contemporaries." Liu Chih-chi's ubiquitous self-consciousness about setting the record straight about what is true and false and what is right and wrong in history certainly struck a sympathetic note in Liu Tsung-yüan. And Liu Tsung-yüan's statement about doing what Confucius did without the self-perfection of Confucius in his letter to Wu Wu-ling (LHTCC, p. 388) echoed Liu Chih-chi almost verbatim.

85. See "Letter in Answer to Tu Wen-fu," LHTCC, pp. 365-66; and "Letter in Answer to Wei Chung-li on the Way of Being a Teacher" (ibid., pp. 357-59), in which Liu enumerated the respective qualities a student should seek to cultivate by reading the Five Classics. He also specifically mentioned what one might conceivably glean from the histories, the Li-sao, and such pre-Ch'in works as the Mencius, Hsün-tzu, Lao-tzu, and Chuang-tzu to enrich one's own literary style—a position quite incongruous with Han Yü's emphasis on purging from one's ideas and style all that is un-Confucian.

86. Feng Yu-lan (vol. 2, chap. 10), for instance, omitted Liu Tsung-yüan completely, and regarded Han Yü only as a distant precursor of Sung Neo-Confucianism.

CHAPTER 3

1. According to Kuo Shao-yü (vol. 2, p. 28), the practice of anthologizing and annotating ku-wen began with Lü Tsu-ch'ien of the Southern Sung dynasty. Lü's Ku-wen kuan-chien (Keys to ku-wen) discussed the writings of the same eight writers later anthologized by Mao K'un. The Ssu-k'u ch'üan-shu tsung-mu t'i yao (p. 1468) lists a Chu Yu of the early Ming, who, even before Mao K'un, brought the works of the eight T'ang-Sung masters together in an anthology. Chu's work, entitled Pa hsien-sheng wen chi (Collected writings of the eight masters), was no longer extant at that time. Min-tse in his recent history mentions Chu Yu but not that Chu's work is lost.

2. For Li Ao and Huang-fu Shih, see Kuo Shao-yü, vol. 1, pp. 258-64. For a partial translation of Li Ao's "Recovery of the Nature," see Wing-tsit Chan, pp. 456-59.

3. Kuo Shao-yü, vol. 1, pp. 284-85. Nienhauser (P'i Jih-hsiu, pp. 52-68) has a chapter on P'i Jih-hsiu's prose but discusses mostly P'i's proto-Neo-Confucian ideas.

4. One indirect reference to this can be seen in Fan Chung-yen (989-1052), Preface to the Collected Works of Yin Shih-lu of Honan, 6:10a:

But ever since Yang Ta-nien [Yang Yi, 947-1020] paced unchallenged in the world with his talent for practical writing, students, in the hope of emulating him, have begun to carve and chisel their own expressions and no longer have time for the ancients. The more extreme ones devote themselves to the cultivation of literary embellishment only. They break the ancient odes into bits and pieces and say perversely that the ancient *tao* is no longer suited for use. Thus, for a long time, the ancient *tao* has been neglected, and no one has studied it.

See also Ou-yang Hsiu's Preface to his *Nei-chih chi* (Collected court documents), in which he mentions that the "four-six style" of parallel prose had come to be accepted as the standard for court documents (*OWWC*, *chüan* 43:2–3).

5. Lo Ken-tse, *Wan-T'ang Wu-tai*, p. 2.

6. "Postscript to an Old Edition of Han [Yü]'s Works," *OWWC*, 73:9b–10a.

7. Liu K'ai was a great admirer of both Han Yü and Liu Tsung-yüan. He once named himself Chien-yü (shouldering [Han] Yü) and styled himself Shao-hsien (*hsien* can also be read *yüan*, meaning inheriting [Liu Tsung-] yüan); later he changed his name to K'ai and his style to Chung-t'u (meaning that he was the pathfinder of the Confucian way for his contemporaries). See Kuo Shao-yü, vol. 1, p. 307.

8. Liu K'ai, "Ying tse," 1:11a.

9. The reference is to Han Yü's "Epitaph for Fan Shao-shu of Nan-yang," *HCLWC*, p. 311.

10. Wang Yü-ch'eng, "Letter in Answer to Chang Fu," 18:11b–12b. The passage attributed to Han Yü is a paraphrase of a passage in Han Yü's "Letter in Answer to Liu Cheng-fu," *HCLWC*, p. 121.

11. Ou-yang Hsiu refers to *hsin* as a value criterion in a great number of his essays. See, e.g., "On Orthodoxy," *OWWC*, 16:2b–10b; "On the *Ch'un-ch'iu*," ibid., 18:5a–11b; "Explanation of the Wei State and Liang States," ibid., 17:8a–9b; "Questions on the Book of Changes," ibid., 8:1a–4a; "A Proposed Epitaph for the Nei-tien Ch'ung-pan Hsüeh," ibid., 24:5a–7a; "First Letter to the *Hsiu-ts'ai* Yüeh," ibid., 69:10a–11b; "Second Letter to the *Hsiu-ts'ai* Yüeh," ibid., 66:5b–7b.

12. "First Letter to the *Hsiu-ts'ai* Yüeh," ibid., 69:10a–11b.

13. "Second Letter to the *Hsiu-ts'ai* Yüeh," ibid., 66:5b–7b.

14. "Valediction to Hsü Wu-tang on His Returning South," ibid., 43:2a–3b. The idea of *pu-hsiu* is also expressed in Ou-yang Hsiu's preface to the collected poems of Mei Sheng-yü indirectly through the argument that *kung* alone is insufficient for the attainment of *pu-hsiu*. See note 17 below.

15. Although Ou-yang Hsiu never discoursed at length on the relationship between literature and *ch'ang*, his position on the subject is rela-

tively clear since *ch'ang* is the principle behind the immortality of the Six Classics and, by extension, behind any human pursuit of lasting value. *Ch'ang*, therefore, is a universal idea with Ou-yang Hsiu; it can be found underlying many of his other ideas. In his "Pi shuo" (On the writing brush), there is a passage called "There is no constant name for the *tao*," (*Tao wu ch'ang-ming shuo*), which gives some indication of how he envisioned *ch'ang* in its changeable application:

> The *tao* has no constant name, hence it is more exalted than all beings. The sovereign has a constant way [of governing], hence he is the most exalted man in the four seas. That which has no constant [name] manifests its efficacy by its response to the fulfillment of the various beings; and that which has a constant way finds the basis [of its action] in adhering to the *tao*. (ibid., 129:4b)

16. "Second Letter to the *T'ui-kuan* Shih [Chieh]," ibid., 66:10b–11a.

17. Preface to the *Collected Poems of Mei Sheng-yü*, ibid., 42:10b–11a.

18. "Poems Composed at a Gathering at the Ministry of Rites," ibid., 43:7a.

19. "Postscript to the *Li-chih-p'u*," ibid., 73:13a–b.

20. See Ou-yang Fa et al., "Deeds [of Ou-yang Hsiu]," ibid., appendix c.5.

21. "Draw water from the spring" (*jang ch'üan*) is a pun on the name of the spring (*Jang ch'üan*).

22. Giles (p. 177) translated *she-che chung* as "Every archer hits his mark" in his "The Old Drunkard's Arbor." The present translation follows the notes given in Hsü Han-feng, p. 219; and Yu-liang, p. 36. The reason for my selection of the present translation is that the pitch-pot game seems to be a more appropriate companion to chess playing than archery, which would require a more spacious setting than what is likely to have been available around the pavilion. Egan (pp. 215–17) has a complete translation of the piece. He identifies the game as a drinking game invented by Ou-yang Hsiu with "a target with pictures of eight animals drawn in a circle around a ninth" (see note on p. 247).

23. *OWWC*, 39:14b–15b.

24. Even modern critics like Le Gros Clark share this opinion: "And yet Su obviously found wine an aid to his inspiration. For like Ou-yang Hsiu, he regarded the source of his drunkenness 'not in the wine that he drank, but among the mountains and streams.' Wine was but the means to the attainment of joy in landscape which was the 'work of the heart.' Encouraged by it, he was able to soar to untold heights of poesy and imagination" (p. 33). One of Su Shih's poems that LeGros Clark quoted in support reads:

How much have I already drunk today?
Ah! I feel I can escape the fetters of mortality.
I fling away my staff and rise.
Away with all your cares and worries, lads!
I soar over running deer on mountain peaks,
And join the leaping monkeys on overhanging cliffs.
Thence do I plunge into the billowing clouds of a vast ocean,
Heaven in tumult!

25. See note 24 above.

26. See note 24 above. In 1036, at the age of 30, when he was first sent away from the capital to Yi-ling, Ou-yang Hsiu wrote his good friend Yin Shih-lu:

> A scholar-official would rather die than compromise his moral righteousness. He would walk up to it [death] in quick steps just as he would to a seat or a bed. . . . I found many examples of famous men of old who, when defending a cause, were ardent and fearless of death, as if they really understood the principle of righteousness. But once arrived at the place of their exile, they began to nourish grievances; they complained and sighed, and they vented in writing their sense of the unbearable grief of a man in adversity. Their hearts were moved to joy and sorrow just like any common man; even Han Wen-kung [Han Yü] was not exempt from this predicament. I have mentioned this to An-tao and admonished him not to complain in his writings. If you observe my words closely, you will no doubt understand how my heart takes to such matters. In recent ages, there have also been men who were demoted and sent away because they criticized state affairs. Yet they acted either arrogantly and overfreely or wildly and drunkenly, claiming that they were born to do great deeds and not trivial ones. Hence, when I was first parted from you, I pledged to be even more assiduous in attending to my duties, and not to drink. And to date I have kept my word in both these respects. (*OWWC*, 67:10a–11b)

27. For information on the political circumstances that led to Ou-yang Hsiu's exile to Yi-ling, see James T. C. Liu, pp. 30–35.

28. "Tsui-weng yin ping hsü," *OWWC*, 15:7a–b. Since this poem, like the one following, clearly recalls Ou-yang Hsiu's feelings of the Ch'u-chou period, as reflected in a poem written in 1046 shortly after he arrived there, I have brought the three poems together to discuss their contents as well as to compare them with "The Old Tippler's Pavilion."

29. For information on the political intrigues that led to the Ch'u-chou exile, see James T. C. Liu, pp. 65–68.

30. "Tseng Shen Po-shih ko," *OWWC*, 7:1a–b.

31. "T'i Ch'u-chou Tsui-weng-t'ing," ibid., 53:13b–14a.

32. The meaning of joy in "The Old Tippler's Pavilion" can be better appreciated when read together with its companion piece, "Record of the Pavilion of Abundance and Joy," which was written in the same year, 1046 (ibid., 39:13a–14b).

33. That Ou-yang Hsiu is word conscious is best illustrated by his "On the Epitaph for Yin Shih-lu," ibid., 73:5a–7a, in which he discussed the reason and meaning behind his choice of certain words. That *yeh* is consciously repeated in "The Old Tippler's Pavilion" to express a positive conception is supported by another interesting short prose work of Ou-yang Hsiu, "Proposed Epitaph for Shih Man-ch'ing," ibid., 24:1a–3a. In this work, he employed some 30 negative particles to present a talented, idiosyncratic poet and military strategist whom he greatly loved and admired, but who, being a habitual drunkard and an eccentric, could occupy only a negative position in Ou-yang Hsiu's moral scheme. The interplay between Ou-yang Hsiu's admiration for his friend and his impartial moral disapproval of his friend's behavior is reflected in the inconspicuous and unobtrusive use 30 times of negative particles. For a translation, see Egan, pp. 53–56.

34. Ohmann (p. 232) says: "Whatever complex apprehension the critic develops of the whole work, that understanding arrives mundanely, sentence by sentence. For this reason, and because the form of a sentence dictates a rudimentary mode of understanding, sentences have a good deal to do with the subliminal meaning (and form) of a literary work. They prepare and direct the reader's attention in particular ways."

35. See esp. "The Landscape at Fu-ch'a" and "The Hall of Beauty and Goodness (Yu-mei-t'ang)," *OWWC*, 40:5a–8a.

36. See note 19 above. For other references to the idea of *pu-chien*, see "Yün tsung hsü," ibid., 42.1a–2a; Preface to the Collected Works of Chien-su-kung Hsüeh, ibid., 44:6a–7a; and note 35 above.

37. Su Shih, "[*Tz'u* to the tune of] Shui-tiao ko-t'ou," in Lung Yü-sheng, p. 108.

38. The Ch'ing scholar Huang Tsung-hsi (1610–95) described the difference in the *ku-wen* style of T'ang and Sung writers in the following terms:

After the T'ang dynasty, *ku-wen* underwent a monumental change. Before the T'ang its diction tends to be ornate, whereas after the T'ang its diction tends to be unadorned; before the T'ang its sentences are short, whereas after the T'ang its sentences are long; before the T'ang its [style] is like a lofty mountain with deep valleys, whereas after the T'ang its [style] is like a level plain with open fields. Such is their clear-cut dividing line.

## CHAPTER 4

1. Hatch, pp. 900–968. Hatch's informative biography on Su Shih's political career and his discussion of Su Shih's thinking *vis-à-vis* Buddhist philosophy treat in detail and with great sensitivity the many intellectual and philosophical tendencies in Su Shih's thinking. I find his interpretation of Su Shih's "philosophy of accommodation" (pp. 947–53) as opposed to the Buddhist philosophy of deliverance and Su Shih's "art of response" in matters practical and artistic (pp. 947–53) of particular relevance and interest to my own overview here.

2. Kuo Shao-yü, vol. 1, pp. 340–41.

3. De Bary et al., p. 512.

4. Ibid., pp. 515–20.

5. Ibid., pp. 520–25, esp. p. 521.

6. Through his philosophy of accommodation and his "art of response," Su Shih was able, in Hatch's words, to "reduce the problem of [how to nurture life] to harmony and repose.... Buddhism becomes a strategy in the nurture of life because emptiness of mind and emotional detachment were an aid in response to things even should one choose not to deny them. The literature in which Su Shih transformed the spontaneity of nature into a life of art is built around the 'thoughtlessness' of response, raising the alternative to the overregulation of the social ethics" (p. 949).

7. Legge, *She King*, p. 256: "That, as a stream ever coming on / such is thine increase."

8. Su Ch'e, "Epitaph for Master Tung-p'o," in *STPC*, vol. 1, *ts'e* 2, p. 50.

9. *STPC*, *ch'ien-chi*, *ts'e* 5, *chüan* 24, p. 25.

10. For *hsin* and *ch'i*, see "Notes on the Peony" (1072), ibid., *ch'ien-chi*, *ts'e* 5, *chüan* 25, p. 36:

The peony has been held in high esteem by the world for more than three hundred years. Its exceeding beauty is a peerless sight. In recent years, it further developed a hundred different looks; there are numerous instances where it [is seen] going after novelty [*hsin*] and unusualness [*ch'i*] in order to court the favor of the time. This is a clever and obsequious species of plant.

For *kao* and *hua*, see Preface to the *Collected Poems of Master Fu-yi* (1074), ibid., *ch'ien-chi*, *ts'e* 5, *chüan* 24, p. 39:

Once my father ... said to me, "From now on, writings are going to grow even more skillful, and the *tao* is going to disintegrate. Men of letters aspire to the distant and neglect what is near; they value the flower [*hua*: ornate appearance] and deprecate the fruit [*shih*: substance]. ... The poetry and prose of Master Fu-yi were composed with a purport. ... The master had no word to spare on lofty [*kao*] idle talk or on decorative verbal games."

Note that the concept of *hsin* is applicable not only to *kung* but also to *yi*. When novelty later becomes the characteristic of *yi* in Su's thinking on the art of painting, we have artworks of the highest merit (*shen-yi*, "creative and preeminent") rather than mere novelty of expression. The bifurcation of Su Shih's critical scheme between *yi* and *kung* is best seen in the contrast between "novelty and the unusual" in appearance and "originality" (*hsin-yi*). Su used the latter term to describe the paintings of Sun Wei and Wu Tao-tzu. See text below and note 14.

11.  *STPC, ch'ien-chi, ts'e* 5, *chüan* 24, p. 37. By "lack of understanding" (*pu-t'ung*), Su Shih probably meant the lack of understanding of the underlying principle of things. See his "Letter Presented to Prime Minister Tseng" (1057) in which the expressions *t'ung* and *pu-t'ung* also occur (ibid., *ch'ien-chi, ts'e* 5, *chüan* 28, p. 94):

The most difficult task in the process of learning is not to have personal bias. The most difficult task in the process of doing away with personal bias is [to attain a total] understanding of the underlying principle of things. Hence, if a person lacks the understanding of the underlying principle of things, even if he wishes to be without personal bias, it would be quite impossible. He will consider what he himself likes good and what he himself dislikes bad. In this way, his trust in himself becomes a form of misjudgment. Therefore, [one should] live in quietude and away from worldly intrusion in order to observe the changes in things; one should comprehend their underlying principle and then form his unbiased judgment [of right and wrong, and of good and bad]. Whatever does not conform to the latter, he will not adopt even though it may come from the sayings of the alleged worthies in the ancient time.

12.  Ch'ien Chung-shu, Foreword to Le Gros Clark, p. xviii.
13.  The importance of *yi* in painting had already been underlined by Chang Yen-yüan of the T'ang dynasty. In discussing the six techniques of painting, Chang said, "To represent the external form [of things], likeness is necessary. Likeness depends on capturing the entire structure and spirit [of the object]. Both structure and spirit and likeness of form stem from

the formulation of *yi*, which is realized by the application of the brush" ("On the Six Techniques of Painting," in *Li-tai ming-hua chi*, p. 51).

Su Shih often noted the significance of *yi* for painting, for example, in "Postscript to the Paintings of P'u Yung-sheng," "Postscript to a Study of Seal Characters, in Verse," "Postscript to the Mountain Villa Painting of Li Po-shih," and "Postscript to the Calligraphy of the Six T'ang Masters," *STPC, ts'e* 5, *chüan* 23, pp. 30, 32–34.

The significance of *yi* for literary writings was emphasized in his famous "Letter in Answer to Hsieh Min-shih." A more colorful rendition of the notion can be found in the following passage by Su Shih, which appears in *Yün-yü yang-ch'iu, chüan* 3:

> In the village of Tan-erh, there are only a few hundred households. Its people can obtain everything they need from the market and are quite self-sufficient. However, the things they want are not obtained for free. They have to have one thing before they can get them. And that one thing is money.
>
> Writings are analogous to this. The myriad events scattered in the Classics, the histories, and the works of the philosophers are not to be obtained gratuitously either. One has to have one thing to procure them with, and only then can he appropriate them for his own use. And that one thing is *yi*.
>
> Possessing no money, one cannot get the things he needs; lacking *yi*, one cannot make use of material for writing. This is an essential aspect of literary composition.

14. Le Gros Clark, p. 18.

15. Cf. Chang Yen-yüan, *Li-tai ming-hua chi*, p. 51: "The third [technique] is to shape the form [of the object in the painting] in accordance with the objects [in nature]; the fourth [technique] is to give the object the color that is proper to its kind."

16. In Chinese art criticism, there is an established practice of evaluating artworks by classification. In Chang Yen-yüan's *Fa-shu yao-lu (ts'e* 71–74), for example, there is a class of special merit called *yi p'in* that caps the other nine divisions of *shang, chung,* and *hsia* of calligraphic art. Hsia Wen-yen also spoke of three classes of painting. His classification, however, seemed to have derived, on the one hand, from the six techniques of painting of Chang Yen-yüan and, on the other hand, from the classification of calligraphic art into three classes—*shen p'in, miao p'in, neng p'in*— by Chang Huai-kwan of the T'ang dynasty. *Shen* seems to imply an artistic achievement that approximates natural creation; *yi* suggests works so exceptional and excellent that they form a school by themselves. For example, Hsia Wen-yen described *shen p'in* as follows: "When the spirit

and expression [of a painting] are so vivid and alive that it seems to have come from the hand of nature and its art seems to lie beyond human perception, then we have a painting of the *shen* category" (1 : 1a).

*Yi p'in* in painting is described in the following terms by T'ao Tsung-yi: Huang Tzu-chiu's "landscape paintings are executed in the spirit of Tung and Chü. They form a school by themselves and hence can be considered as of the *yi* category" ("Keys to Landscape Painting," *ts'e* 122, 8 : 1a). Hsia Wen-yen defined *miao p'in* and *neng p'in* as follows: "Paintings that are superior in their brush work, harmonious in their coloring and shading, and suggestive in their moods belong to the *miao* [excellent] category. Paintings that are mimetic in form and keep within the confines of ruler and compass belong to the *neng* [skilled] category" (1.1a).

17. *STPC, ch'ien-chi, ts'e* 5, *chüan* 24, p. 30.

18. Ibid.: "One day, [Sun Chih-wei] dashed into the monastery in a great hurry, and hastily asked for a brush. With sleeves flying in the wind, he finished [a painting of water] in an instant. [The water in the painting] flowed and cascaded, rose and turned with such forcefulness that it seemed to sweep away any house with it. When Chih-wei died, his brush technique died with him."

19. *CCTPWC*, p. 51.

20. *STPC, hou-chi, chüan* 14, pp. 12–13.

21. An explicit allusion to the master carver and the ideal of skill can be found in "Postscript to the Paintings of Wu Tao-tzu" (ca. 1085), ibid., *ts'e* 5, *chüan* 23, p. 34.

22. Ibid., p. 33. The allusion to the axe thief seems to be to an anecdote in the *Lieh-tzu* about the effect of a person's bias on his perception of persons and things in the outside world:

There is a person who lost his axe. He thought it was his neighbor's son [who took his axe]. When he watched the son's gait, it was that of an axe thief; [when he watched] the son's looks, they were those of an axe thief; [when he watched] his speeches, they were those of an axe thief; [when he watched his] movements and manners; nothing he saw was not that of an axe thief. Shortly afterwards, he went digging in a valley and found his axe. One day he saw his neighbor's son again, and the latter's movements and manners no longer resembled those of an axe thief. (pp. 173–74)

See also Graham, p. 180.

23. *STPC, ch'ien-chi, ts'e* 4, *chüan* 20, p. 11: "Only when a person is no longer bound by the *yi* or the self is he able to communicate with things in the sphere of feelings." For the idea of having no personal bias (*wu ssu*), see "Letter Presented to Prime Minister Tseng," cited in note 11 above.

In "Postscript to the Mountain Villa Painting of Li Po-shih," Su Shih said, "When he [Li Po-shih] was living in the mountains, he was detached from all things. Therefore his spirit could communicate with all things, and his intelligence penetrated the workings of all artisans" (ibid., *ts'e* 5, *chüan* 23, p. 34).

When we compare these three passages with the work cited in note 22, we can see that to be one with nature in one's understanding, it is imperative that the subjective self not intrude. The notion that personal bias in a person's understanding of things and his feelings about them contorts his communication with nature and that the bias is inevitably reflected in one's work is further supported by Su Shih's comment on Chang Chih's cursive-style calligraphy in his "Postscript to the Calligraphy of the Six T'ang Masters":

> Calligraphy resembles the man. . . . The cursive-style calligraphy of Chang *ch'ang-shih* is one with nature, without bias or partiality. At points, his artistic touch is more explicit. But the form and substance, idea and expression, are completely integrated and hence perfectly self-sufficient. (His cursive-style calligraphy] is known as creative and preeminent. (ibid., p. 33)

24. Ibid., *hou-chi*, *chüan* 14, pp. 12-13.

25. See "Letter Presented to Prime Minister Tseng," ibid., *chüan* 28, *ts'e* 5, p. 94. See also "original idea" in the "Postscript to the Paintings of P'u Yung-sheng," translated earlier in the text.

26. The "Rhymeprose" has been translated many times. The justification for another translation here is primarily a matter of comparative interest. First, there is the basic problem of whether the text reads "one" Taoist priest or "two" Taoist priests in Part II of the *fu*. Second, there is the question of aesthetic distancing between Su Shih as the poet of the *fu* and Master Su as the *persona* in the *fu*. All previous translations have one Taoist priest and use "I" or "I, Su" to translate "Su-tzu" in the *fu*, which collapses the effect of the *persona*. The *persona* puts distance between Su Shih the poet and Master Su the *persona* and separates the poetic vision from the daily life led by the poet. This poetic distancing of a moment of insight into man and his world from the reality of daily existence is similar in method and effect to Ou-yang Hsiu's invocation of the Old Tippler to voice his insight into life and its vicissitudes in "The Old Tippler's Pavilion." To equate the two blurs the line between literature and life. Other variants between my translation and other translations on details of lesser importance are noted below.

Other translations can be found, in the order of their publication dates, in Le Gros Clark, pp. 126-41; Watson, *Su Tung-p'o*, pp. 87-93; A. C.

Graham in Birch, *Anthology*, pp. 381–84; Chai and Chai, pp. 51–55; and Shih-shun Liu, pp. 261–67.

27.  The constellations *tou niu* are variously translated as the Dipper and the Ox, in the constellation of Sagittarius (Le Gros Clark, p. 129 note); the Archer and the Goat (Watson, *Su Tung-p'o*, p. 87); and the Dipper and the Herdboy Star (Graham in Birch, *Anthology*, p. 381). After consulting a scholar in astronomy who seemed to think that the orbits of the Dipper and the Ox made it impossible for the moon to appear between them, I first resolved on translating *tou niu* as the Milk Dipper and the Archer—a translation that in realistic terms gives the moon more room to move around in than would the Archer and the Goat—and then reluctantly yielded to dictionary usage and settled on the Dipper and the Herdboy like Graham.

Wang Li, in his chapter "Astronomy, Calendar, Musicology" in *Ku-tai Han-yü*, points out that the 28 constellations in Chinese usage constitute a manner of defining the horizon and directions in stellar rather than in geographical terms. *Tou niu* belongs to the group of seven constellations that defines the northern horizon, corresponding to the area of Chiang-hu and Yang-chou in geographical terms (pp. 784, 790)—where the boat ride took place. Hence, it probably conforms more to the Chinese use of tropes in literary works to take *tou niu* as meaning the northern horizon, which, in combination with "over the eastern hill," defines where Su Shih was: he was looking northeastward to the moon from the foot of the Red Cliff. This is how Wang Po in his "T'eng-wang-ko hsü" defines the location of T'eng-wang-ko: "Hsing fen Yi-Chen, ti-chieh Heng-Lu," with the constellations Yi and Chen matching the state of Ch'u in ancient China, which became Chin-chou later on.

In any event, Su Shih could not have meant the moon's lingering between the Dipper and the Herdboy to be interpreted literally. Such an interpretation would yield a visually constricted picture, totally incongruous with the boundless effect in time and space he creates with the whole of the first part. From Wang Po's example and Su Shih's here, we can see that the use of constellations and of geographical areas to define a location falls into the literary and stylistic convention of a rhymeprose. The literary convention has some realistic basis but is not intended to be read primarily in realistic terms.

28.  In 1079, when Su Shih was going from Hsü-chou to Hu-chou, he went on a boating excursion with Wang Tzu-li and Wang Tzu-ch'in, who played the flute. See *STPC*, *ts'e* 2, "Nien-p'u," p. 23.

29.  Le Gros Clark (p. 131) notes that this poem appears in the *Wen Hsüan*, *chüan* 27, and is ascribed to Ts'ao Ts'ao.

30.  The allusion to the water endlessly flowing is to the *Analects*, 9:16: "Once when the Master was standing by a stream, he said, 'Could one but

go on and on like this, never ceasing day or night'" (Waley, *Analects*, p. 142).

31. *STPC, ts'e* 4, *chüan* 19, p. 112.

32. "Record of the Fang-ho Pavilion" (1078), ibid., *ts'e* 6, *chüan* 32, pp. 31–32. According to this work, Su Shih was in the mountains at P'eng-ch'eng and saw two cranes kept by a hermit.

33. Le Gros Clark translates "a Taoist priest" (p. 137) and considers "two Taoist priests" to be of "no significance in the story... unless Su Shih had in mind the story of Pen-ching Ch'an-shih" (p. 140, note 10). Watson translates "a Taoist immortal" with no note or explanation (*Su Tung-p'o*, p. 92). Graham translates "a Taoist monk" with no note or explanation (Birch, *Anthology*, p. 384).

34. *STPC, ts'e* 4, *chüan* 19, p. 113.

35. Ibid. The SPTK edition has one priest; the SPPY edition and the Shanghai Shang-wu yin-shu-kuan 1933 edition have two priests. A comparison of the publication history of the various editions shows that the SPPY version seems to be the earliest one; "one priest" is to all appearances a misguided emendation.

The SPPY movable-type edition of the *Tung-p'o ch'üan-chi*, also known as *Tung-p'o ch'i-chi*, in 110 *chüan* is based on a Sung edition commissioned by Emperor Hsiao-tsung, which has a preface by Su Ch'iao dated 1173.

The SPTK edition of *Ching-chin Tung-p'o wen chi shih-lüeh* in 60 *chüan* with commentaries by Lang Yi is a photoreprint of another Sung edition, which has a preface dated 1191 — 18 years later than Su Ch'iao's preface. Lang Yi's commentary immediately following the text "one Taoist priest" reads: "Many editions had 'dreamt two Taoist priests.' It should be one Taoist priest. I suspect the former of being a copyist's error." This summarizes fairly well how the variant reading of "one priest" originated. Lang Yi also quoted I Iu Tzu's *Ts'ung-hua hou-chi*, 28:2b, but only in part, to support his own emendation. The partial quote, however, clearly indicates that in Sung times, especially during the Northern Sung, "two priests" was a common reading.

The 1933 Shanghai Shang-wu yin-shu-kuan edition (reissued Shanghai: 1958; and Taipei: 1967) followed the Ming edition of *Ch'ung-k'an Su Wen-chung-kung ch'üan-chi*, which has a preface by Li Shao dated 1456. This Ming edition adhered to the "two priests" reading, which Li Shao said was preserved in many of the mutilated copies of Su's works that he had consulted.

Many other Ming and Ch'ing editions of Su Shih's works in the Harvard-Yenching Library at Cambridge, Mass., such as *Su Ch'ang-kung wen-chi*, compiled by Chang P'u (Ming dynasty), 5:5a; *Tung-p'o ch'üan-*

*chi*, edited by Chang Yang-cheng (Ming), 33:12a; *Su Wen-chung-kung wen-ch'ao*, edited by Mao K'un (Ming), 28:7a; *Hsi-sheng Tung-p'o wenhui*, published jointly by Mao K'un and others (Ming), 33:5a; and *Tungp'o ch'üan-chi*, Tao-kuang *jen-ch'en* ed. (Ch'ing), 2:12b, have "one priest." But it is questionable whether their reading is derived from sources more reliable than the one conjectural statement in Lang Yi's commentary.

Jonathan Chaves has brought to my attention that two Taoist priests appear in many paintings of the "Rhymeprose," including the set of paintings by Ch'iao Chung-ch'ang of the Sung dynasty, which is now in the Crawford Collection in New York. (See frontispiece.)

In this chapter, I have tried to offer an interpretation of the ideas (*yi*) involved in the variant reading of "two Taoist priests." Artistically and conceptually speaking, "two Taoist priests" offers a more satisfactory and interesting reading of the two prose poems. Textually, there is also sufficient evidence to make the reading an acceptable, even preferable, one. Until evidence more substantial than the statement in Lang Yi's commentary is found for the "one priest" reading, I shall follow the earliest dated text of the SPPY edition and read "two Taoist priests."

36. Legge, *Taoism*, p. 197.

37. Beardsley, pp. 403–9.

38. Hu Tzu, *Ts'ung-hua hou-chi*, 28:3a–b.

39. Brouwer, p. 80. I am grateful to Dr. Hao Wang for his explanation of Brouwer's theory of "two-oneness." The parallels between Eastern and Western perceptions of the interrelations among number, change, and time are thought-provoking.

Brouwer explains Kant's intuitionism, which associates geometry with space and arithmetic with time, and reviews the development of non-Euclidean geometry; "the position of intuitionism," he then concludes, "has recovered by abandoning Kan's aprivity of space but adhering the more resolutely to the aprivity of time" (pp. 78–80). This was immediately followed by the quoted passage in my text.

According to Dr. Wang, Kant's original considerations were not as purified as Brouwer's. For example, he theorized with the famous example $7 + 5 = 12$ rather than further reducing it to the underlying move from one integer to the next, a move whose essence is Brouwer's idea of two-oneness. (The Chinese $2–4–8$ sequence probably will also be regarded by modern Western mathematicians as not purified enough.) Kant did, for instance, say: "Only in time can two contradictorily opposed predicates meet in one and the same object, namely, one after the other" (*Critique of Pure Reason*, A32 or B49). Here, of course, Kant had in mind the possibility of change, which can only take place in time.

When the notions of time and change are analyzed down to their most fundamental components, we seem to arrive at a minimum duality of one and two (Chang Tsai, for example, studied the idea of the duality of one and two in the instance of the *two* ends of *one* stick). Two contradictory properties in one object are possible only at two moments. The two moments both belong to one stream of time. The two properties both belong to the one (changing) object. Whereas Brouwer uses this idea to move in the more abstract bare bone of what underlies arithmetic and the integers, Su Shih further magnified the duality of one and two by adding yet another concrete image to render the duality doubly conspicuous. Of course, the change of one object from a crane into a priest already reveals duality in time and in change. The change of one crane into two priests corresponds more closely to the purer move from the integer 1 to the integer 2.

As we experience "one after the other," we think of the "one" and "the other" together as a two. In this way, we also get the number 2 from the number 1 when we abstract from the content of our consciousness and concentrate only on the time components in "one after the other," i.e., the two moments of time, "one after the other." Hence 2 is after 1 in two ways: it corresponds to the togetherness of the two moments, and it is a new number following 1 as the next moment (the second) and as the successor of 1 in the sequence of integers. These ways may be seen as represented respectively by the simpler transformation of one crane into two cranes and the more complex transformation of one crane into two priests.

CONCLUSION

1. *Ch'üan Han wen*, 26: 5a–9b.

2. Liu Chih-chi, 10a.

3. Ou-yang Hsiu did not put equal emphasis on the role of *yi* in art, although he was quite aware of its presence in current discussion of arts, particularly with regard to painting. For example, he said in "Scrutinizing Paintings," *OHCC*, p. 1047: "Spare and tranquil, such a state is difficult to paint. . . . Hence those creatures that fly and run with varying speed and do not have depth in their state of being are easy to render visible." When relating *yi* to literary expression, Ou-yang Hsiu was more direct and did not seem to make the graded distinction of *yi-fa-kung* that Su Shih did. He said, for instance, "People say that in writing poetry, one does not pursue good phrases but only seeks good ideas. My opinion is that if the idea is good, the phrase will also be good" (ibid., p. 1030). Sometimes, he was even derogatory toward writers and poets who emphasized *yi*: "The vigorous style of Li [Po] and Tu [Fu] is no longer present. [Modern writers] strive to compete in subtlety in perception [*yi*]. The more stubborn ones take even greater pains at formulating their ideas. Once they get an idea, they will spare no effort at chiseling and carving" (ibid., p. 1037).

4. The concept of *ch'i* is used to address different questions in T'ang and Sung intellectual thought and literary theories. *Ch'i* was used by T'ang *ku-wen* theorists to address the question of differences in natural endowment in men, which together with heart or universal mind (*hsin*), provides the basis for a rationalization of the differences in the tonality of their writings (see the discussion of the background of the *ku-wen* movement in the Introduction). In early Neo-Confucian thinking during the Northern Sung, *ch'i* is used to address the ontological question of being (*yu: wu*) in conjunction with the concept of *shu* (the mathematical principle behind change or an abstraction of the phenomenon of being in mathematical terms) and to reorient the practice of seeing in the phenomena of life and death a metaphor for transiency and impermanence expressing nothingness or emptiness (*wu*) to a practice of seeing them in terms of continuous transformation expressing the infinite progression of generation and dissolution in terms of ongoing phases of the universal movement of *ch'i*.

This new perception of reality certainly affected the lyric vision and mimetic principle inherent in the writings of contemporary Sung poets and writers. We have seen, in our analysis of the "Rhymeprose on the Red Cliff," for instance, how Su Shih's concept of "two-oneness" in this work reverberates with echoes of the thought of the contemporary Neo-Confucian thinker Chang Tsai. Moreover, his theory of perceptive mind (*yi*) and freedom from personal bias (*wu ssu*) contrasts strongly with the T'ang writer Liu Mien's theory of heart or universal mind (*hsin*) and emotion (*ch'ing*) in a definition of *wen* and *ku-wen*.

How Neo-Confucian thought affected the theoretical outlook and literary style of contemporary poets and writers is a fascinating but unexplored topic. I have attempted only some very elementary connections in my chapters on Sung theories and practices of *ku-wen* and *wen*.

The best discussion of Chang Tsai's theory of *ch'i* and of "two-oneness" that has come to my attention is in Chang Tai-nien, *Chung-kuo che-hsüeh ta-kang*, esp. pp. 109–26. In another book on Chinese philosophy, Chang Tai-nien scrutinized the theory of *ch'i* in Chang Tsai's philosophy and came to the conclusion that Chang Tsai thought that *wu* was not the basis of the material world, even though it was a manifestation of *ch'i* and *ch'i* affirmed the material base and the realm of being (*yu*). See *Chung-kuo che-hsüeh fa-wei*, pp. 87–134. Chang's chapter "The Philosophy of Chang Heng-ch'ü [Chang Tsai]" is much more comprehensive than the treatment of Chang Tsai's ideas in Hou Wai-lu's *Chung-kuo ssu-hsiang*, although I was somewhat disappointed not to find a discussion of the connection between *ch'i* and *shu* in Chang Tsai's thought. I have for some time speculated that the concept of *shu* in early Neo-Confucian thinking (Chou Tun-yi, Chang Tsai) in some way had succeeded in abstracting the concept of time that underlay the Buddhist and Taoist theories of dissolution, death, and impermanence and had supplied a new basis for perceiving being and life by integrating *shu* with the timeless concept of generation—*sheng-sheng*—from the *Yi ching*. Being untrained in the discipline of philosophical inquiry, I have not proceeded further into the question.

5. Hernadi, pp. 6–7. Margouliès, in the introduction to his *Le Kou-wen chinois* (pp. vi–xxiii), discussed *ku-wen* as a sort of genre, using the *Ku-wen kuan-chih* as representative of what he had in mind as *ku-wen* and not restricting the term to the kind of *ku-wen* defined by Han Yü in his program.

6. Hightower, "The *Wen-hsüan*." Hightower noted that the development of genre theory in China has been closely associated with anthology making: "The sixth century *Wen hsüan*, with its preface, marks a significant stage in the process" (p. 512). "Later anthologists continued to reshuffle the terms, culminating in the thirteen classes of Yao Nai's *Ku-wen tz'u lei-tsuan*, a list as influential as that of the *WH*, though still far from ideal" (pp. 776–78). See also Edwards, "Classified Guide." Wu Ch'u-tsai included rhymeprose in his *Ku-wen kuan-chih*, an inclusion that implies that his conception of *ku-wen* might include all forms of "ancient writings."

7. The consideration of *fu* and *tz'u* as subcategories of *ku-wen* is mainly derived from the practice of anthologists. See, e.g., Mao K'un, Yao Nai, and Wu Ch'u-ts'ai.

8. Tieghem's formulation (quoted in Hernadi, "Chapter Two: The Writer and the Reader," p. 22) is particularly sympathetic to the methodological approach of literary histories toward the concept of genre.

9. The T'ang-Sung School in Ming times continued the didactic tradition as well as the tradition of discussing subjects of everyday or of personal significance in a more sensual style. It is a curious phenomenon that Ming literary theories emphasized the notion of *fa* (technique), which was then thought to be the distinguishing characteristic of T'ang-Sung prose and poetry. This notion of *fa*, insofar as I understand it from Ming usage, refers to a technique of capturing in one's own work the perceived originality of the ancients as formerly done by exemplary T'ang-Sung *ku-wen* writers. See Min-tse, vol. 2, pp. 648–703.

# SELECTED BIBLIOGRAPHY

THE BIBLIOGRAPHY consists largely of works cited or mentioned in the present book and is not intended to be a complete bibliography of T'ang-Sung *ku-wen* literature. Sources for the major texts can be found in the list of abbreviations below. I have used the more commonly available editions for easy reference. The other sources are grouped in three sections: (1) primary sources; (2) secondary sources in Chinese, mostly studies by modern scholars of the four *ku-wen* masters; and (3) sources in Western languages, some of which are translations that I have consulted or cited. Although I completed the manuscript in 1982, I have updated the Bibliography to include works published through 1983.

The following abbreviations appear in the Bibliography and the Notes:

| | |
|---|---|
| *AM* | *Asia Major* |
| *BSOAS* | *Bulletin of the School of Oriental and African Studies* |
| *CCTPWC* | *Ching-chin Tung-p'o wen-chi shih-lüeh* 經進東坡文集事略 (Collected works of [Su] Tung-p'o, with commentaries, presented to the throne). SPTK. |
| *CLEAR* | *Chinese Literature: Essays, Articles, Reviews* |
| CTCC | Chu-tzu chi-ch'eng 諸子集成 |
| CTMS | Ching-tai mi-shu 津逮祕書 |
| *CTS* | *Chiu T'ang shu* 舊唐書 |
| *CTW* | *Ch'üan T'ang wen* 全唐文 (Complete prose writings of the T'ang Dynasty). Ed. Hsü Sung 徐松. Kuang-ya shu-chü Kuang-hsü *hsin-chou* (1901) edition 廣雅書局光緒辛丑本. |

HCLSHN    *Han Ch'ang-li shih hsi-nien chi shih* 韓昌黎詩繫年集釋 (Collected poems of Han Ch'ang-li in chronological order, with commentaries). Ed. Ch'ien Chung-lien 錢仲聯. Peking, 1957.

HCLWC    *Han Ch'ang-li wen-chi chiao-chu* 韓昌黎文集校注 (Collected prose works of Han Ch'ang-li, with commentaries). Ed. Ma T'ung-po 馬通伯. Shanghai, 1952.

HJAS    *Harvard Journal of Asiatic Studies*

HTS    *Hsin T'ang shu* 新唐書. PNP.

HYHP    *Hsin-ya hsüeh-pao* 新亞學報

JOS    *Journal of Oriental Studies*

LHTCC    *Liu Ho-tung ch'üan-chi* 柳河東全集 (Complete works of Liu [Tsung-yüan] of Ho-tung). Taipei, 1960.

OHCC    *Ou-yang Hsiu ch'üan-chi* 歐陽修全集 (Complete works of Ou-yang Hsiu). Taipei, 1960.

OWWC    *Ou-yang Wen-chung-kung wen-chi* 歐陽文忠公文集 (Collected works of Ou-yang Wen-chung-kung). SPTK.

PNP    Po-na-pen 百衲本

SF    Shuo fu 說郛

SPPY    Ssu-pu pei-yao 四部備要

SPTK    Ssu-pu ts'ung-k'an 四部叢刊

STPC    *Su Tung-p'o chi* 蘇東坡集 (Collected works of Su Tung-p'o), Taipei, 1967.

TSCC    Ts'ung-shu chi-ch'eng 叢書集成

PRIMARY SOURCES

Chang Huai-kuan 張懷瓘. *Shu tuan* 書斷 (Evaluation of calligraphy). Pai-chüan hsüeh-hai 百川學海, ts'e 23.

Chang Yen-yüan 張彥遠. *Fa shu yao-lu* 法書要錄 (The essentials of calligraphy and painting). CTMS, ts'e 71-74.

———. *Li-tai ming-hua chi* 歷代名畫記 (Famous paintings through the ages). TSCC.

Chao Te-lin 趙德麟. *Hou-ch'ing-lu* 侯鯖錄 (Delicacies for the nobility), SF, vol. 20.

Chao Yen-wei 趙彥衛. *Yün-lu man-ch'ao* 雲麓漫鈔 (Random jottings at Yün-lu [referring to events of ca. 1170 onward]). Peking, 1958.

Ch'en Ching-yün 陳景雲. "Han-chi tien-k'an" 韓集點勘 (Punctuating the collected works of Han [Yü]). In idem, *Wen-tao shih-shu* 文道十書 (Ten articles on the principles of literature). 6 ts'e. 1754.

Ch'en Tzu-ang 陳子昂. *Ch'en Po-yü wen-chi* 陳伯玉文集 (Collected works of Ch'en Po-yü). SPTK.

Ch'ien Ch'ien-yi 錢謙益. *Mu-chai ch'u-hsüeh-chi* 牧齋初學集 (Reading notes of the Mu-chai). SPTK.

Ch'ien Ta-hsin 錢大昕. *Ch'ien-yen-t'ang wen-chi* 潛研堂文集 (Collected works of the Ch'ien-yen studio). Shanghai, 1935.

*Chiu T'ang shu* 舊唐書 (Old T'ang history). Shanghai, 1934. Erh-shih-wu shih edition 二十五史本.

*Chou shu* 周書 (History of the Chou). PNP.

Chu T'ing-yü 朱廷玉. *Wu-pai-chia yin-chu Ch'ang-li hsien-sheng chi* 五百家音註昌黎先生集 (Collected works of Mr. Ch'ang-li [Han Yü] annotated by 500 scholars). Liang-yi-t'ang edition 兩儀堂本.

*Ch'üan Chin wen* 全晉文 (Complete writings of the Chin Dynasty). Ed. Yen K'o-chün 嚴可均. Kuang-ya edition 廣雅本.

*Ch'üan Han wen* 全漢文 (Complete writings of the Han Dynasty). Ed. Yen K'o-chün 嚴可均. Peking, 1958.

*Ch'üan Hou-Han wen* 全後漢文 (Complete writings of the Later Han Dynasty). Ed. Yen K'o-chün 嚴可均. Kuang-ya edition 廣雅本.

*Ch'üan Shang-ku San-tai Ch'in-Han San-kuo Liu-ch'ao wen* 全上古三代秦漢三國六朝文 (Complete writings of the ancient period, the Three Dynasties, the Ch'in and the Han, the Three Kingdoms, and the Six Dynasties). Ed. Yen K'o-chün 嚴可均. Peking, 1958.

*Chuang-tzu* 莊子. CTCC.

*Chuang-tzu chi-chieh* 莊子集解 (*Chuang-tzu* with collected commentaries). Ed. Wang Hsien-ch'ien 王先謙. Shanghai, 1933.

Fan Chung-yen 范仲淹. *Fan Wen-cheng-kung chi* 范文正公集 (Collected works of Fan Wen-cheng-kung). SPTK.

*Hou-Han shu* 後漢書 (History of the Later Han dynasty). PNP.

Hsia Wen-yen 夏文彥. *T'u-hui pao-chien* 圖繪寶鑑 (A treasured mirror of pictorial art). Yüan Chih-cheng *ping-wu* (1366) edition 元至正丙午刻本.

*Hsün-tzu chi-chieh* 荀子集解 (*Hsün-tzu* with collected commentaries). Ed. Wang Hsien ch'ien 王先謙. Taipei, 1965.

Hu Tzu 胡仔. *T'iao-hsi yü-yin ts'ung-hua* 苕溪漁隱叢話 (Chit-chats of the hermit-fisherman of T'iao-hsi). Peking, 1962.

―――. *T'iao-hsi yü-yin ts'ung-hua hou chi* 苕溪漁隱叢話後集 (More chit-chats of the hermit-fisherman of T'iao-hsi). Peking, 1962.

Huang Tsung-hsi 黃宗羲. "Nan-lci kcng-hsü tzu-hsü" 南雷庚戌自序 (Author's preface to the *Nan-lei [wen-an]*). In *Nan-lei wen an, I* 南雷文案(一) (Literary works of Nan-lei, part I). In *Li-chou yi-shu hui k'an* 梨洲遺書彙刊 (Works by [Huang] Li-chou, collected and published posthumously). Shanghai, 1910.

Hung Hsing-tsu 洪興祖. *Han-tzu nien-p'u* 韓子年譜 (A chronology of Master Han's life and works). 5 *chüan*. Hong Kong, 1969.

*Hung ming chi* 弘明集 (Texts to propagate and elucidate [Buddhist doctrines]) SPTK.

Kan Pao 干寶. *Sou-shen chi* 搜神記 (Records of searching out spirits). Sao-yeh shan-fang edition 掃葉山房本, 1928.

Kao Pu-ying 高步瀛. *T'ang Sung wen chü-yao* 唐宋文舉要 (Selected prose works of T'ang and Sung writers). 3 vols. Shanghai, 1962.

Ku-wen yüan 古文苑 (Garden of ancient literature). SPTK.

Ku Yen-wu 顧炎武. *Jih-chih-lu* 日知錄 (Daily reading notes). Hupeh, 1872.

Li Chao 李肇. *Kuo-shih pu* 國史補 (Supplement to [T'ang] dynasty history). Shanghai, 1957.

*Li chi* 禮記. Shih-san-ching chu-shu edition 十三經注疏本, 1815.

Li Fang 李昉, ed. *T'ai-p'ing yü-lan* 太平御覽 (Encyclopedia presented to the throne in the T'ai-p'ing era [of the Sung dynasty]). Peking, 1960; reprint of 1060 edition.

Li Fu-yen 李復言. *Hsü yu-kuai lu* 續幽怪錄 (More records of the hidden and the supernatural). SF, *ts'e* 119.

Li Po 李白. *Fen-lei pu-chu Li T'ai-po shih* 分類補注李太白詩 (The poetry of Li T'ai-po, categorized and annotated). SPTK.

―――. *Li T'ai-po ch'üan-chi* 李太白全集 (The complete works of Li T'ai-po). SPPY.

Li Shang-yin 李商隱. *Li Yi-shan shih wen chi* 李義山詩文集 (Collected poetry and prose of Li Yi-shan). Kuo-hsüeh chi-pen ts'ung-shu edition 國學基本叢書.

*Lieh-tzu* 列子. Commentary by Chang Chan 張湛. Taipei, reprint of Kuang-hsü *chia-shen* (1894) edition 光緒甲申本.

Liu Chih-chi 劉知幾. *Shih t'ung* 史通 (Understanding of history). Peking, 1961; facsimile of 1577 edition.

Liu Hsiang 劉向. *Shuo yüan* 說苑 (Garden of anecdotes). Han-Wei ts'ung-shu edition 漢魏叢書本.

Liu Hsieh 劉勰. *Wen-hsin tiao-lung* 文心雕龍 (The literary mind and the carving of dragons). Ed. Fan Wen-lan 范文瀾. Hong Kong, 1960.

Liu K'ai 柳開. *Ho-tung chi* 河東集 (Collected works [of Liu K'ai] of Ho-tung). SPTK.

Liu Yü-hsi 劉禹錫. *Liu Meng-te wen-chi* 劉夢得文集 (Collected prose of Liu Meng-te). SPTK.

*Lun yü* 論語 (Analects). Taipei, 1956.

Lung Yü-sheng 龍榆生, ed. *T'ang Sung ming-chia tz'u hsüan* 唐宋名家詞選 (Selections from famous T'ang-Sung *tz'u* song writers). Shanghai, 1956.

Mao K'un 茅坤, ed. *T'ang Sung pa ta chia wen ch'ao* 唐宋八大家文鈔 (Prose of the eight T'ang-Sung masters). Wan-li *chi-mao* (1579) hsü (preface) k'o-pen 萬歷己卯序刻本.

*Mao shih* 毛詩 (*Shih ching* with commentaries by Mao Heng 毛亨). SPTK.

Niu Seng-ju 牛僧孺. *Hsüan-kuai-lu* 玄怪錄 (Records of the dark and the supernatural). SF, *ts'e* 119.

*Pei shih* 北史 (History of the northern dynasties). PNP.

Shao Po 邵博. *Shao-shih chien-wen hou-lu* 邵氏見聞後錄 (A supplementary volume to the miscellaneous notes of Mr. Shao). TSCC.

*Ssu-k'u ch'üan-shu tsung-mu t'i-yao* 四庫全書總目提要 (General catalogue of the Ssu-k'u ch'üan-shu). Peking, 1965.

Ssu-ma Ch'ien 司馬遷. *Shih chi* 史記 (Records of the Grand Historian). SPPY.

Ssu-ma Kuang 司馬光. *Tzu-chih t'ung-chien* 資治通鑑 (A comprehensive mirror to political government). Peking, 1957.

Su E 蘇鶚. *Tu-yang tsa-pien* 杜陽雜編 (Miscellaneous notes on the Tu-yang region [in Shensi]). Changsha, 1939.

*Sui shu* 隋書 (History of the Sui dynasty). PNP.

*T'ang hui-yao* 唐會要 (T'ang institutions). Shanghai, 1955.

*T'ang wen ts'ui* 唐文粹 (The best of T'ang prose). SPTK.

T'ao Ch'ien 陶潛. *Sou-shen hou-chi* 搜神后記 (More records of searching out the spirits). Sao-yeh shan-fang edition 掃葉山房本, 1928.

T'ao Tsung-yi 陶宗儀. *Ch'o-keng-lu* 輟耕錄 (Thoughts while taking a break from ploughing the land). CTMS, *ts'e* 121–26.

Tuan Ch'eng-shih 段成式. *Yu-yang tsa-tsu* 酉陽雜俎 (Miscellaneous bits of Yu-yang Mountain [in Szechwan]). Shanghai, 1937.

Wang Fu-chih 王夫之. *Tu T'ung-chien lun* 讀通鑑論 (On reading [Ssu-ma Kuang's *Tzu-chih*] *t'ung-chien*). SPPY.

Wang T'ang 王讜. *T'ang yü-lin* 唐語林 (Forest of T'ang anecdotes). Shanghai, 1939.

Wang Yü-ch'eng 王禹偁. *Hsiao-hsü chi* 小畜集 (Hsiao-hsü's collected works). SPTK.

*Wen-hsüan* 文選 (The anthology). Taipei, 1959.

Wu Ch'u-ts'ai 吳楚材. *Ku-wen kuan-chih* 古文觀止 (The best of *ku-wen*). Shanghai, 1956.

Wu Kuang-sheng 吳光昇, ed. *Liu-chou hsien chih* 柳州縣志 (Gazetteer of Liu-chou prefecture). N.p., 1932; reprint of 1754 edition.

Yao Fan 姚範. *Yüan-ch'un-t'ang pi-chi* 援鶉堂筆記 (Yüan-ch'un-t'ang reading notes). 1835.

Yao Nai 姚鼐. *Ku-wen tz'u lei-tsuan* 古文辭類纂 (Ancient writings by category). Shanghai, 1935.

*Yi-wen lei-chu* 藝文類聚 (Collected writings by category). Peking, 1965.

*Yün-yü yang-ch'iu* 韻語陽秋 (Critical notes on poetic and prose styles). Comp. Ke Ch'iu-fang 葛丘方. 4 *ts'e*. Ming woodblock edition.

SECONDARY SOURCES IN CHINESE

Chang Shih-chai 章實齋. *Wen-shih t'ung-yi* 文史通義 (A comprehensive study of historical and literary forms). Shanghai, 1934.

Chang Shih-chao 章士釗. *Liu-wen chih-yao* 柳文指要 (An outline of the essentials in the writings of Liu Tsung-yüan). 3 vols. Peking, 1971.

Chang Tai-nien 張岱年. *Chung-kuo che-hsüeh fa-wei* 中國哲學發微 (Primary theses in Chinese philosophy). Shansi, 1981.

————. *Chung-kuo che-hsüeh ta-kang: Chung-kuo che-hsüeh wen-t'i shih* 中國哲學大綱:中國哲學問題史 (Outline of Chinese philosophy: A history of Chinese philosophy by topics). Peking, 1982.

Chao Chi-pin 趙紀彬. "Liu Yü-hsi ho Liu Tsung-yüan wu-shen-lun ssu-hsiang yen-chiu" 劉禹錫和柳宗元無神論思想研究 (Studies of the atheistic thinking of Liu Yü-hsi and Liu Tsung-yüan). *Che-hsüeh yen-chiu* 哲學研究, 1957, no. 10 (May), 50–72.

Ch'en Teng-yuan 陳登原. "Han Yü p'ing" 韓愈評 (A critique of Han Yü). *Chin-ling hsüeh-pao* 金陵學報 (Chengtu), 2, no. 2 (1932): 275–319.

Ch'en Yin-k'o 陳寅恪. "Lun Han Yü" 論韓愈 (A critique of Han Yü). *Li-shih yen-chiu* 歷史研究 (Peking), 1954, no. 2: 105–14.

————. "Lun *Tsai-sheng-yüan*" 論再生緣 (On *Tsai-sheng-yüan*). In idem, *Han-liu-t'ang chi* 寒柳堂集 (Collected works of the Cold Willow Studio). Shanghai, 1980, pp. 1–96.

Ch'ien Chi-po 錢基博. *Han Yü chih* 韓愈志 (Six treatises on Han Yü). Rev. ed. Shanghai, 1958.

Ch'ien Mu 錢穆. "Han Liu chiao-yi" 韓柳交誼 (The friendship between Han [Yü] and Liu [Tsung-yüan]). In idem, *Chung-kuo wen-hsüeh chiang-yen-chi* 中國文學講演集 (Lectures on Chinese literature). Hong Kong, 1963, pp. 102–4.

————. "Tsa-lun T'ang-tai ku-wen yün-tung" 雜論唐代古文運動 (The *ku-wen* reform movement in the T'ang dynasty). *HYHP*, 3 (1957): 123–68.

Chin Chung-shu 金中樞. "Sung-tai ku-wen yün-tung chih fa-chan yen-chiu" 宋代古文運動之發展研究 (A study of the development of the *ku-wen* movement in the Sung). *HYHP*, 5, no. 2 (1963): 79–146.

Chou K'ang-hsieh 周康燮, ed. *Liu Tsung-yüan yen-chiu lun chi* 柳宗元研究論集 (Critical studies of Liu Tsung-yüan: Collected essays). Hong Kong, 1973.

Ch'ü Wan-li 屈萬里. "T'eng-wang-ko hsü ti liang-ko wen-t'i" 滕王閣序的兩個問題 (Two problems in [Wang Po's] preface to the T'eng-wang Tower). *Ta-lu tsa-chih* 大陸雜誌, 16, no. 9 (1958): 1–6.

Feng Yu-lan 馮友蘭. *Chung-kuo che-hsüeh shih* 中國哲學史 (History of Chinese philosophy). Shanghai, 1934. English version: *A History of Chinese Philosophy*. Tr. Derk Bodde. Princeton, N.J., 1952–53.

Hou Wai-lu 侯外廬. *Chung-kuo ssu-hsiang t'ung-shih* 中國思想通史 (A comprehensive intellectual history of China). 4 vols. Peking, 1956–60.

————. "Liu Tsung-yüan ti wei-wu-chu-yi che-hsüeh ssu-hsiang ho she-hui ssu-hsiang" 柳宗元的唯物主義哲學思想和社會思想 (Liu Tsung-yüan's materialist philosophy and social thinking). *Che-hsüeh yen-chiu* 哲學研究, 1964, no. 6 (Aug.): 59–78. Reprinted in Chou K'ang-hsieh, pp. 1–21.

————, ed. *Chung-kuo ku-tien san-wen yen-chiu lun-wen-chi* 中國古典散文研究論文集 (Critical studies of Chinese classical prose: Collected essays). Peking, 1959.

Hsü Han-feng 徐翰逢. *Ku-tien shih-wen hsüan-shih* 古典詩文選釋 (Annotated selections of classical poetry and prose). Hong Kong, 1955.

Huang Yün-mei 黃雲眉. *Han Yü, Liu Tsung-yüan wen-hsüeh p'ing-chia* 韓愈柳宗元文學評價 (A critical evaluation of the literary works of Han Yü and Liu Tsung-yüan). Shantung, 1980; reissue of 1957 edition.

Jao Tsung-yi 饒宗頤. "Han Yü Nan-shan-shih yü T'an Wu-ch'an yi Ma Ming *Fo So-hsing-tsan*" 韓愈南山詩與曇無讖譯馬鳴佛所行讚 (Han Yü's debt to the Chinese translation of Aśvaghoṣa's *Buddha Carita* by T'an Wu-ch'an). *Chūgoku bungaku hō* 中国文学報 (1963): 82–102.

Ku Chieh-kang 顧頡剛. *Ch'in-Han fang-shih yü ju-sheng* 秦漢方士與儒生 (Taoist magicians and Confucian scholars in Ch'in-Han times). Shanghai, 1978. First published under the title *Ch'in-han hsüeh-shu shih-lüeh* 秦漢學術史略 (A synopsis of the philological studies of the Ch'in and Han). Shanghai, 1935.

Ku Yi-sheng 顧易生. *Liu Tsung-yüan* 柳宗元. Shanghai, 1961.

————. "Shih lun Han Yü shang ch'i chi Han wen yü tz'u fu p'ien-wen ti kuan-hsi" 試論韓愈尚奇及韓文與詞賦駢文的關係 (A tentative study of Han Yü's emphasis on the "extraordinary" and of the relationship between his prose and *tz'u, fu*, and parallel prose). *Wen-hsüeh yi-ch'an tseng-k'an* 文學遺產增刊, no. 10 (1962): 66–73.

————. "Su Shih ti cheng-chih t'ai-tu chi yu-kuan tso-p'in" 蘇軾的政治態度及有關作品 (Su Shih's political attitude and related works). *Wen yi lun-tsung* 文藝論叢, no. 5 (Oct. 1978): 290–330.

Kung Shu-chih 龔書熾. *Han Yü chi ch'i ku-wen yün-tung* 韓愈及其古文運動 (Han Yü and his *ku-wen* movement). Chungking, 1945.

Kuo Hsi-liang 郭錫良. "Han Yü tsai wen-hsüeh yü-yen fang-mien ti li-lun ho shih-chien" 韓愈在文學語言方面的理論和實踐 (The theory and practice of Han Yü in literary writing and literary language). *Yü-yen hsüeh lun-ts'ung* 語言學論叢, 1957, no. 1: 51–74.

Kuo Shao-yü 郭紹虞. *Chung-kuo wen-hsüeh p'i-p'ing shih* 中國文學批評史 (History of Chinese literary criticism). 2 vols. Shanghai, 1943, 1947.

Kuo Yü-heng 郭予衡. "Chieh-ch'u ti san-wen-chia Han Yü" 杰出的散文家韓愈 (The outstanding prose stylist Han Yü). *Wen-hsüeh p'ing lun ts'ung-k'an* 文學評論叢刊, 1979, no. 2: 296–315.

Li Ch'ang-chih 李長之. *Han Yü*. Chungking, 1945.

Li Chia-yen 李嘉言. "Han Yü fu-ku yün-tung ti hsin t'an-so" 韓愈復古

運動的新探索 (New inquiries into the classical revival movement of Han Yü). *Wen-hsüeh* 文學, 2 (1934): 1076–84.

Lin Shu 林紓. *Han Liu wen-chang yen-chiu-fa* 韓柳文章研究法 (A methodological study of the prose style of Han Yü and Liu Tsung-yüan). Shanghai, 1924.

Liu K'ai-jung 劉開榮. *T'ang-tai hsiao-shuo yen-chiu* 唐代小說研究 (A critical study of T'ang dynasty fiction). Shanghai, 1947.

Liu Kuo-ying 劉國瀛. *T'ang-tai ku-wen yün-tung lun kao* 唐代古文運動論稿 (A preliminary study of the T'ang *ku-wen* movement). Shansi, 1984.

Liu Tzu-chien 劉子建. *Ou-yang Hsiu ti chih-hsüeh yü ts'ung-cheng* 歐陽修的治學與從政 (Ou-yang Hsiu's scholarship and political career). Hong Kong, 1963.

Lo Ken-tse 羅根澤. *Chung-kuo wen-hsüeh p'i-p'ing shih, II* 中國文學批評史(二) (A history of Chinese literary criticism, part II). Shanghai, 1958.

———. *Sui T'ang wen-hsüeh p'i-p'ing shih* 隋唐文學批評史 (A history of literary criticism in the Sui-T'ang period). Chungking, 1943.

———. *Wan-T'ang Wu-tai wen-hsüeh p'i-p'ing shih* 晚唐五代文學批評史 (A history of literary criticism in the late T'ang and Five Dynasties periods). Chungking, 1943, 1945; Shanghai, 1947.

Lo Lien-t'ien 羅聯添. *Han Yü* 韓愈. Taipei, 1977.

———. *Han Yü yen-chiu* 韓愈研究 (A critical study of Han Yü). Taipei, 1973.

———. *Liu Tsung-yüan shih-chi hsi-nien chi tzu-liao lei-pien* 柳宗元事蹟繫年暨資料類編 (The deeds of Liu Tsung-yüan in chronological order and a listing by kind of research materials [on Liu]). Taipei, 1981.

Min-tse 敏澤. *Chung-kuo wen-hsüeh li-lun p'i-p'ing shih* 中國文學理論批評史 (A history of Chinese theories of literature and literary criticism). 2 vols. Peking, 1981.

Shih Tzu-yü 施子愉. *Liu Tsung-yüan nien-p'u* 柳宗元年譜 (A chronology of Liu Tsung-yüan's life and works). Wuhan, 1958. Reprinted in Chou K'ang-hsieh, pp. 1–23.

Shimizu Shigeru 清水茂. "Liu Tsung-yüan ti sheng-huo t'i-yen chi ch'i shan-shui yu-chi" 柳宗元的生活體驗及其山水遊記 (The life experience of Liu Tsung-yüan and his records of excursions in nature). Tr. Hua Shan 華山. *Wen-shih-che shuang-yüeh-k'an* 文史哲雙月刊, 1957, no. 4. Reprinted in Chou K'ang-hsieh, pp. 59–83. Originally published in *Chūgoku bungaku hō* 中国文学報, no. 2 (April 1955): 45–74.

Sun Ch'ang-wu 孫昌武. *Liu Tsung-yüan chuan lun* 柳宗元傳論 (A biographical and critical study of Liu Tsung-yüan). Peking, 1982.

Ts'en Chung-mien 岑仲勉. "T'ang-chi chih-yi" 唐集質疑 (Questioning the T'ang anthology). *Chung-yang yen-chiu-yuan Li-shih yü-yen-so chi-k'an* 中央研究院歷史語言所集刊, 9 (1947): 1–82.

Tuan Hsing-min 段醒民. *Liu Tzu-hou yü-yen wen-hsüeh t'an-wei* 柳子厚寓言文學探微 (Research into Liu Tsung-yüan's allegorical writings). Taipei, 1978.

Wang Li 王力. *Ku-tai Han-yü* 古代漢語 (Ancient Chinese). 2 vols. Peking, 1962.

Wang Ming-sheng 王鳴盛. *Shih-ch'i shih shang-ch'üeh* 十七史商榷 (Notes on the seventeen dynastic histories). In *Kuang-ya ts'ung-shu* 廣雅叢書.

Wu Keng-shun 吳庚舜. "Kuan-yü T'ang-tai ch'uan-ch'i fan-jung ti yüan-yin" 關於唐代傳奇繁榮的原因 (Concerning the causes of the flourishing of *ch'uan-ch'i* in the T'ang). *Wen-hsüeh yen-chiu chi-k'an* 文學研究集刊, 1964, no. 1: 70–100.

Wu Wen-chih 吳文治. *Liu Tsung-yüan p'ing-chuan* 柳宗元評傳 (A critical biography of Liu Tsung-yüan). Peking, 1962.

———. "Liu Tsung-yüan wu-shen-lun ssu-hsiang ch'u-t'an" 柳宗元無神論思想初探 (A preliminary exploration of Liu Tsung-yüan's atheistic thought). *Hsin-chien-she* 新建設, May 1957. Reprinted in Chou K'ang-hsieh, pp. 33–36.

———, comp. *Ku-tien wen-hsüeh yen-chiu tzu-liao: Liu Tsung yüan chüan* 古典文學研究資料: 柳宗元卷 (Materials for research on classical literature: Volume on Liu Tsung-yüan). Peking, 1964.

Yeh Chia-ying 葉嘉瑩. "Ts'ung Yüan Yi-shan lun shih chüeh-chü t'an Hsieh Ling-yün ho Liu Tsung-yüan ti shih yü jen" 從元遺山論詩絕句談謝靈運和柳宗元的詩與人 (An essay on the poetry and the personality of Hsieh Ling-yün and Liu Tsung-yüan, using the "Quatrain on Poetry" by Yüan Yi-shan as my point of departure). *Dou-sou* 抖擻, no. 15 (1976): 1–21.

Yu Kuo-ch'en 游國琛. *Su T'ung-po sheng-p'ing chi ch'i tso-p'in shu-p'ing* 蘇東坡生平及其作品述評 (On the life and works of Su Tung-p'o). Taipei, 1965.

Yu-liang 友諒. *Ku-tien shih-wen yen-tu sui-pi* 古典詩文研讀隨筆 (Reading notes on a study of [selected] classical poetry and prose). Hong Kong, 1962.

SOURCES IN WESTERN LANGUAGES

Aristotle. *Introduction to Aristotle*. Ed. Richard McKeon. New York, 1947.

Beardsley, Monroe. *Aesthetics: Problems in the Philosophy of Criticism*. New York, 1958.

Birch, Cyril, ed. and comp. *Anthology of Chinese Literature*, vol. 1. New York, 1965.

———, ed. *Studies in Chinese Literary Genres*. Berkeley, Calif., 1974.

Bodde, Derk. "Chinese 'Laws of Nature': A Reconsideration." *HJAS*, 39 (1979): 139–55.

————. "'Laws of Nature' in Chinese Thought." *HJAS*, 20 (1957): 709–27.

Brouwer, L. E. J. "Intuitionism and Formalism." Speech delivered Oct. 14, 1912. Tr. Arnold Dresden. *Bulletin of American Mathematics Society*, 20 (Nov. 1913). Reprinted in P. Benacerraf and H. Putnam, eds., *Philosophy of Mathematics*, pp. 81–96. London, 1983.

Chai, Ch'u, and Chai, Winberg, eds. *A Treasury of Chinese Literature*. New York, 1965.

Chan, Wing-tsit. *A Source Book in Chinese Philosophy*. Princeton, N.J., 1963.

Chatman, Seymour, and Levin, Samuel R., eds. *Essays on the Language of Literature*. New York, 1967.

Chaves, Jonathan. *Mei Yao-ch'en and the Development of Early Sung Poetry*. New York, 1976.

Ch'en Yin-k'o. "Han Yü and the T'ang Novels." *HJAS*, 1 (1934): 39–43.

Chou Yi-liang. "Tantrism in China." *HJAS*, 8 (1945): 241–333.

De Bary, William Theodore, et al., eds. *Sources of Chinese Tradition*. New York, 1960.

Dubs, Homer H., tr. *The Works of Hsün-tzu*. Taipei, 1966; originally published in London, 1928.

Edwards, E. D. *Chinese Prose Literature of the T'ang Period*. 2 vols. London, 1937–38.

————. "A Classified Guide to the Thirteen Classes of Chinese Prose." *BSOAS*, 12 (1947): 770–78.

Egan, Ronald C. *The Literary Works of Ou-yang Hsiu (1007–72)*. Cambridge, Eng., 1984.

Feng Yu-lan. *A History of Chinese Philosophy*. 2 vols. Tr. Derk Bodde. Princeton, N.J., 1952–53.

Fowler, Alistair. *Kinds of Literature*. Cambridge, Mass., 1980.

Franke, Herbert, ed. *Sung Biographies*. 4 vols. Wiesbaden, 1976.

Fusek, Lois, tr. *Among the Flowers (The Hua-chien-chi)*. New York, 1982.

Giles, Herbert. *Gems of Chinese Literature*. London, 1884.

Goodrich, Chauncey S. *Biography of Su Ch'o*. Berkeley, Calif., 1953.

Graham, A. C., tr. *Lieh-tzu*. London, 1960.

Hartman, Charles. "*Alieniloquium*: Liu Tsung-yüan's Other Voice." *CLEAR*, 4, no. 1 (Jan. 1982): 23–74.

————. "Historical and Literary Background." In Nienhauser et al., pp. 15–25.

Hatch, George C. "Su Shih." In Franke, vol. 3, pp. 900–968.

Hawkes, David, tr. *Ch'u Tz'u: The Songs of the South*. Boston, 1962.

Hernadi, Paul. *Beyond Genre (New Directions in Literary Classification)*. Ithaca, N.Y., 1972.

Hightower, James R. "Ch'ü Yüan Studies." In *Silver Jubilee Volume of* the *Zinbun-Kagaku-Kenkyusyo, Kyoto University*, pp. 192–223. Kyoto, 1954.

——. "Han Yü as Humorist." *HJAS*, 44 (1984): 5–27.

——. "Lament for the Unemployed Gentleman [by Ssu-ma Ch'ien]." *HJAS*, 17 (1954): 197–200.

——. *The Poetry of T'ao Ch'ien*. Oxford, 1970.

——. "Some Characteristics of Parallel Prose." In *Studia Serica Bernhard Karlgren Dedicata*, pp. 60–91. Copenhagen, 1959.

——. *Topics in Chinese Literature*. Cambridge, Mass., 1966.

——. "The Wen-hsüan and Genre Theory." *HJAS*, 20 (1957): 512–33.

Kant, Immanuel. *Logic*. Tr. Robert Hartman and Wolfgang Schwartz. Indianapolis and New York, 1974.

Lamont, H. G. "An Early Ninth Century Debate on Heaven: Liu Tsung-yüan's *T'ien-shuo* and Liu Yü-hsi's *T'ien-lun*." Part I, *AM*, 18 (1973): 181–208; part II, *AM*, 19 (1974–75): 57–84.

Le Gros Clark, Cyril Drummond. *The Prose Poetry of Su Tung-p'o*. New York, 1964; reprint of 1934 edition.

Legge, James, tr. *The Chinese Classics*. 5 vols. London, 1861–71; reissued, Oxford, 1893, Hong Kong, 1960. Vol. 1: *Confucian Analects*; vol. 2: *The Works of Mencius*; vol. 3: *The Shoo King*; vol. 4: *The She King*; vol. 5: *The Ch'un-ts'ew with the Tso-chuan*.

——. *The Li Ki*. Oxford, 1885.

——. *The Texts of Taoism*. Oxford, 1891.

Lin Yu-tang. *The Gay Genius: The Life and Times of Su Tung-p'o*. New York, 1947.

Liu, James J. Y. *Chinese Theories of Literature*. Chicago, 1975.

——. "Li Shang-yin's Poem 'The Memorial Inscription by Han Yü.'" *East-West Center Review*, 1 (1964). 13–19.

——. *The Poetry of Li Shang-yin*. Chicago, 1969.

——. "Toward a Synthesis of Chinese and Western Theories of Literature." *Journal of Chinese Philosophy*, 4 (1977): 1–24.

Liu, James T. C. *Ou-yang Hsiu: An Eleventh-Century Neo-Confucianist*. Stanford, 1967.

Liu Shih-shun, tr. *Chinese Classical Prose: The Eight Masters of the T'ang-Sung Period*. Hong Kong, 1979.

Locke, Majorie A. "The Early Life of Ou-yang Hsiu and His Relation to the Rise of the Ku-wen Movement of the Sung Dynasty." University of London, Ph.D. diss., 1951.

Ma, Y. W. "Prose Writings of Han Yü and Ch'uan-ch'i Literature." *JOS*, 7 (1969): 195–227.

Mair, Victor H. "Scroll Presentation in the T'ang Dynasty." *HJAS*, 38 (1978): 35–60.

Margouliès, G. *Le Kou-wen chinois*. Paris, 1925.

Maritain, Jacques. *Creative Intuition in Art and Poetry.* New York, 1953.

Needham, Joseph. "Human Law and the Laws of Nature in China and the West." In idem, *Science and Civilization in China,* vol. 2, pp. 518–83. Cambridge, Eng., 1953.

Neighbors, Lloyd. "Fables and Biographical Sketches." In Nienhauser et al., pp. 80–90.

Nienhauser, William. "An Allegorical Reading of Han Yü's 'Mao Ying Chuan' (Biography of Fur Point)." *Oriens Extremus,* 23, no. 2 (Dec. 1976): 153–74.

———. "Landscape Essays." In idem et al., pp. 66–79.

———. "Life and Works." In idem et al., pp. 26–44.

———. *P'i Jih-hsiu.* Boston, 1979.

——— et al., eds. *Liu Tsung-yüan.* New York, 1973.

Ohmann, Richard. "Literature as Sentences." In Seymour Chatman and Samuel R. Levin, eds., *Essays on the Language of Literature,* pp. 231–38. New York, 1967.

Owen, Stephen. *The Great Age of Chinese Poetry, the High T'ang.* New Haven, Conn., 1981.

———. *The Poetry of Meng Chiao and Han Yü.* New Haven, Conn., 1975.

Pulleyblank, Edwin G. *The Background of the Rebellion of An Lu-shan.* London, 1955.

———. "Liu K'o, a Forgotten Rival of Han Yü." *AM,* 7 (1959): 145–60.

———. "Neo-Confucianism and Neo-Legalism in T'ang Intellectual Life, 755–806." In Wright, pp. 77–114.

Schafer, Edward. *Pacing the Void.* Berkeley, Calif., 1977.

Solomon, Bernard, tr. *The Veritable Record of the T'ang Emperor Shun-tsung (Han Yü's Shun-tsung Shih-lu).* Cambridge, Mass., 1955.

Twitchett, Denis, ed. *The Cambridge History of China,* vol. 3, *Sui and T'ang China, 589–906, Part 1.* Cambridge, Eng., 1979.

Waley, Arthur. *The Poetry and Career of Li Po, 701–62 A.D.* London, 1950.

———, tr. *The Analects of Confucius.* London, 1938.

Watson, Burton, tr. *The Complete Works of Chuang-tzu.* New York, 1968.

———. *Records of the Grand Historian.* 2 vols. New York, 1961.

———. *Su Tung-p'o: Selections from a Sung Dynasty Poet.* New York, 1965.

Wright, Arthur, ed. *The Confucian Persuasion.* Stanford, 1960.

Yang, Hsien-yi, and Yang, Gladys, tr. "Epitaph for Liu Tzu-hou." *Chinese Literature,* 1959, no. 2 (Feb.): 81–84.

———. "A Farewell to Li Yuan." *Chinese Literature,* 1959, no. 2 (Feb.): 75–76.

———. "A Farewell to Meng Chiao." *Chinese Literature,* 1959, no. 2 (Feb.): 73–75.

# INDEX

In this index an "f" after a number indicates a separate reference on the next page, and an "ff" indicates separate references on the next two pages. A continuous discussion over two or more pages is indicated by a span of page numbers, e.g., "pp. 57–58." *Passim* is used for a cluster of references in close but not consecutive sequence.

Library of Congress Cataloging-in-Publication Data

Chen, Yu-shih.
  Images and ideas in Chinese classical prose.
    Bibliography: p.
    Includes index.
    1. Chinese prose literature—T'ang dynasty,
618–907—History and criticism.   2. Chinese prose
literature—Sung dynasty, 960–1279—History and
criticism.   I. Title.
PL2409.C45 1988        895.1'8308'09        87-26720
ISBN 0-8047-1409-6 (alk. paper)